Lecture Notes in Computer Science 7709

Commenced Publication in 1973
Founding and Former Series Editors:
Gerhard Goos, Juris Hartmanis, and Jan van Leeuwen

Tai-hoon Kim   Young-hoon Lee
Wai-chi Fang (Eds.)

Future Generation Information Technology

4th International Conference, FGIT 2012
Gangneug, Korea, December 16-19, 2012
Proceedings

 Springer

Volume Editors

Tai-hoon Kim
GVSA and University of Tasmania, Hobart, TAS, Australia
E-mail: taihoonn@hanmail.net

Young-hoon Lee
Hannam University, Daejeon, South Korea
E-mail: yhlee@hnu.kr

Wai-chi Fang
National Chiao Tung University, Hsinchu, Taiwan, ROC
E-mail: wfang@mail.nctu.edu.tw

ISSN 0302-9743   e-ISSN 1611-3349
ISBN 978-3-642-35584-4   e-ISBN 978-3-642-35585-1
DOI 10.1007/978-3-642-35585-1
Springer Heidelberg Dordrecht London New York

Library of Congress Control Number: 2012953706

CR Subject Classification (1998): H.4, C.2, D.2, H.3, I.2, H.5

LNCS Sublibrary: SL 3 – Information Systems and Application, incl. Internet/Web
and HCI

Typesetting: Camera-ready by author, data conversion by Scientific Publishing Services, Chennai, India

Printed on acid-free paper

Springer is part of Springer Science+Business Media (www.springer.com)

Foreword

Future-generation information technology is an area that attracts many academics and industry professionals. The goal of the FGIT conference is to bring together researchers from academia and industry as well as practitioners to share ideas, problems, and solutions relating to the multifaceted aspects of this field.

We would like to express our gratitude to all of the authors of submitted papers and to all attendees for their contributions and participation.

We acknowledge the great effort of all the Chairs and the members of the Advisory Boards and Program Committees of the above-listed event. Special thanks go to SERSC (Science & Engineering Research Support Society) for supporting this conference.

We are grateful in particular to the following speakers who kindly accepted our invitation and, in this way, helped to meet the objectives of the conference: Zita Maria Almeida do Vale, Hai Jin, Goreti Marreiros, Alfredo Cuzzocrea and Osvaldo Gervasi.

We wish to express our special thanks to Yvette E. Gelogo for helping with the editing of this volume.

December 2012   Chairs of FGIT 2012

Preface

We would like to welcome you to the proceedings of the 4th International Mega-Conference on Future Generation Information Technology (FGIT 2012), which was held during December 16–19, 2012, at the Korea Woman Training Center, Kangwondo, Korea.

FGIT 2012 provided a chance for academics and industry professionals to discuss recent progress in related areas. We expect that the conference and its publications will be a trigger for further research and technology improvements in this important field. We would like to acknowledge the great effort of all the Chairs and members of the Program Committee.

We would like to express our gratitude to all of the authors of submitted papers and to all attendees for their contributions and participation. We believe in the need for continuing this undertaking in the future.

Once more, we would like to thank all the organizations and individuals who supported this event and helped in the success of FGIT 2012

December 2012   Tai-hoon Kim on behalf of the Volume Editors

Organization

Honorary Chair

Young-hoon Lee   Hannam University, Korea

Steering Co-chairs

Tai-hoon Kim   Hannam University, Korea
Wai-chi Fang   National Chiao Tung University, Taiwan

International Advisory Board

Haeng-kon Kim   Catholic University of Daegu, Korea
Tughrul Arslan   Engineering and Electronics, Edinburgh
                                 University, UK
Adrian Stoica   NASA Jet Propulsion Laboratory, USA
Yanchun Zhang   Victoria University, Australia
Stephen S. Yau (Chair)   Arizona State University, USA
Sankar K. Pal   Indian Statistical Institute, India
Jianhua Ma   Hosei University, Japan
Aboul Ella Hassanien   Cairo University, Egypt

Program Chair

Dominik Slezak   Infobright , Poland and Canada

Program Co-chairs

Byeong-Ho Kang   University of Tasmania, Australia
Akingbehin Kiumi   University of Michigan-Dearborn, USA
Byungjoo Park   Hannam University, Korea
Xiaofeng Song   Nanjing University of Aeronautics and
                                 Astronautics, China
Kyo-il Chung   ETRI, Korea
Kirk P. Arnett   Mississippi State University, USA
Frode Eika Sandnes   Oslo University College, Norway

Publicity Co-chairs

Junzhong Gu	East China Normal University, China
Hideo Kuroda	Nagasaki University, Japan
Dae-sik Ko	Mokwon University, Korea
Minsuk O.	Kyunggi University, Korea
Robert C.H. Hsu	Chung Hua University, Taiwan
Aboul Ella Hassanien	Cairo University, Egypt

Publication Co-chairs

Bongen Gu	Chungju National University, Korea
Younghwan Bang	KITECH, Korea

Table of Contents

Frequency Sharing Method for High Frequency Ocean Surface Radar Using Matched Filtering and Orthogonal Waveforms

In-Sik Choi[1], Seung-Jae Lee[1], Joo-Hwan Lee[2], and Young-Jun Chong[2]

[1] Department of Electronic Engineering, Hannam University
133 Ojung-dong, Daeduk-Gu, Daejeon 306-791, Republic of Korea
recog@hannam.ac.kr, sensor@hnu.kr
[2] Radio & Telecommunications Convergence Research Laboratory,
Radio Technology Research Department
ETRI, 138 Gajeongno, Yuseong-gu, Daejeon 305-700, Republic of Korea
{Joohlee,yjchong}@etri.re.kr

Abstract. In this paper, we propose a new frequency-reuse method which shares the frequency band in high frequency ocean surface radar (HFOSR). Our technique uses matched filtering and two orthogonal waveforms considering the distance between two radars. The orthogonal waveforms are the up-chirp and down-chirp signals, which have the same center frequency and the same bandwidth. In South Korea, there are 16 ocean surface radars which use the 13, 25 and 42 MHz operating frequencies. They are currently using 14 different frequency channels to reject mutual interference. Our method uses only six different frequency channels, thus reducing the number of frequency channels by eight and freeing those resources for other uses or services.

Keywords: ocean surface radar, frequency reuse, orthogonal waveforms, chirp signals, mutual interferences.

1 Introduction

High frequency ocean surface radar (HFOSR) is a good electromagnetic sensor for measuring the distribution of the radial component of ocean surface currents over a wide area in a short time [1]. There is increasing interest for HFOSR to support environmental, oceanographic and meteorological phenomena, climatology, and disaster-mitigation operations [2].

In South Korea, HFOSR is used to observe oil spills, outflows from dikes, and to prevent accidents in the six sea regions (Kangwon province, Busan city, Yeosu bay, Jeju Island, Seamangeum, and Kunsan city). There are 16 HFOSR systems in South Korea and their operating frequency are different within a close area due to mutual interference.

Recently, there has been many studies about the frequency-reuse technology for HFOSR. In the patent [3], Codar Ocean Sensors proposed the frequency sharing method via GPS time modulation multiplexing. This system uses the GPS time synchronization and frequency modulated continuous wave (FMCW) waveforms. The

T.-h. Kim, Y.-h. Lee, and W.-c. Fang (Eds.): FGIT 2012, LNCS 7709, pp. 1–6, 2012.

low-pass filtering in the receiver separates one radar's echo information while discarding all of the interfering direct signals from the other radars.

In this paper, we propose a new frequency-sharing method which uses matched filtering in the receiver and the orthogonal linear frequency modulation (LFM) waveforms instead of FMCW waveforms. In addition, the proposed method does not require the GPS synchronization process that is necessary with Codar Ocean Sensors. Our method uses only six frequency channels, thus reducing the required number of frequency channels by eight compared to the current method, which requires 14 different frequency channels.

2   HF Ocean Surface Radar in South Korea

When the transmitted radar wavelength is equal to half of the wavelength of the ocean surface wave, a strong reflected signal will be returned in the backscattering direction. This phenomenon is known as "Bragg scattering". In HFOSR using Bragg scattering, the frequency range of 3 to 50 MHz is very useful for measuring ocean surface waves driven by wind.

Fig. 1 shows the locations of the 16 HFOSR systems operating in South Korea [2]. Their coverage can be divided into six regions of, such as Kangwon province, Busan city, Yeosu bay, Jeju Island, Seamangeum, and Kunsan city.

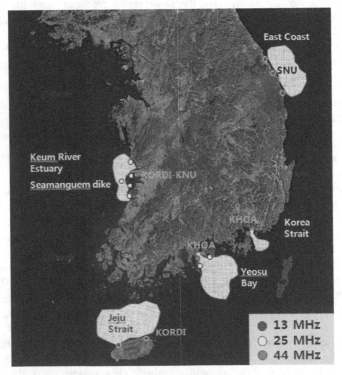

Fig. 1. Locations of HFOSRs in Korea

Table 1 shows the operating frequencies and maximum detection ranges of the 16 HFOSRs in South Korea [2]. As shown in the table, the 16 radars use different operating frequencies in the same regions. Five radars use the 13 MHz band, seven radars utilize the 25 MHz band and four radars use the 43 MHz band. Maximum detection range is dependent on the operating frequency, and the bandwidths are directly related to the range resolution. Generally, FMCW chirps are used as HFOSR waveforms.

Table 1. Information of HFOSRs in South Korea

Station	Center Frequency	Maximum range [km]	Bandwidth[kHz]
Dong-hae	$f_{13MHz}(A)$	70	50
Sam-chuck	$f_{13MHz}(B)$	70	50
Ul-jin	$f_{13MHz}(A)$	70	50
Geo-je	$f_{44MHz}(A)$	10	300
Yeoun-do	$f_{44MHz}(B)$	10	300
Seo-sang	$f_{44MHz}(C)$	18	300
Hong-hyen	$f_{24MHz}(A)$	25	100
Hang-il-am	$f_{24MHz}(B)$	25	100
O-dong-do	$f_{44MHz}(D)$	18	350
Bu-an	$f_{24MHz}(A)$	23	100
Seo-chon	$f_{24MHz}(C)$	45	100
Bi-eong	$f_{24MHz}(D)$	45	100
Sin-si	$f_{24MHz}(E)$	23	100
Ga-ruck	$f_{24MHz}(F)$	23	100
Ae-wol	$f_{13MHz}(C)$	80	50
Kim-young	$f_{13MHz}(D)$	80	50

3   Proposed Method and Results

In this paper, we consider a HF radar system that utilizes a correlation processor receiver (i.e., a matched filter). It is well known that the LFM up-chirp signal and LFM down-chirp signal are orthogonal, meaning that the matched filter output of the up-chirp signal and the down-chirp signal is zero.

The LFM up-chirp waveform has the following form:

$$s(t) = \exp(j2\pi(f_0 t + \frac{\mu}{2} t^2)) \tag{1}$$

where f_0 is the chirp start frequency, $\mu = B / \tau_0$, τ_0 is the pulse width, and B is the bandwidth.

Similarly, the LFM down-chirp signal expressed as follows:

$$s(t) = \exp(j2\pi(f_0 t - \frac{\mu}{2} t^2)) \tag{2}$$

Fig. 2 shows the matched filter output of the LFM up-chirp and down-chirp signals. The convolution of the up-chirp transmitted signal and the up-chirp received signal contains large echo signals corresponding to the target locations. However, the convolution of the down-chirp transmitted signal and the up-chirp received signal is nearly zero. Therefore, we can share the center frequency and instantaneous bandwidth of HFOSRs using this orthogonal property.

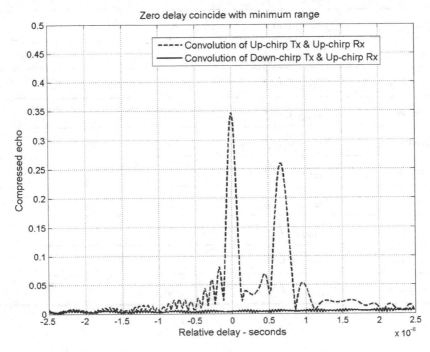

Fig. 2. Convolution of the LFM up-chirp and down-chirp signals

Table 2 shows the proposed frequency and waveform allocation of the 16 HFOSRs in South Korea. We can share the operating frequency within the same area using the orthogonal waveforms. Therefore, there are six frequency channels in total. Thus, eight frequency channels are freed for use by other services.

Table 2. Proposed frequency and waveform allocation

Station	Center Frequency	Waveform
Dong-hae	$f_{13MHz}(A)$	Up-Chirp
Sam-chuck	$f_{13MHz}(A)$	Down-Chirp
Ul-jin	$f_{13MHz}(B)$	Up-Chirp
Geo-je	$f_{44MHz}(A)$	Up-Chirp
Yeoun-do	$f_{44MHz}(A)$	Down-Chirp
Seo-sang	$f_{44MHz}(A)$	Up-Chirp
Hong-hyen	$f_{24MHz}(A)$	Up-Chirp
Hang-il-am	$f_{24MHz}(A)$	Down-Chirp
O-dong-do	$f_{44MHz}(A)$	Down-Chirp
Bu-an	$f_{24MHz}(B)$	Up-Chirp
Seo-chon	$f_{24MHz}(A)$	Up-Chirp
Bi-eong	$f_{24MHz}(A)$	Down-Chirp
Sin-si	$f_{24MHz}(C)$	Up-Chirp
Ga-ruck	$f_{24MHz}(C)$	Down-Chirp
Ae-wol	$f_{13MHz}(A)$	Up-Chirp
Kim-young	$f_{13MHz}(A)$	Down-Chirp

4   Conclusion

In this paper, we proposed a novel frequency-sharing method which uses matched filtering and orthogonal waveforms. Using the proposed frequency and waveform allocation method, eight frequency channels are freed in the South Korea at the HF frequency band. These frequency channels can be used for either public or military purposes. Our method can also be applied to other radar systems such as weather radar, military radar, or automobile radar.

Acknowledgment. This work was supported by the Electronics and Telecommunications Research Institute (ETRI) Research Fund (No. 5011-2012-0050). This work was partially supported by the Basic Science Research Program through the National Research Foundation of Korea (NRF) funded by the Ministry of Education, Science & Technology (No. 2012-009094).

References

1. Nadai, A., Kuroiwa, H., Mizutori, M., Sakai, S.: Measurement of Ocean Surface Currents by the CRL HF Ocean Surface Radar of FMCW Type. Part 2. Current Vector, Journal of Oceanography 55, 13–30 (1999)
2. Song, K.-M., Cho, C.-H., Jung, K.T., Lie, H.-J.: Report on the Present Condition and Operating of High Frequency Ocean Surface Radars in Korea. Journal of Korean Society of Coastal and Ocean Engineers 22, 437–445 (2010)
3. Barrick, D.E., Lilleboe, P.M., Teague, C.C.: Multi-station HF FMCW radar frequency sharing with GPS time modulation multiplexing. United States Patent No. US 6,856,276 B2 (2005)

Vertical Handover Security in 4G Heterogeneous Networks: Threat Analysis and Open Challenges

Naïm Qachri[1], Olivier Markowitch[1], and Jean-Michel Dricot[2],*

[1] Université Libre de Bruxelles
Faculty of Sciences – Computer Science Departement
CP 212, boulevard du Triomphe, 1050 Brussels, Belgium
[2] Université Libre de Bruxelles
Ecole Polytechnique – OPERA Dpt. – Wireless Communications Group
CP 165/51, Avenue Roosevelt 50, 1050 Brussels, Belgium
nqachri@ulb.ac.be

Abstract. In this paper, we propose a review of the mechanisms and procedures to securely manage vertical handovers in heterogeneous networks. The purpose of the paper is to position the heterogeneous networks in the context of wireless security and to describe the possible attacks that come along with this new kind of infrastructure. From a critical analysis of the literature, this paper focuses on the new security challenges that surround the different entities involved in the handover management.

Keywords : Network security, LTE, heterogeneous network, handover mechanisms, mobile networks.

1 Introduction

Heterogeneous Networks (HetNets) is the future of long term evolution of the fourth generation networks (4G-LTE advanced). It is a concept where a telecommunication operator can expand the access to its network by integrating two or more different technologies. For instance, HetNets encompass well-known technologies such as 3G, WiFi, and WiMax to further improve the Quality of Service (QoS) and available bandwidth.

The heterogeneous networks have their specific infrastructures that imply new weaknesses due to diversity of the technologies used to connect the network. Several and distinct security protocols and cryptographic primitives must cohabit, each technology having its weaknesses and legacies. Also, the topology of the deployment changes and the security is no longer *on the last mile*. For instance, most Wi-Fi access points will be deployed in the personal environment of the customers. Identically, femtocells – a small and low-power base station for cellular networks – are deployed in companies and private spaces. Formally, the multi-RAT (Radio Access Technology) devices are within the user premises and the classical security model has to be changed. In HetNets, one cannot consider

---

* Contact author.

T.-h. Kim, Y.-h. Lee, and W.-c. Fang (Eds.): FGIT 2012, LNCS 7709, pp. 7–14, 2012.

the infrastructure as securely managed by the main provider only therefore new challenges arise. Among them, there is the vertical handover, a mechanism to maintain seamlessly the data transmission of a session during a change of point of access sometimes technologically different from the previous point of access.

Contribution: This paper presents a preliminary threat analysis of the vertical handovers within heterogeneous networks from a security point of view. This work is the mandatory preliminary analysis to provide the correct model of assessment for the secure handover mechanisms (present and future) for HetNets.

The remaining of this paper is organized as follows. The Section 2 introduces the HetNet architecture and a definition of the different handovers. Section 3 presents the existing security standards in mobile networks, with a specific focus on this related to vertical handover. Next, in Section 4, new attacks specific to HetNets are presented. In Section 5, a novel meta-model for the security analysis of heterogeneous is presented. Section 6 concludes the paper.

2 The HetNet Architecture and Definitions

A HetNet is a new paradigm to integrate wireless technologies in a converged network. Its general architecture is represented in Fig. 1. More precisely, it can be observed from Fig. 1 that HetNets include three main elements: (i) the access to the network for the mobile device, (ii) the transport of the communication through the IP-based architecture dedicated to the technology, and (iii) the routing of the IP packets within the core network. The different entities/actors of the Next-generation heterogeneous network architecture are defined hereunder.

- The *mobile node* (MN, or UE for user equipment) is the mobile device connecting to the network.
- A *point of access* (PoA) is the point where a mobile node connects to the core network or the backhauling. For instance, it corresponds to the access point in the Wi-Fi terminology or the point of presence (PoP) in the user premises in 3G/4G/LTE.
- The *authentication center* (AuC) is the element where a MN is authenticated to the core network. In 3GPP systems, it is often co-located with the Home Local Register (*HLR*).
- The *serving PoA* (SPoA) is the point of access from where the mobile node comes during the handover.
- The *transferring PoA* (TPoA) is the point of access to which the mobile node connects during the handover.

It is important to note that the communications between the entities of a telecommunication network are realised by using dedicated and abstract interfaces. For instance, the X2 interface allows eNodeB base stations to communicate autonomously and performs tasks related to the handover.

Finally, the different possible handovers taking place in an heterogeneous network can be defined as follows:

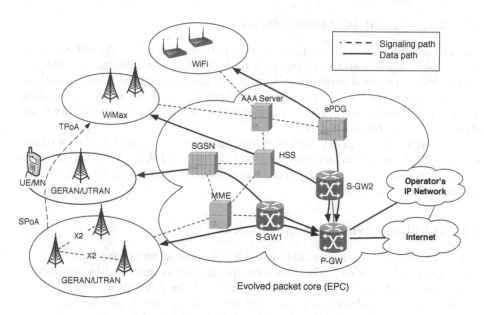

Fig. 1. Next-generation heterogeneous network architecture

Definition 1. *A* hard handover *is the migration of a communication from a point of access (SPoA) to the network to another one (TPoA) with a complete disconnection from the old point of access and a connection to the TPoA from the mobile device.*

Definition 2. *A* soft handover *is the migration of a communication from a point of access to the network to another one without disconnecting the mobile node.*

Definition 3. *An* horizontal handover *occurs when an handover is processed between two point of access with the same technology.*

Definition 4. *A* vertical handover *occurs when an handover is processed between two point of access from two different technologies.*

We now provide the reader with the existing security solutions in mobile and data networks.

3   Existing Security Standards for Mobile Networks

The ITU-T X.800/X.805 recommendations define most of the potential threats present in mobile networks: (i) *denial of service* which is the destruction of information and/or network resources; (ii) *corruption/modification* through the unauthorized tampering with an asset; (iii) *removal/destruction* or theft of information or resources : (iv) *information disclosure* consisting of an unauthorized access to the information or assets; (v) *unavailability* of the network services ; and (vi) *accountability* which translates into an overbilling of the customer.

3.1 2G, 3G, and 4G Mobile Networks

The 2G architecture was based on A5/2 and A5/1 encryption algorithms which were rapidly broken and were replaced by the A5/3 algorithm in 3G systems. Furthermore, a mutual authentication protocol has replaced the previous authentication protocol. However, a weakness still remains and lies in the negotiation of the chosen encryption algorithm before a session, giving an opportunity to an attacker to compromise the device.

The 3GPP release 11 [1] aims at integrating the 4G technology but without specifically changing the security architecture. The HLR or AAA server keeps the same responsibilities, and, even if the femtocells are introduced, the PoA's is still supposed to be trusted.

3.2 Wi-Fi and WiMax Data Networks

The IEEE 802.11 standard was designed to provide wireless extensions to Ethernet local area networks. The handover mechanism is managed by means of a *distribution system* (DS) that is not in charge of the AAA protocols. The evolution of the technology has introduced the authentication severs like Radius through IEEE 802.1X [2]. The last draft of the IEEE 802.11 standard [2] includes a convergence with 3GPP standards with, e.a., the EAP-SIM protocol for authentication and key agreement protocol. The IEEE 802.16 WiMAX [3] uses the same security mechanisms and protocols as IEEE 802.11 (excepted the choice of some cryptographic encryption algorithms).

3.3 Related Works Specific to Handover Security

The authors in [4, 5] propose a simple framework to manage handovers. Their solution is similar to the EAP framework but the study of the security assets management for vertical handover is not presented. Furthermore, the use of an additional server dedicated to handovers management (like a Radius server) is inefficient in terms of signalling.

In [6, 7], the authors discuss about handover, but do not make a difference between vertical and horizontal handovers, which is misleading with respect to the security assets management. For instance, 3DES in its two keys version needs a 112 bit key length while AES requires 128 bits and it is unclear how the protocols manages this key length difference. Furthermore, a third party is involved in [6], which in turns, generates additional signalling load.

The IEEE 802.21 standard [8] aims at providing a media independent handover (MIH) mechanism. It consists in the addition of an intermediary layer between the OSI Layers 2 and 3. This new layer is in charge of interfacing the different technologies (e.g., WiFi, WiMax, 3G). Also, it describes clearly primitives that the future releases of the 3GPP and IEEE standards for wireless technologies must integrate in order to provide media-independent functionalities. The efficiency of the framework has been evaluated in [9, 10] but not its security. The authors in [11] have studied the security mechanisms of MIH between Wi-Fi and WiMAX using an EAP framework and the IKEv2 authentication protocol.

However, the analysis of the security efficiency is superficial and the authors make the misleading assumption that the handover is secure because it is build on an addition of secure building blocks.

A unified authentication protocol is detailed in [12] with a focus on the security assets of the 4G architecture. Unfortunately, the analysis of the security is relatively informal and does not consider the possible corruption of some entities in the network, like the base stations.

Finally, the proposal of the 3rd Generation Partnership Project consortium (3GPP) is to establish secure VPN tunnels between the UE in an untrusted WLAN and the core network. Unfortunately, this will not protect the system against new sets of attacks, such as those oriented towards the non-trusted base stations.

4 Analysis of the New Challenges and Attacks in HetNets

The HetNets represent a paradigm shift in mobile network architectures by the massive addition of non-trusted entities such as femtocells or wifi access points. By studying the security models and mechanisms of HetNets, the main entities of the networks can be identified from the whole entities involved in the communication. The derived meta-model is presented in Fig. 2. Based on this meta-model, we now present the most relevant attacks that are specific to future HetNets.

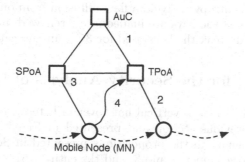

Fig. 2. Generic network model of vertical handover in heterogeneous network

Attacks from a Malicious Node − In HetNets, it is possible for an attacker to capture the traffic that is encrypted with different algorithms during the handover. Therefore, cryptanalytic attacks can take place and allow to recover the session keys. In practice, most of the attacks of a malicious node take place on the channel 4 and channel 2 from Fig. 2.

We now present another attack. Let us consider that the handover mechanisms forwards to the TPoA the encryption and authentication keys through the channel 3, but not the sequence number.[1] A malicious node that has stored the session of communication will be able to replay the session stored (e.g., from

---

[1] A sequence number is a unique numerical value that is incremented at each secure packet exchange.

an eavesdrop on the channel 4), with a sequence number reseted, without needing the security assets. The replay will use the same encryption keys from the SPoA, before the mobile node migrates. It will then create a denial of service for the original mobile node.

Attacks from a Corrupted Point of Access – In classical 3G/4G architecture, the infrastructure is considered secure. In HetNets, the SPoA could duplicate the security assets and eavesdrop the conversation between the TPoA and the core network in order to capture the communication (Information Disclosure). This attack affects the channels 1 and 3. Other attacks from a corrupted PoA will be a variant of Denial of Service attack. None of the solutions presented in Section 3.3 prevent that specific threat.

Attacks from a Malicious Node Cooperating with a Point of Access – A malicious nodes can create over-billing attacks by sending to the malicious node the security assets after the handover. Subsequently, the malicious node can initiate, with the help of corrupted SPoA, a double handover that will consists in cloning a session of communication without giving to the cloned node the entire authentication informations.

Flaw Diffusion, Cryptographic Primitives – The heterogeneity and the legacy leads to a natural diversity of cryptographic primitives and protocols. For instance, a handover can take place between WiMAX (which works on 3DES) and a 3G TPoA (working with KASUMI) and the encryption keys must be rekeyed with enough entropy to avoid a flaw diffusion from one primitive to the other. More precisely, if the keys are inadequately renewed, breaking the 3DES encryption key would break the keys used for 3G communications.

5   Meta-Model for the Security Analysis of LTE HetNets

Our generic network model of vertical handover in heterogeneous network was introduced in the previous section and presented in Fig. 2. A novel security analysis is required since all the propositions presented in Section 3 put their trusts on the network channels 1 and 3, and the entities AuC, SPoA and TPoA are considered to be ultimately secure. In an HetNet, the use of elements outside of the core networks brings possible corruptibility, as demonstrated in Section 4.

Novel Security Model – We propose a preliminary meta-model that includes the actual entities and channel for legacy purposes. The following trusts are introduced. First, the AuC remains the most trusted entity; it has to verify the legitimacy of the different PoA's that are connected to the core network. Next, the PoAs trust their communication channels, but not each other due to their potential corruptibility. This point is extremely important since, in the 4G architecture, the base stations (i.e., the eNodeB) will be allowed to self-optimize and exchange informations autonomously by means of a dedicated interface, referred to as "X2 interface".

Finally, The mobile node must be equally considered as trusted or untrusted and both scenarios must be specifically assessed.

Meta-Protocol – Most of the presented protocols exhibit similar behaviors and can be summarized by a generic meta-protocol presented in [5] and in Fig. 3. This meta-protocol represents a generic signalization required by any kind of handover in a mobile network.

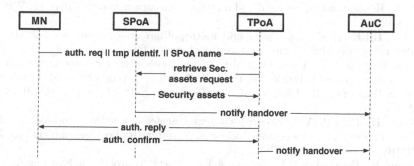

Fig. 3. The meta-protocol to manage a vertical or horizontal handover [5]

This meta-protocol is a first step towards a formal analysis of the security in HetNets. However, it should be extended to encompass the management of the security assets (e.g., the secret keys) as well. Also, the trust on the channel of communication and the entities must be carefully re-defined.

Several open questions remain. For instance, the IEEE 802.11 standard does not implement a complete rekeying during a handover management. Also, the rekeying between 3G and WiMAX exists for technologies using the same algorithms and do not consider different keys lengths. Finally, the deployment of femtocells for LTE cannot guarantee that the points of access are not corrupted.

6 Conclusions and Future Works

This paper has presented a preliminary analysis of the security of vertical handover mechanisms in the context of 4G/HetNets. Security flaws and HetNet-specific attacks have been presented and a novel threat model was introduced. The presented framework is generic and can be used to build efficient and secure mechanism that manage the vertical handover in heterogeneous networks. This work is currently being extended in order to propose novel lightweight handover mechanisms and protocols that will be based on our meta-protocol and formally analyzed.

Acronyms

GERAN GSM Edge Radio Access Network – **UTRAN** Universal Terrestrial Radio Access Network – **NodeB** UMTS base station – **MME** Mobility Management Entity – **HSS** Home Subscriber Server – **ePDG** Evolved Packet Data Gateway – **SGSN** Serving GPRS Support Node – **AAA** authentication, authorization and accounting – **S-GW** Serving gateway – **P-GW** Packet Data Network Gateway – **UE** user equipment.

References

1. 3GPP. 3rd generation partnership project; technical specification group services and system aspects; 3gpp system architecture evolution (sae); security architecture, release 11 (June 2012)
2. IEEE, IEEE standard for local and metropolitan area networks - part 11: Wireless lan's (2012)
3. IEEE, IEEE standard for local and metropolitan area networks - part 16: Air interface for broadband wireless access systems (2009)
4. Park, S., Kim, P.S.: A new vertical handover mechanism for convergence of wired and wireless access networks. In: Park, Y.-J., Choi, Y. (eds.) Proc. of ICOIN 2009 Proceedings of the 23rd Intl. Conf. on Information Networking, pp. 102–107. IEEE (2009)
5. Wang, H., Prasad, A.R.: Security context transfer in vertical handover. In: 14th IEEE Proceedings on Personal Indoor and Mobile Radio Communications 2003 PIMRC 2003, pp. 2775–2779 (2003)
6. Marin, R., Fernandez, P.J., Gomez, A.F.: 3-Party Approach for Fast Handover in EAP-Based Wireless Networks. In: Meersman, R. (ed.) OTM 2007, Part II. LNCS, vol. 4804, pp. 1734–1751. Springer, Heidelberg (2007)
7. Lim, S.-H., Bang, K.-S., Yi, O., Lim, J.: A Secure Handover Protocol Design in Wireless Networks with Formal Verification. In: Boavida, F., Monteiro, E., Mascolo, S., Koucheryavy, Y. (eds.) WWIC 2007. LNCS, vol. 4517, pp. 67–78. Springer, Heidelberg (2007)
8. IEEE, IEEE standard for local and metropolitan area networks - part 21: Media independent handover services (2008)
9. Dutta, A., Das, S., Famolari, D., Ohba, Y., Taniuchi, K., Fajardo, V., Lopez, R.M., Kodama, T., Schulzrinne, H.: Seamless proactive handover across heterogeneous access networks. Wirel. Pers. Commun. 43(3) (November 2007)
10. Lampropoulos, G., Salkintzis, A.K., Passas, N.: Media-independent handover for seamless service provision in heterogeneous networks. IEEE Communications Magazine 46(1), 64–71 (2008)
11. Sun, H.-M., Chen, S.-M., Chen, Y.-H., Chung, H.-J., Lin, I.-H.: Secure and efficient handover schemes for heterogeneous networks. In: Proceedings of the 2008 IEEE Asia-Pacific Services Computing Conference, APSCC 2008, pp. 205–210. IEEE Computer Society, Washington, DC (2008)
12. Krichene, N., Boudriga, N.: Securing roaming and vertical handover in fourth generation networks. In: Proceedings of the 2009 Third International Conference on Network and System Security, NSS 2009, pp. 225–231. IEEE Computer Society Press, Washington, DC (2009)

Three-Dimensional Stacked Memory System
for Defect Tolerance

Haejun Seo[1], Yoonseok Heo[2], and Taewon Cho[1]

[1] Department of Electronics Engineering, College of Electrical & Computer Engineering,
Chungbuk National University, ChungBuk, Korea
{hjseo,twcho}@chungbuk.ac.kr
[2] Faculty of Electrical & Electronic Engineering, Chungcheong University,
ChungBuk, Korea
hys@ok.ac.kr

Abstract. This paper presents a method for constructing a memory system using defective memory chips comprising faulty storage blocks. The three-dimensional memory system introduced here employs a die-stacked structure of faulty memory chips. Signals lines passing through the through-silicon-vias (TSVs) connect chips in the defect tolerant structure. Defective chips are classified into several groups each group comprising defective chips having faulty blocks at the same location. A defect tolerant memory system is constructed using chips from different groups. Defect-free storage blocks from spare chips replace faulty blocks using additional routing circuitry. The number of spare memory chips for defect tolerance is $s= \lceil (k \times n) / (m - k) \rceil$ to make a system defect tolerant for $(n + s)$ chips with k faulty blocks among m independently addressable blocks.

Keywords: Defect tolerance, DFB(Defect Free Block), TSV(Through Silicon Via), IAB(Independently Addressable Block), spare chips.

1 Introduction

The probability of defect occurrences increases as VLSI feature size keeps shrinking with nano-scale process. Multi-layered chip stacking becomes a promising breakthrough implementing high capacity memories. Defect of inner dies of a package affects fatal influence on system operation resulting in failure of costly die stacked systems. Defect tolerant structure has been concerned in terms of contribution to improve yield. Defect tolerance will be continuously studied as slight defect is fatal to system operation with the development of nanotechnology and chip stacking structure. In deep submicron structure, it is expected that cost for additional function for defect tolerance to be minimal. The semiconductor memory is the most successful application of shrinking technology. Yield improvement is the most integral part to win tough semiconductor market competition. It is not possible to meet the market price without any plan for defect tolerance. A typical way to tolerate defects is to replace defective elements with spares. Substantial effort has been devoted to get defect free memory systems with reasonable amount of redundancy [1].

T.-h. Kim, Y.-h. Lee, and W.-c. Fang (Eds.): FGIT 2012, LNCS 7709, pp. 15–24, 2012.

Semiconductor chip stacking technology draws serious attention as a promising tool to reduce package volume with substantial speed and power improvement [2]. The key point of the chip stacking technology is connection with through silicon via (TSV) between inter chips [3]. It is possible to make connection from upper to bottom of a memory chip economic and reliable [4]. Figure 1 illustrates inter-die wire. Wires of large number between the dies are possible, and this can be connected over several dies by TSV. If the stacking structure is applied to high capacity memory system, new method for defect tolerance is demanded.

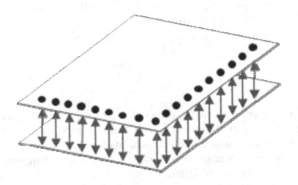

Fig. 1. Inter-die wire between stacked chips

This paper presents a method for defect tolerance in three dimensional architecture employing structure of stacked memory chips. Conventional two dimensional defect tolerance addresses reconfiguration of storage blocks within a chip. Another approach is to use spare chip to reconfigure the addressing scheme to replace faulty storage blocks. A three dimensional architecture introduces a defect-free chip as a spare to replace defective memory blocks of a stacked memory system [7]. The proposed scheme is to build up a defect-tolerant memory system using defective memory chips. The memory system works as if it does not have any logical faults from faulty chips. Defective chips are selected by a defined way, stacked and interconnected using TSVs, and then routing logic replaces signals from defective locations with the ones from spares. Defective chips even after repair are grouped into classes considering the number of defective blocks and the addresses of defective blocks. A chip classification rules, memory system structure and routing logic and the estimation of the number of spare chips will be discussed with some evaluations.

This paper is organized as follows: Section 2 describes TSV technology necessary to convert conventional 2-D structure into 3-D along with a process to construct 4 normal memory chips from 4 defective memory chips and a defect-free memory chip. Section 3 presents a structure built from defective chips only. Section 4 analyzes the system to yield the number of redundant chips to make the whole system logically normal.   Section 5 concludes with brief evaluation.

2   Memory Stacking and Defect Tolerance

2.1   Chip-Stacking Technology

Chip stacking is a simple way to build a high capacity memory system without introducing costly next generation semiconductor process and device technology. Figure 2 depicts an example of memory system with multiple die layers. The jth storage block of the ith chip of a stacked memory system can be represented as a pair (i, j). This type of chip stacking has been announced by Samsung in 2006 for high capacity flash memory system in a package [5]. Many systems including not only memories but also most system on chip applications will employ this three-dimensional package in near future [6].

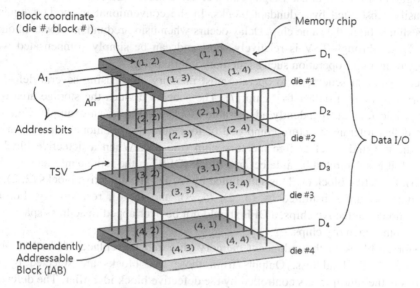

Fig. 2. Memory stacking using TSV

2.2   Implementation of TSV Technology

Through silicon via (TSV) is the key technology necessary to build a stacked memory chip system using multi layers of dies. When dies are stacked to form a circuit entity, effective interconnection is required to pass through a silicon body of a chip since active circuit structure is formed on one-side of die surface. The TSV provides with reliable electrical connection between the top and the bottom sides of a silicon die. The TSV is formed by drilling the dies chemically. Currently TSV is implemented using cylindrical copper filling with diameter of 5 to 20 μm. TSV technology is now being spread out to commercial products with stable fabrication process.

TSV technology gives a number of advantages. Signal transmission through TSV is much faster than conventional chip I/O due to shorter signal traveling distance, and thereby high speed operation is possible. Smaller footprint size allows massive inter-die interconnections with smaller area overhead. Signals from smaller local circuit blocks can be exchanged among stacked dies resulting in practical three-dimensional circuit structure. It reduces power consumption substantially eliminating input and output pads which need excessive operating energy. Heat dissipation problems are mitigated significantly. Each die of a system may carry exotic characteristics secured by its own optimized process technology.

2.3   Conventional Defect-Tolerance Method

TSV interconnection among stacked memory chips allows straightforward reconfiguration for cell block assignment. Defective blocks are efficiently intercepted and easily substituted by redundant blocks. In the conventional method, redundant blocks should be in the same chip. Delay occurs when using redundant blocks in other chips. Delay through TSV is relatively short and can be simply compensated with strategy of memory operation such as memory interleaving.

A conventional scheme is to operate most memory chips using several defective memory chips and a defect free chip [7]. The scheme divides the storage area of a memory into four independently addressable blocks (IABs) as an example. Figure 3 shows defect tolerant structure composed of four defective memory chips (from die #1 to die #4) and a defect free memory chip (die #5). When a defective block is accessed, it is substituted by a defect free block (DFB) in the redundant memory chip (die #5). Defective block (1, 1) is substituted by (5, 1). The defective blocks (2, 2), (3, 3), and (4, 4) are substituted by (5, 2), (5, 3), and (5, 4), respectively. For the composition of defective chips, a DFB should not be overlapped in address space with DFBs in other memory chips.

A storage block in the redundant memory chip and its replaced defective block share the identical address. Outputs from those two blocks are selected by the switches in the multiplexers controlled by the defective block identifier. The defective block identifier reads incoming address and sends routing signals to four multiplexers. The multiplexers then switch off the data from a defective block, and send out the ones from the spare die.

The design shown in Figure 3 implements defect tolerance with four defective memory chips and one defect free memory chip. A defect free memory chip should be included so that it can be used to replace faulty memory blocks of the defective chips. The address spaces of the four defective blocks must not be overlapped. Next section explains a system with defective memory chips, and thereby contributes to yield improvement by making defective chips useful.

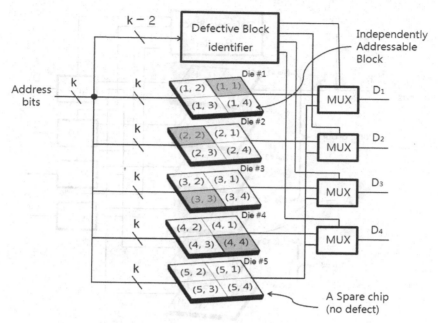

Fig. 3. Defect tolerant system with defective memory chips and a defect free chip [7]

3   Memory System Using Only Defective Memories

The new defect tolerant memory system is to use defective memory chips only in implementing normal memory operation. It is assumed that each chip has one defective storage block. No defect-free chips are involved in this proposed design. A design is illustrated for demonstration purposes, where 6 defective memory chips used to yield a memory system equivalent to the one having four defect-free chips. The four of the six chips comprise defective storage blocks. Addresses of defective storage blocks differ from each other. The remaining two chips are spares.

3.1   System Architecture

The six chip system employs TSVs for inter-chip connection as shown in Figure 4. Chips are number from the top layer to the bottom: Die #1 through Die #6. The number of storage blocks of a chip is assumed to be four. We call this four dies as a working group of the system. Memory chips of Die #1 to Die #4 are selected to have the different addresses of defective blocks from each other, while Die #5 and Die #6 may have the same defective locations as the ones in Die #1 through Die #4. In Figure 4, the locations of defective blocks (1, 1), (5, 1) and (2, 2), (6, 2) are overlapped.

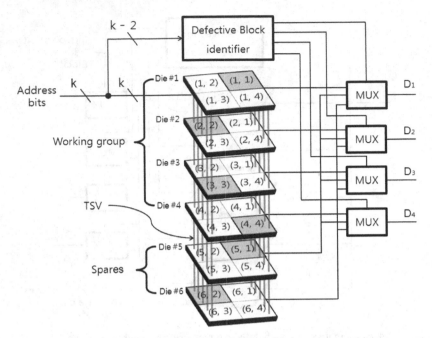

Fig. 4. Defect tolerant system using only defective memory chips

In the defect tolerant system a working group of four memory chips, normally operate with other two spare defective chips. When defective blocks in the working group are addressed, the outputs from the blocks are switched off, and replaced by the outputs from the defect free blocks in the memory chip #5 and #6. In the case of overlapped defective blocks, the defective block (1, 1) is substituted with (5, 2) and (2, 2) is substituted with (6, 1) to minimize the distance between those chips. Similarly, (3, 3) is and (4, 4) substituted with (5, 3) and (6, 4), respectively. In this case, the distance between the chips is 2 layers.

TSVs connect the stacked chips. Due to TSV, signal and data transmission can be easily performed. While the peripheral circuitry in a conventional system carries out data transmission, the proposed system performs direct signal and data transmission through TSV. However, for (1, 1) and (5, 1), it is expected that there might be the delay of transmission.

3.2   Defect Tolerance Process

Two stage allocation steps assign DFBs in the spare chips to defective blocks in the working group chips: allocation of defective blocks that have DFB with the same address in the spare chips; allocation of remaining defective IABs. For example, the first stage of the allocation assigns blocks (1, 1) and (2, 2) of Figure 5(a) to (5, 2) and (6, 1), respectively. Then the second stage allocates the remaining two defective blocks (3, 3) and (4, 4) of Figure 5(b) to (5, 3) and (6, 4), respectively.

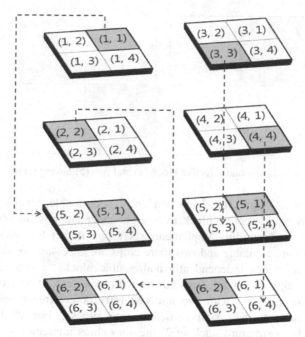

Fig. 5. The case when defective block is overlapped (a) and the process of defect tolerant if it's not (b)

4   Number of Chips for Redundancy

The number of redundant chips depends on the number of defective storage blocks of each chip in the system. The estimation begins with a system comprising four memory chips, and then extended to the system with 2^n chips. Each chip assumes to have four independently addressable storage blocks and one of its storage blocks to be defective.

Consider the case of 1 defective block per chip. Twelve DFBs are available among sixteen IABs in four memory chips, since each chip comprises three defect free blocks and one defective block. Four additional defect free blocks are necessary to implement sixteen defect free blocks. The number of spare chips is two, since a spare chip has three DFBs. Assume that a system comprises eight stacked memory chips and each chip has eight IABs. The system should implement thirty two defect free blocks, but comprises twenty four defect free blocks. Two spare chips are necessary to supply additional eight defect free blocks.

The estimation can be extended to the cases of two defective blocks per chip. There are two defective blocks from four independently addressable blocks of a chip. The case of four IABs per chip needs eight additional DFBs to cover the nominal memory address space. Four additional chips are needed. A structure comprising eight blocks per chip should implement thirty two defect free blocks, but obtains sixteen defect free blocks are available in the working group. For defect tolerance, sixteen defect free blocks are needed which is equivalent to eight memory chips.

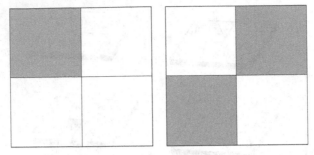

Fig. 6. The case when there's one defective block (a) and two (b) having 4 blocks per one chip

Consider cases of eight to 2^n independently addressable blocks per chip. A structure that has one defective block from eight independently addressable blocks comprising eight memory chips implements sixty four defect free blocks. Fifty six defect free blocks are available and two spare chips are necessary to add eight defect free blocks. With sixteen independently addressable blocks, a structure comprises sixteen memory chips and obtains two hundred fifty six defect free blocks. Because the working group provides with two hundred forty defect free blocks, two spare chips are necessary to add sixteen defect free blocks. For 2^n independently addressable blocks, a structure stacking 2^n memory chips implements 2^{2n} defect free blocks. It yields $(2^{2n} - 2^n)$ independently addressable blocks. Let m and s denote the number of IABs in a memory and the number of spare chips. The estimation of $s(2^n - 1) \geq 2^n$ is used to decide the number of spare memory chips to add $2^{2n} - (2^{2n} - 2^n) = 2^n$ defect free blocks. Here m denotes the number of spare memory chips. Defect tolerance can be accomplished when the number of defect free blocks in spare chips is more than the number of defect free blocks to be added. For $s = 1$, $(2^n - 1) \geq 2^n$ then it is not satisfied. For $s = 2$, $(2^{n+1} - 2) \geq 2^n$ then it is satisfied, hence the number of spare chips to be added is two.

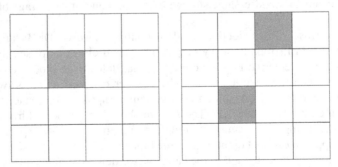

Fig. 7. The case when there's one defective block (a) and two (b) having 16 blocks per one chip

Assume that there are two defective blocks for each chip. A structure comprising eight memory chips with eight independently addressable blocks implements sixty four defect free blocks. Forty eight defect free blocks can be obtained and three spare chips are necessary to add sixteen defect free blocks. A system with sixteen independently addressable blocks implements two hundred fifty six blocks and obtains two hundred twenty four defect free blocks. To add thirty two defect free blocks, three spare chips are necessary. For 2^n independently addressable blocks, a system implements 2^{2n} defect free blocks. The system yields $2^{2n} - 2^{n+1}$ defect free blocks. The system needs $2^{2n} - (2^{2n} - 2^{n+1}) = 2^{n+1}$ defect free blocks. Estimation of $s(2^{n+1} - 2) \geq 2^{n+1}$ decides the number of spare chips. For s=3, $(3 \times 2^{n+1} - 6) \geq 2^{n+1}$ then it is satisfied and the number of spare chips is three.

Assume k defective blocks are in each memory chip. The system with k defective blocks implements 2^{2n} defect free blocks, and obtains $2^{2n} - k \cdot 2^n$ defect free blocks. The number of defect free blocks to be added is $k \cdot 2^n$ and thereby k+1 spare chip is necessary. Also for $s < 2^n$, the case of the number of stacked chips is much less than the number of independently addressable blocks, the number of spare chips are calculated as follows. Here $\ulcorner x \urcorner$ represents the ceiling function on x. Table 1 summarizes the number of spare chips reflecting the number of defective storage blocks.

$$S = \ulcorner (k \times n) / (m - k) \urcorner \tag{1}$$

The number of IABs in a memory chip exceeds thousands in typical large capacity memories. While the stacking technology can handle several dozen dies at most. For k defective storage area per chip, k+1 spare chips make working group defect tolerant with large capacity memories with sparse defects. Note that the addresses of defective blocks should be different each other within a working group.

Table 1. The number of spare chips reflecting the number of defective storage blocks

Defective storage blocks	1 block / chip			2 blocks / chip			3 blocks / chip			..	k blocks / chip
IAB / chip	8	16	2^n	8	16	2^n	8	16	2^n		2^n
Stacked dies	8	16	2^n	8	16	2^n	8	16	2^n		2^n
Total IAB / sys.	64	256	2^{2n}	64	256	2^{2n}	64	256	2^{2n}		2^{2n}
DFB / sys.	56	240	$2^{2n} - 2^n$	48	224	$2^{2n} - 2^{n+1}$	40	208	$2^{2n} - 3 \cdot 2^n$		$2^{2n} - k \cdot 2^n$
DFB needed	8	16	2^n	16	32	2^{n+1}	24	48	$3 \cdot 2^n$		$k \cdot 2^n$
Spare chips / sys.	2	2	2	3	3	3	5	4	4		k+1

5   Conclusion

Defect tolerance presented in this paper addresses the redundancy structure in building a memory system with chips each comprising defective storage blocks. The memory chips are stacked and interconnected using through silicon vias to form a three dimensional structure. Defective blocks of working memory space are replaced with defect free storage blocks of spare chips. Signals among chips are transmitted through TSV nets to prevent excessive delay or power dissipation. The number of memory spare chips is that $S = \lceil (k \times n) / (m - k) \rceil$ for the memory stacked system with $(n + s)$ defective chips each comprising k defective storage blocks among its m storage blocks. This scheme allows defective chips can be used to build a complete memory system without significant performance degradation, and thereby enhances manufacturing yield. The scheme can be extended to three dimensional memory test and fault tolerance.

References

1. Niggemeyer, D., Otterstedt, J., Redeker, M.: A defect-tolerant DRAM employing a hierarchical redundancy scheme, built-in self-test and self-reconfiguration. In: Proceedings, International Workshop on Memory Technology, Design and Testing, pp. 33–40 (1997)
2. Venkatasubramanian, G., Boykin, P.O., Figueiredo, R.J.: Design of high-yield defect-tolerant self-assembled nanoscale memories. In: IEEE International Symposium on Nanoscale Architecture (NANOARCH 2007), pp. 77–84 (2007)
3. Motoyoshi, M.: Through-silicon via (TSV). Proceedings of the IEEE 97(1), 43–48 (2009)
4. Yasufuku, T., et al.: Effect of resistance of TSV's on performance of boost converter for low power 3D SSD with NAND flash memories. In: IEEE International Conference on 3D System Integration (2009)
5. Jang, D.M., et al.: Development and Evaluation of 3-D SiP with Vertically Interconnected Through Silicon Vias (TSV). In: Proc. IEEE Int'l Electronic Components and Tech. Conf., pp. 847–850 (2007)
6. Gerke, D.: NASA 2009 Body of Knowledge (BoK): Through-Silicon Via Technology, JPL Publication 09-28 11/09, NASA WBS: 724927.40.43, JPL Project Number: 103982, Task Number: 03.03.15, download (April 1, 2010), http://nepp.nasa.gov
7. You, Y., Han, S.: Design methodology of normal memory systems design methodology with defective memories, Korean Patent Number 0336434 (2002)

VCPU Shaping for Supporting Latency Sensitive Workloads

Byung Ki Kim[1,*], Chuck Yoo[2], and Young Woong Ko[1]

[1] Dept. of Computer Engineering, Hallym University, Chuncheon, Korea
{bkkim,yuko}@hallym.ac.kr
[2] Dept. of Computer Science and Engineering, Korea University, Seoul, Korea
hxy@os.korea.ac.kr

Abstract. In virtual machine environments, it is difficult to allocate CPU resource in a timely manner when lots of domains are in BOOST priority. In this paper, we present a virtual machine scheduling scheme based on VCPU shaping and efficiently deals with multi BOOST problem. We evaluate our prototype in terms of latency over diverse workloads. Our experiment result shows that the proposed realtime priority scheme effectively allocates CPU resources for low latency guest domain over varying workloads.

Keywords: Xen, realtime, scheduler, QoS, resource monitor.

1 Introduction

Today, computer systems are becoming more complex and more powerful, merging various functionalities into a single platform. Virtualization is an emerging technology that can provide scaling computer system efficiently and reduce running/management costs by running multiple OSs simultaneously on a single computer. From the perspective of server consolidation, virtualization technology provides many benefits. Virtualization helps to improve utilization of the existing infrastructure and to save money by reducing energy consumption. When there are fewer physical server machines, it leads to decreased energy consumption. To take advantage of this potential, there has been considerable effort to exploit virtualization technology in a realtime system [1][2][3]. Particularly, there are a variety of possible requirements when handling real-time applications in a virtualization environment, such as streaming servers, telephony servers, and game servers. However, supporting realtime guarantees is not easy because it is difficult to predict guest domains CPU requirement exactly. Therefore, to guarantee the real-time execution of a task, it is necessary to deal with the workload of guest domain exactly. In this paper, we present a virtual machine scheduling

* This work was supported by the National Research Foundation of Korea(NRF) grant funded by the Korea government(MEST) (No. 2011-0029848), and Basic Science Research Program through the National Research Foundation of Korea(NRF) funded by the Ministry of Education, Science and Technology(2010-0005442).

T.-h. Kim, Y.-h. Lee, and W.-c. Fang (Eds.): FGIT 2012, LNCS 7709, pp. 25–32, 2012.
© Springer-Verlag Berlin Heidelberg 2012

scheme based on realtime priority and efficiently deals with multi BOOST problem. The multi BOOST problem arises from allowing multiple domains to be boosted equally without considering its characteristics. This results in increased latency for time sensitive domains because the credit scheduler is not aware of urgency among tasks within different guest domains.

2   Related Works

Many research results on virtual machine are roughly focused on improving I/O performance, network response, CPU allocation, resource monitoring and real time guarantee. [2] suggested a soft real-time scheduler for the Xen hypervisor by modifying a credit scheduler to calculate scheduling priorities dynamically. They defined a laxity value that provides an estimate of when tasks need to be scheduled next. When a VCPU of a real-time domain is ready, it is inserted where its deadline is expected to be met. This approach allows low-latency tasks to be executed in a timely manner. However, it cannot guarantee realtime workloads because it does not provide an admission control mechanism. Therefore, if the workloads increase, it cannot meet the deadline of realtime tasks. Vsched[3] is a user-level scheduling tool using a periodic realtime scheduling model. Vsched does not run directly on the hardware but rather on the top of a host operating system. Their approach is quite straightforward to describe realtime workloads because a domain is regarded as a process. However, to support real-time workloads accurately, the host operating system should support realtime characteristics such as a fine-grained preemption mechanism, prevention of priority inversion, and fast interrupt handling, among others. RT-Xen[4] introduces a hierarchical realtime scheduling framework in Xen. The key idea with RT-Xen is to provide a sporadic server root scheduler for Xen that is compatible with a RM scheduling and it uses 1 ms scheduling resolution while incurring moderate overhead. However, RT-Xen cannot support an admission control mechanism for a realtime domain. Therefore, with excessive workloads, it is difficult to guarantee realtime workloads.

3   Support for Latency Sensitive Domain

Xen's credit scheduler is a proportional fair share CPU scheduler. It allows domain fairly share the CPU resource depend on *weight*. To minimize the I/O latency, credit scheduler introduced BOOST mechanism for I/O intensive domains which are sleep and wake very often. Also, it features global load balancing across physical cores on a multi-core processor. Credit load balancer tries to reduce idle state of each PCPU. The BOOST mechanism improved I/O performance in Xen. When a domain blocks and wakes up often credit scheduler temporally boosts the priority of awaking VCPUs. If this VCPU consumes a non negligible amount of CPU(normally 10ms), its priority will be reset to UNDER. If on the other hand the VCPU consumes little CPU and is blocking and awoken a lot (doing

I/O for example), its priority will remain boosted, optimizing it's wake-to-run latencies. This BOOST mechanism allows wake-to-run latency sensitive VCPUs to preempt more CPU resource intensive VCPUs without impacting overall system fairness.

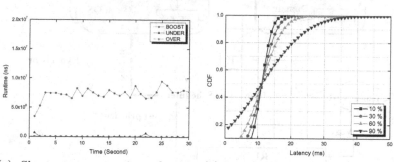

(a) Short term running domain scheduling information   (b) Latency depending on workload

Fig. 1. Latency increased by other boosted domain

The boosted priority normally staying BOOST for 10ms. If their are domains with periodic tasks which works for short-term period(under 10ms) and blocks periodically. These domain are likely to be boosted. As shown in Figure 1(a), the domain with periodic task has been scheduled with BOOST priority. If there are domains with similar workload, credit scheduler will schedule these domains with BOOST priority. In this case, there is CPU contention which impacts the I/O response time. It is known that the credit scheduler has shortcoming to support latency sensitive domains although I/O intensive domain has BOOST priority. This is not able to support latency sensitive domains. When the CPU intensive domains are working periodically, both I/O and CPU intensive domains are boosted. It induces CPU contention because of multiple boosted priority. In this reason, the credit scheduler is insufficient to support a time-sensitive domains due to its latency caused by boosted multi-domain. Note that split drivers require an additional scheduling delay between the driver domain and a guest domain when a domain requests I/O interrupt. Although credit has BOOST priority to improve I/O performance it is not sufficient for latency sensitive domains. The major limitation is credit scheduler allows multiple domains to be boosted equally without considering its characteristics. This results in increased latency for time sensitive domains because the credit scheduler is not aware of urgency among tasks within different guest domains. In this section we analyze the circumstance that xen scheduler cannot support time sensitive domains, and propose a mechanism to keep the latency low.

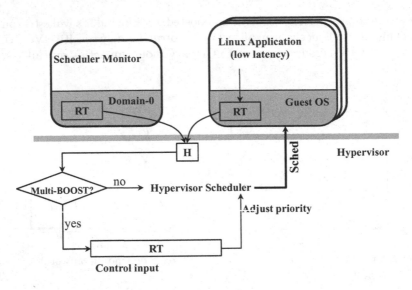

Fig. 2. System architecture

4   Scheduling Latency in Xen

To schedule VCPU on time, VMM should provide admission control mechanism in real time. Figure 2 shows the overall architecture of the proposed system. We propose a scheduler monitoring tool to support latency sensitive domain. The proposed system is composed of three parts; first, QoS monitor module in guest operating system checks whether realtime tasks miss their deadline. If there is deadline miss in a certain level, QoS monitor geneate urgent message VMM scheduler through hypercall. In this work, we made additional hypercall interface to request RT priority. Second, Scheduler monitoring tool in domain-0 oversees domain's behavior to detect the multi-BOOST. Third, in hypervisor, we implemented control module which receives hypercall from guest operating system and domain-0. The control module receives the hypercall from guest operating system then credit scheuler chanage the domain priority RT.

To show the scheduling latency over the xen credit scheduler, we measured packet arrival latency at time sensitive domain using ping. Five domains are running over the Xen : domain-0, domain 1 for latency-sensitive I/O domain, domain 2 to 4 for CPU-intensive task, that is calculating MD-5 hash for every 10 ms(30 % CPU load). Then, external server receives the ping from latency-sensitive I/O domain (ping interval is fixed to 10ms). Our xen machine has the 2 physical cores so the domains' VCPUs are migrating across the physical cores by the credit load balancing.

Figure 1(b) show the cumulative latency distribution for three thousand of packet arrival time on external server from guest domain. When cpu-intensive domains block and wake periodically their scheduling priority is BOOST. In this worst case, the latency intensive domains have to contend with the cpu-intensive domains. As the cpu utilization increasing by the multi-boosted domains, the latency for time sensitive domain is increasing.

The delay is not only caused by delayed domain but also domain-0. Figure 3 presents examples of delay caused by multi-BOOST in detail. Here, time sensitive domains about to send a packet to external server. Time sensitive domains are delayed by boosted domains. Also, domain-0 is delayed by other boosted domains. In this multi-BOOST situation, to improve I/O latency, domain-0 has to be compartmentalized in to other boosted domains.

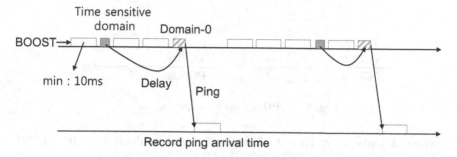

Fig. 3. Scheduling delays by Multi-BOOST

To resolve this problem we introduce VCPU shaping scheme and new RT(Real-Time) priority for the highest priority in credit scheduler. In this work, the proposed system can predict if a VCPU is CPU-intensive or I/O-intensive by using Xen monitoring tools. We assume CPU-intensive VCPU has possibility of multi-BOOST when there are lots of CPU-intensive VCPU. So, the proposed system check CPU-intensive VCPU ratio during system running using Xen monitoring tools[5]. If the ratio is greater than multi-BOOST level, we protect latency sensitive workloads from general workloads by using realtime priority. We added a new hypercall interface to hypervisor that can change the domains' priority to RT. When a urgent domain call *change_rt* hypercall xen scheduler change the domains' priority RT to avoid race conditions caused by multiple BOOST. This mechanism potentially give rise to starvation to other domains. But the credit scheduler share the CPU resource proportionally. When the urgent domain, which has RT priority, use more than 10ms credit scheduler change its priority to normal priority.

4.1 Experimental Setup

In this section, we describe the experiments that evaluate the response time for latency sensitive domains. We built 10 CPU-intensive domains and the latency sensitive domain. All domains have only one VCPU. CPU-intensive domains calculate MD5 hash for every 10 ms periodically. Latency sensitive domain sends a ping to external server for every 10 ms. We record the packet arrival time on external server. The latency is a interval of packet arrival time.

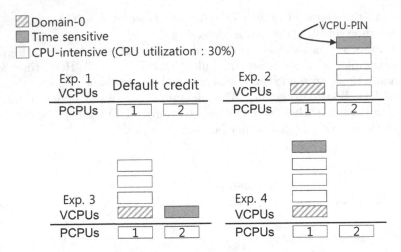

Fig. 4. VCPU set up for experiments

Experiment Category. Exp. 1 : Latency induced by default credit : 3 CPU-intensive domains consume 30% of CPU. All the domains including domain-0 are migrating across the PCPUs by credit load-balancing.

Exp. 2 : Domain-0 is pinned on PCPU-1 which is not busy. Three of CPU-intensive domains are pinned on PCPU-2. PCPU-2 has 90% of CPU utilization. Time sensitive domain is pinned on PCPU-2.

Exp. 3 : Three of CPU-intensive domains are pinned on PCPU-2. We make PCPU-1 busy where the domain-0 is pinned. In this case the driver domain contend with CPU-intensive domains. Time sensitive domain is pinned on PCPU-2 which is not busy.

Exp. 4 : All the domains are pinned on PCPU-1.

5   Result and Evaluation

We measure the latency experiments Exp. 1 through Exp. 4. We plot this in Figure 5(a) for the default credit scheduler and modified VCPU configurations. Each experiment result is varying. Following Exp. 2, latency sensitive domain is pinned on the PCPU-2. There are race condition caused by multi BOOST. The PCPU-1 is not busy. On the other hand, When the latency sensitive domain requests the hardware interrupts, Domain-0 is able to handle this I/O request timely manner. Although there is no race condition on PCPU-1, the reason of increasing latency is scheduling delay by multi BOOST. In the result of Exp.2, we can indicate that Domain-0 is ready to handle I/O requests but the latency domain is have to be scheduled on time. In this case, time sensitive domain can send a hypercall to hypervisor to change this domains' priority RT. In this Figure 5(b), the latency is improved drastically. This result shows the multi BOOST can impact the performance of latency sensitive domain. To reduce the latency, latency sensitive domain has to be compartmentalize into the highest priority

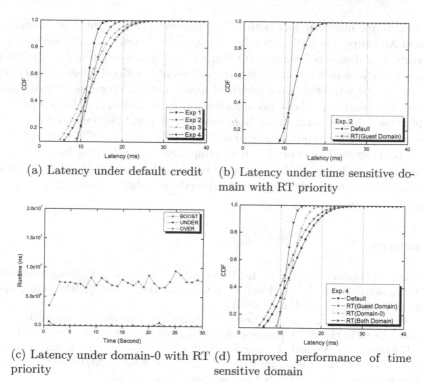

(a) Latency under default credit

(b) Latency under time sensitive domain with RT priority

(c) Latency under domain-0 with RT priority

(d) Improved performance of time sensitive domain

Fig. 5. Result of latency sensitive domain

as RT. We also measure the situation that domain-0 is on the busy PCPU. As following the result of Exp. 3, the latency is increasing too despite latency sensitive domain is using a whole PCPU. This result in Figure 5(c) presents that domain-0 is not sufficient for processing I/O requests from guest domains.

To support latency sensitive domains' I/O requests, domain-0 is need to be scheduled with the highest priority. Compare this result to Exp. 2 its latency is worse. Time sensitive domain is ready to run, but the domain-0 is suffer from race condition. Both domain-0 and time sensitive domains' priority is important to support latency sensitive domains' I/O performance. Exp. 4 explain how the performance of latency is recovering. With the default credit scheduler, Exp. 4 results the worst performance. As shown in the Figure 5(d), proposed mechanism enables the hypervisor support the time sensitive domains. Firstly, time sensitive domains has to be scheduled on time. Secondly, to handling I/O request from time sensitive domain, domain-0 also has to be scheduled promptly.

6   Conclusion

To allocate hardware resources to virtual machines efficiently, it is important to characterize the behavior of virtual machines to improve responsiveness. Virtual machine monitor must support both CPU intensive and I/O intensive domains. Although Xen supports CPU-intensive domains fairly well, it has drawback for supporting I/O domains because I/O domain requires low latency, high bandwidth and provides isolated execution regardless of workload effect of other domains. In this paper, we propose a virtual machine characterizing scheme using Xentrace that analyzes scheduling information from Xentrace information and determines scheduling parameters. Here, we designed and implemented monitoring tools and VCPU shaping mechanism for predicting the CPU usage of each domain. We described an effort for supporting time sensitive domain. The credit scheduler is not sufficient for latency sensitive domain because of multi BOOST. We introduced a new scheduling priority on credit scheduler to compartmentalize the urgent domain.

References

1. Barham, P., Dragovic, B., Fraser, K., Hand, S., Harris, T., Ho, A., Neugebauer, R., Pratt, I., Warfield, A.: Xen and the art of virtualization. ACM SIGOPS Operating Systems Review 37(5), 164–177 (2003)
2. Lee, M., Krishnakumar, A., Krishnan, P., Singh, N., Yajnik, S.: Supporting soft real-time tasks in the xen hypervisor. ACM Sigplan Notices 45, 97–108 (2010)
3. Lin, B., Dinda, P.: Vsched: Mixing batch and interactive virtual machines using periodic real-time scheduling. In: Proceedings of the 2005 ACM/IEEE Conference on Supercomputing, pp. 8–21. IEEE Computer Society (2005)
4. Xi, S., Wilson, J., Lu, C., Gill, C.: Rt-xen: Towards real-time hierarchical scheduling in xen. In: Proceedings of the ACM International Conference on Embedded Software (EMSOFT) (2011)
5. Kim, B.K., Jang, J.H., Hur, K.W., Lee, J.G., Ko, Y.W.: Monitoring and feedback tools for realtime workloads for xen virtual machine. In: Proceedings of the International Conference on IT Convergence and Security 2011, pp. 151–161. Springer, Netherlands (2011)

Architecture for Convegence Mobile Cooperation Service Using Components Integration

Haeng-Kon Kim

School of Information Technology, Catholic University of Deagu, Korea
hangkon@cu.ac.kr

Abstract. In this paper, we describe the AMS(Architecture for Mobile Service) methodology to guide the reflexive development of architectures from the mobile convergence software requirements. In particular, we are detailing the first step of this methodology, the definition of the convergence goals model whose constituents are the fundamental basis for the overall process defined in AMS proving its suitability for obtaining traceable components integration architectural models. It provides our work either to its ability to specify and manage positive and negative interactions mobile services among goals or to its capability to trace low-level details back to high-level concerns. AMS using components integration is a model informing an convergence architecture to design mobile service environments: it combines inference capabilities with the management of contextual components information that is modulated according to the strMobile Applications(MA)ture of physical and logical spaces of mobile service architectures.

Keywords: Convergence Architecture, Mobile Service Integration, Mobile computing, Mobile Cooperation, Contextual Information, Agent Based Architectures.

1   Introduction

Research on computer supported cooperative work recognized from the very beginning two main cooperation modalities - face-to-face and remote cooperation - and tried to understand their nature and to support them through effective applications. More recently, the concept of local mobility has been Mobile Applications(MA) as an in-between modality between face-to-face and remote cooperation, and as something that may cause the interruption of cooperative activities [1], but also as a property of most work situations [2]. Of course, this effects another fundamental aspect of cooperation, that is *continuity* both in the physical space (no matter if a person stays at her desktop or gets up and walks to another room, her work must be supported without discontinuity) and in the logical context of action (for example, if a person is working on a document with a coworker, they don't have to abandon their activity to find information related to the document). The design of mobile-computing environments to support cooperation requires a reference model able to take into account the above specifications and in particular the notions of community and flexible peripheral participation. To our knowledge Mobile Applications (MA) model has not yet been

T.-h. Kim, Y.-h. Lee, and W.-c. Fang (Eds.): FGIT 2012, LNCS 7709, pp. 33–43, 2012.

proposed, since the cooperation dimension is usually totally disregarded or left implicit and community is not a first class object.

On the other hands, mobile service architecture describes and demonstrates the content of created mobile applications. The form of software descriptions varies. Diverse need of information and requirements of architecture have caused variety in mobile service architecture definitions. One definition of the mobile service architecture is to describe the relationship between static and dynamic parts of the software. Different technologies, which are handled, especially from mobile service architecture point, were spreading to industrial use. In addition there are continually developed more complicated applications that include thousands of lines of code and that are complicated to maintain and to reuse. These are the real-world problems and demands that caused the emergence of different mobile service architecture and will develop in the world of changing technologies and system requirements. In that way mobile service architecture definition can nowadays be seen as a critical part of the development of the mobile service applications. Borderline between architecture and Mobile Applications (MA) of lowest part of mobile service is thin, which may make designing mobile service architecture some overlapping. One definition could be that mobile service architecture includes those features of software that do not change during the software process [3].

The aim of this paper is to give a contribution in this direction by defining an approach to conceive cooperative work that is inspired by the mobile computing paradigm and by proposing a new model as a basic step toward architecture. We also describe the design of collaborative mobile-computing environments to adequately support. In our view, the shift from the desktop computer metaphor to the mobile computing one is promising in the aim to support cooperative work with a smooth form of coordination; in fact, people become able to act and interact, in a more natural and instinctive manner, within a computational environment that is aware of persons and activities and that is able to adapt the support it provides to the changing context. To reach this goal the integration of the themes of cooperation and the mobile computing paradigm has to be strengthened, more than it is currently.

Based on the business cases we have analyzed, we have made the following assumptions about the mobile applications, as the online connection to the host is slow and the mobile device has very limited local memory. Using these assumptions, we have implemented a lightweight mobile application architecture design that provides an efficient SOA back-end connection solution with a minimal cost and hardware requirements. In our architecture, the business objects are serialized, compressed and transmitted to the client side in the form of a compressed message. Our architecture provides an asynchronous remote invocation mechanism to support on-demand requests of server-side. The client sends update requests to the server as compressed SOAP messages. The server responds to remote calls from the mobile client as well as sends real-time alerts and data-updates notifications to the client side.

2   Related Works

2.1   Mobile Computing and Cooperation

Mobile computing (MC) is still more an idea than a reality since embedding computation into real everyday objects is not a simple task from the technical point of view and it is usually achieved either in prototypes or quite expensive devices. However, the rapidity and unpredictability of the technological evolution suggest playing with this idea to be ready when it becomes feasible and be able to master the implications in application design. So, in the following we will consider some of the implications of MC without been too MA constrained by the current technological achievements. We suppose that each object can have specialized computational capabilities making them reactive and proactive in relation to actors and/or other objects that are close of in their surroundings. This distributed computing power is connected through a wireless network that supports bi-directional information flows towards and from more traditional computational nodes. The MC literature is generally more focused on the individual dimension, and only recently it contained an explicit suggestion to consider cooperation in MA environments[4]. A way to connect MA and cooperation is through the notion of context, since MA and context-aware computing share the same goal to make the environment "alive" and its context an important part of what determines the application's behavior[5]. More specifically, we like the idea to view context not as a representational problem but as an interactional problems as context has to be seen as a relational property that holds between objects or activities; something may or may not be contextually relevant in relation to some particular activity; the scope of contextual features is defined dynamically; context is an occasioned property, relevant to particular settings, particular instances of action, and particular parties to that action; finally, context is not out there rather it arises from the activity.

2.2   Mobile Applications

Mobile Applications are a natural extension to the current wired infrastructure. In the enterprise, a variety of people including road warriors, sales and service professionals, are being equipped with on-the-go computing capabilities using mobile technologies for the entertainment, education, communication, work, and other ares.   These pieces of information can be recognized by MA technologies able to identify and locate documents and people on the one hand, and by technologies managing the information constituting the logical space of collaboration (competencies, duties, roles, etc.) on the other hand. Irrespective of its current situation, each person has to behave so that the meeting is anyhow MA. Here, the technology has to support different degrees of participation of the community members to the cooperative process going on in the meeting. Moreover, the environment has to support the quiet development of the meeting itself. As for the last aspect, cellular phones have to be turned to the quiet state when participants enter the room apart from the case of the meeting coordinator that could be contacted by the missing members. Other functionalities can be available that are typical of smart environments.

2.3   Mobile-Computing Environments in Cooperation

The two above described scenarios illustrate some aspects that characterize our understanding on how MA environments can positively affect cooperation. Although we acknowledge the fact that MA as any technology must be properly re-appropriated within the cooperative practices, in the following we summarize the possible advantages Mobile Applications can bring: MA can alleviate the discontinuity due to the local mobility characterizing almost all work situations, since the environment and the smart objects populating it extend the space "around" computation beyond the "desk". In fact, Mobile Applications can allow actor using their physical spaces as flexible contexts for their work without requiring any explicit representation, and by recovering their usual work practices; moreover, Mobile Applications can support individual and cooperative activities in a seamless way by the use, exchange and access to computationally-enriched habitual-use objects: mobile computing could be another choice but, besides usability problems and technological limits (e.g., battery life), the main problem here is that it does not solve the problem of the separation between computation and environment, the latter being only able to guarantee computational access. Finally, Mobile Applications can support the integration of physical and logical contexts of cooperation both in local mobility and remote situations, and consequently allows one to use her augmented environment as a coordination media. In fact, people can achieve coordination without communication by observing and modifying their shared environment: coordination emerges incidentally. Mobile Applications environments add a new "dimension" to coordination without communication because the environment (and its remote representation) can change itself in an autonomous manner, by adapting to the changing situation in which cooperation occurs.

2.4   Mobile Applications Architectures in General

(1) Purpose of the Software Architecture

Modeling and documenting software architecture is important for many reasons. Stakeholders can look at structural features of software with the help of modeling and Documentation. Using architectural model developers can analyze software at very early phase of the software process. Architecture is the first step in designing software itself and it defines stable ground for software development. Different architecture models can be standardized and named, and can be re-used in many subsequent applications. This leads to identification and documentation of general architecture models that are application independent. The architecture models are called architectural styles. Examples for architectural styles are layered architecture and repository architecture. [6,7]

(2) Product line Architecture

The set of software programs, which have similar structure and functionality, are called software product families. The software architecture, which is common to software product family, is often called product line architecture. Layers, components Mobile application architectures and frames have significant role in product line architecture. The use of product line architectures is continuously increasing in software industry. In specific the increasing use of the product line architecture is motivated by the fact that they make reuse of software modules easier, that leads further into more reliable software programs, better time controlled projects, increased productivity of the development, less development risks, easier prototyping etc. [10]

(3) Layered Software Architecture
Layered software architecture means software structure that consists of layers that are logically similar on different abstraction levels. The function of layered software architecture is that higher layer can use services, which lower layer produces. Normally that leads into a situation where the lower layers produce the most common services. On the other hand this means that the higher level the layer is described to the more independent the layer is from the application itself. Layered software architecture can be described in three-layered architectural model, which consists of application layer, middleware layer and platform layer.

Middleware and utility offers platform independent common services like support for user interface. Platform layer offers for example operating system, communication software and other hardware dependent software (drivers etc.). See **Figure 1**.

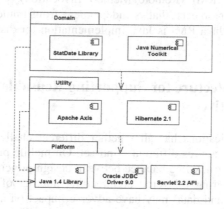

Fig. 1. Three-layer architectural model

Most common structure of layered software architecture is hierarchical and bypassing forbid. Hierarchy means that direction of service request is always from higher level to lower level or service request is send to same level. To forbid bypassing means that service request do not bypass next layer. Structures that allow bypassing are possible but are not so common. See Figure 2.

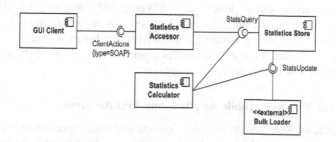

Fig. 2. Mobile Application architectures

Independent layer needs interfaces to serve and request service for. Services are produced to serve higher layer requests that could be used via the interface. This interface is called service interface or utilization interface. Because of the independent nature of the architectures the designers who are specialized in different layers can focus onto their own layers without knowing anything about another layer. Additionally layered software architecture makes understanding of system easier to them who are not so familiar with software designing and implementation for example customers and managers. [4,5]

(4) Distributed Systems
Nowadays more and more applications work in distributed environments either in wired or wireless systems. Due to this new distributed technologies are created and architectural solutions based on these new technologies are developed. The most significant of these technologies are CORBA (Common Object Request Broker Architecture) and Java RMI (Remote Method Invocation). CORBA is common, distribution standard for objects, that is independent from implementation language and operating systems. Java RMI is Java implementation for distribution mechanism of objects.

3   Mobile Architecture for Supporting Reusable and Cooperative

Designing mobile applications has all together different challenges than designing desktop application. It requires different mind-set. On mobile platform everything is limited and one has to struck fine balance between design principles and resources at hand e.g. while considering n-layered architecture, number of layers more than 3 (presentation, business and data) may have adverse impact on application's memory footprint and CPU requirement. Same desktop yardstick will not work on mobile and as an architect switching to mobile; one has to calibrate the experience per mobile platform. This article provides design considerations for mobile application.

3.1   Overview

A mobile application will normally be structured as a multi-layered application consisting of user experience, business, and data layers. When developing a mobile application, you may choose to develop a thin Web-based client or a rich client. If you are building a rich client, the business and data services layers are likely to be located on the device itself. If you are building a thin client, the business and data layers will be located on the server. Figure 1 illustrates common rich client mobile application architecture with components grouped by areas of concern.

3.2   Different Views of Mobile Applications Architectures

Different mobile applications architecture models and their representations have been used in different purposes. When analyzing more precisely the architectures and their representations one dimension is the abstraction level. Higher abstract levels are used mobile application architectures 5 in general description. The abstraction levels of the representations allow to describe the basic functionality and structure of the software

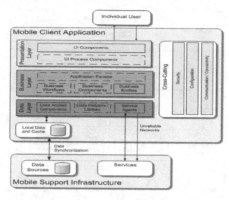

Fig. 3. Cooperative Our Mobile Application Architecture

level by level and that makes it more easy and faster. The view that is under study is dependent of the stakeholder in question, such as end-user, clients, project leader, implementer, manager or salesman, whose interests in software vary quite much. This paper is focused on the mobile application development from the early idea until final product. The five viewpoints are as follow:

- **First** view is the *use case* view where the system is looked at from outside, as the user looks at it. This view emphasizes outer functionality of the system.
- **Second** view is called *logical view* and it describes static software models (classes, interfaces etc.) and dynamic relationship of different software models of the system. This view emphasizes inner functionality of the system.
- **Third** view is called *process view* and this view describes interaction and organization between parallel processes and threads. This view emphasizes performance, scalability and distribution of the system.
- **Fourth** view is called *implementation view*. This view divides system to physical parts (files etc.), which are gathering together to be represented in special way. This view emphasizes controlling of software product.
- **Fifth** view is called *deployment view*. This view describes hardware composition of the system; connections needed by hardware and software modules and processes locate in different hardware component. This view emphasizes distribution of the system, delivery of the system and assembly of the system.

Using software architecture gives quite good new concepts like classes, interfaces, components, modules, sub-systems, inheritance of classes, processes, messages, files, hardware components, communication models etc. Architecture model may concern either static structure of software like classes or dynamic structures like objects. It may also concern static relationships as well as dynamic behavioral models. Architecture can be described either as abstract model, which has not direct relation to software, or as concrete model. An example of applying the views in mobile music service will be presented in **Figure 3**.

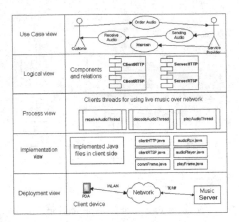

Fig. 4. Five view points for Mobile Application architectures

3.3   Mobile Architecture Design

The following design guidelines provide information about different aspects you should consider when designing a mobile application. Follow these guidelines to ensure that your application meets your requirements and performs efficiently in scenarios common to mobile applications: If the application requires local processing and must work in an occasionally connected scenario, consider designing a rich client. A rich client application will be more complex to install and maintain. If the application can depend on server processing and will always be fully connected, consider designing a thin client. If your application requires a rich user interface (UI), only limited access to local resources, and must be portable to other platforms, design an RIA client. If the mobile device is a stand-alone device, you will not need to account for connection issues. When network connectivity is required, mobile applications should handle cases when a network connection is intermittent or not available. Mobile devices require a simpler architecture, simpler UI, and other specific design decisions in order to work within the constraints imposed by the device hardware. Keep these constraints in mind and design specifically for the device instead of trying to reuse the architecture or UI from a desktop or mobile application. The main constraints are memory, battery life, ability to adapt to difference screen sizes and orientations, security, and network bandwidth. Depending on the application type, multiple layers may be located on the device itself. Use the concept of layers to maximize separation of concerns, and to improve reuse and maintainability for your mobile application. There are several common issues that you must consider as your develop your design. These issues can be categorized into specific areas of the design. The following table 1 lists the common design issues for each category where mistakes are most often made.

Table 1. Design Consideration for Mobile Client Frame

Category	Key consideration issues
Authentication and Authorization	Failing to authenticate in occasionally connected scenarios
Security	Failing to authorize in occasionally-connected scenarios
Communication	Failing to protect sensitive data over the air
Configuration Management	Failing to restore configuration state after a reset
Data Access	Failing to implement data-access mechanisms that work with intermittent connectivity
Exception Management	Not recovering application state after an exception
Logging	Not considering remote logging instead of logging on the device
Porting	Failing to rewrite the existing rich client UI to suit the device
Synchronization	Failing to secure synchronization when communicating
Testing	Failing to appreciate debugging costs when choosing to support multiple device types
UI	Not considering the restricted UI form factor
Validation	Not validating input and data during host PC communication

(1)   Authentication and Authorization

Designing an effective authentication and authorization strategy is important for the security and reliability of your application. Weak authentication can leave mobile vulnerable to unauthorized use. Mobile devices are usually designed to be single-user devices and normally lack basic user profile and security tracking beyond just a simple password. Other common desktop mechanisms are also likely to be missing. The discoverability of mobile devices over protocols such as Bluetooth can present users with unexpected scenarios. Mobile applications can also be especially challenging due to connectivity interruptions. Consider all possible connectivity scenarios, whether over-the-air or hard-wired.

(2)Communication

Device communication includes wireless communication (over the air) and wired communication with a host PC, as well as more specialized communication such as

Bluetooth or Infrared Data Association (IrDA). When communicating over the air, consider data security to protect sensitive data from theft or tampering. If you are communicating through Web service interfaces, use mechanisms such as the WS-Secure standards to secure the data. Keep in mind that wireless device communication is more likely to be interrupted than communication from a PC, and that your application might be required to operate for long periods in a disconnected state.

(3)User Interface

When designing the UI for a mobile application, do not try to adapt or reuse the UI from a desktop application. Design your device UI so that it is as simple as possible, and designed specifically for pen-based input and limited data entry capabilities as appropriate. Consider the fact that your mobile application will run in full-screen mode and will only be able to display a single window at a time. Therefore, blocking operations will prevent the user from interacting with the application. Consider the various screen sizes and orientations of your target devices when designing your application UI.

(4) Mobile Applications Architecture Modeling (part of)

We develop principle mobile applications architecture and shown in figure 4 as part of it. Our architecture will assist mobile cooperation by proposing a model and related architecture to design environments by taking into account the dimension of cooperation. The implementation of the architecture is ongoing: the integration of two preexisting components led to their re-implementation to improve their functionality.

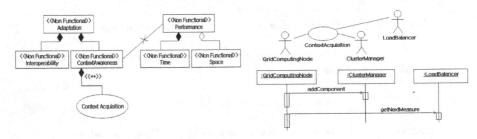

Fig. 5. Modeling examples for Mobile Application architectures

4   Conclusion and Future Works

Mobile device design and development is unique due to the constrained and differing nature of device hardware. We may be targeting multiple devices with very different hardware parameters. We describe the considerations for device-specific capabilities that we can use to enhance our application functionality.

In this paper, we give a contribution in this direction by defining an approach to conceive cooperative work that is inspired by the mobile computing paradigm and by proposing a new model as a basic step toward architecture. We also describe the design of collaborative mobile-computing environments to adequately support. In our view, the shift from the desktop computer metaphor to the mobile computing one is promising in the aim to support cooperative work with a smooth form of coordination.

To reach this goal the integration of the themes of cooperation and the mobile computing paradigm has to be strengthened, more than it is currently. Irrespective of the actual availability of smart objects, the proposed model and architecture has its own value since the considered scenarios can take advantage from its two main features, distributed inference capability and flexible and adaptive management of contextual information, also in presence of more traditional computational devices.

In the future, we are going to develop specific frameworks using the architecture and apply various practical cases to it.

Acknowledgement. This work was supported by the Korea National Research Foundation (NRF) granted funded by the Korea Government (Scientist of Regional University No. 2012-0004489).

References

[1] Windows Embedded Developer Center, http://msdn.microsoft.com/en-us/embedded/default.aspx
[2] Patterns & practices Mobile Client Software Factory, http://msdn.microsoft.com/en-us/library/aa480471.aspx
[3] Microsoft Sync Framework, http://msdn.microsoft.com/en-us/sync/default.aspx
[4] OpenNETCF.Diagnostics.EventLog in the Smart Device Framework, http://msdn.microsoft.com/en-us/library/aa446519.aspx
[5] ASP.NET Mobile, http://www.asp.net/mobile/road-map/
[6] ASP.NET Mobile source code support into Visual Studio (2008), http://blogs.msdn.com/webdevtools/archive/2007/09/17/tip-trick-asp-net-mobile-development-with-visual-studio-2008.aspx
[7] Messeguer, R., Ochoa, S.F., Pino, J.A., Medina, E., Navarro, L., Royo, D., Neyem, A.: Building Real-World Ad-Hoc Networks to Support Mobile Collaborative Applications: Lessons Learned. In: Carriço, L., Baloian, N., Fonseca, B. (eds.) CRIWG 2009. LNCS, vol. 5784, pp. 1–16. Springer, Heidelberg (2009)
[8] Mohagheghi, P., Conradi, R.: Quality, "Productivity and economic benefits of software reuse: a review of industrial studies". Empirical Software Engineering 12(5), 471–516 (2007)
[9] Morán, A.L., Rodríguez-Covili, J., Mejia, D., Favela, J., Ochoa, S.: Supporting Informal Interaction in a Hospital through Impromptu Social Networking. In: Kolfschoten, G., Herrmann, T., Lukosch, S. (eds.) CRIWG 2010. LNCS, vol. 6257, pp. 305–320. Springer, Heidelberg (2010)

An Efficient Layer 2 Routing Algorithm in a Dual-ring Bridged Network for Smart Grid

Seokjoon Hong and Inwhee Joe

Division of Computer Science and Engineering, Hanyang University,
Seoul, 133-791 South Korea
iwjoe@hanyang.ac.kr

Abstract. In a dual-ring bridged network, a bridge with RSTP algorithm may send packets to other bridges inefficiently. An RSTP algorithm has only one spanning tree for data communications. A redundant link in a dual-ring bridged network is wasteful and inefficient. Thus, we propose an algorithm that allocates two spanning trees to two separate rings of the dual-ring using PVST (Per VLAN Spanning Tree). After allocating two spanning trees to each bridge port, a layer 2 routing table is built by exchanging new BPDU messages with other bridges using two spanning trees. By using this routing table, bridges can forward data to the destination bridge with the shortest path. Because the proposed algorithm is compatible with existing RSTP algorithms, the proposed algorithm can be used for bridges in all Ethernet networks including Industrial Ethernet networks. It also can be used for smart grid automation network technology. We provide proof of the efficiency of the proposed algorithm via OPNET simulation results.

Keywords: Dual-ring bridged network, RSTP, VLAN, PVST, End-to-end delay.

1   Introduction

Ethernet is used for various networks such as local area networks (LAN), metro area networks (MAN) and industrial area networks (IAN). An important characteristic of Ethernet is its resilience, i.e., the capability to sustain user traffic in the presence of network faults.

As Ethernet-bridged networks such as MAC learned to rely on flooding mechanisms, Ethernet transport packets began to rely on spanning tree protocols, which prevent data looping. The legacy 802.1d Spanning Tree Protocol (STP) [1] is the first algorithm to prevent data looping and recovery when a link failure occurs. Because of poor convergence speed and inefficient bandwidth allocation, the 802.1w Rapid Spanning Tree Protocol (RSTP) [2] and the 802.1s Multiple Spanning Tree Protocol (MSTP) [3] have been introduced. RSTP offers faster convergence than STP, but also uses a single tree for the entire network, blocking all the links that are not included in the spanning tree. Those redundant links cannot forward traffic at all, which seriously impacts link usage and network performance. MSTP allows a bridge to participate in multiple spanning tree instances, one tree per group of VLANs [4]. Another algorithm

T.-h. Kim, Y.-h. Lee, and W.-c. Fang (Eds.): FGIT 2012, LNCS 7709, pp. 44–51, 2012.

used for efficient bandwidth allocation is PVST (Per VLAN Spanning Tree), which can use multiple links efficiently by allocating a spanning tree per VLAN [5].

Network resilience is also important for Industrial Ethernet networks such as smart grid networks. There are International Electrotechnical Commission (IEC) standards for smart grid implementation. IEC 61850 [6] is an international standard for station-bus application, which lets IEDs (intelligent electronic devices) communicate with each other and with a substation controller. The IEC 62439 standard [7] defines redundancy methods applicable to most industrial networks, which differ in topology and recovery time.

Parallel Redundancy Protocol (PRP) and High Availability Seamless Redundancy (HSR) [8] are the latest additions to the IEC 62439 standard. Designed for mission critical and time sensitive applications such as those found in electric utility protection and control applications, PRP and HSR provide guaranteed behavior under failure conditions and increased network reliability. Higher network uptime translates to reduced outages and maintenance resulting in overall cost savings.

Rapid Ring Recovery (RRR) [9] detects failure and recovery rapidly in Ethernet ring topologies. RRR is based on the novel usage of multiple virtual rings. RRR utilizes all possible VLANs for forwarding traffic. Initially, RRR will choose VLAN to be the primary forwarding topology. When it is detected that a link on the primary VLAN has failed, the RRR-enabled switch on either side of the failure will forward the traffic on an alternative VLAN for the remainder of its journey.

RSTPoR (Simple Protocol Enhancements of RSTP over Ring Topologies) [10] addressed resilience over Ethernet networks using RSTP. It proposed simple protocol modifications of original RSTP to speed up its performance.

In this paper, we propose another efficient routing algorithm for dual-ring bridged network topology. In Section 2, we describe an efficient routing algorithm for a dual-ring bridge network. In Section 3, we evaluate the performance of the proposed algorithm in terms of the end-to-end delay using an OPNET simulation. Finally, we conclude in Section 4.

2   Efficient Routing Algorithm in Dual-ring Bridged Network

In this section, we propose a routing algorithm for a dual-ring bridged network. The existing RSTP (802.1w) algorithm is inefficient for a dual-ring bridged network. The RSTP algorithm builds only one spanning tree for all bridged networks to prevent data loops. Thus, we propose an algorithm that allocates two separate rings of the dual-ring by using a PVST (Per VLAN Spanning Tree) scheme. It also uses a routing table for data forwarding.

Figure 1 shows the main idea of the proposed algorithm. If all bridges are linked with a dual-ring network, the proposed algorithm builds two spanning trees as in Figure 1. It can be implemented via two VLAN allocations for different ports. We propose a lower port that links adjacent bridges to VLAN1 and another port, VLAN2. With two symmetrical spanning trees, all bridges can select the best route, which has the shortest hop to the destination bridge. For example, with one spanning tree, bridge 3 cannot directly forward data to bridge 4. However, if there are two spanning trees for routing as in Figure 1, bridge 3 can forward data to bridge 4 directly.

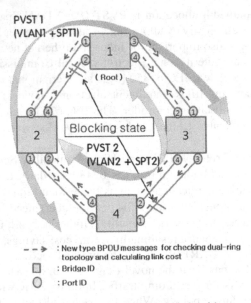

Fig. 1. Main idea of the proposed algorithm

Furthermore, with two symmetrical spanning trees, all bridges can select the shortest path, which has the shortest hop count to the destination bridge. We also propose a scheme for selecting the blocking point of two spanning trees. The scheme selects the lower port of the bridge, which is the farthest bridge from the root, as the blocking port for VLAN1 and selects the lower port of the root bridge for VLAN2. The scheme uses the following formula to select the farthest bridge from the root bridge:

$$q = \left\lceil \frac{m}{2} \right\rceil \tag{1}$$

Here, m is the total hop count with dual-ring topology and q is the hop count from the root bridge. Using this formula, the farthest bridge from the root bridge is the bridge with the largest q. If two bridges have the same q, the bridge with the larger bridge ID can be selected as the farthest bridge.

Figure 2 shows a change in the spanning tree when bridge link failure occurs. If the link failure occurs in a dual-ring topology bridge network, the existing spanning tree is changed to a new spanning tree that considers the failure point a blocked point. Thus, the link failed point is located in the same position as the blocked point with no change in the spanning tree.

The procedure for our algorithm is shown in Figure 3. The algorithm can be implemented with a bridge node and is compatible with the existing RSTP algorithm. First, the proposed algorithm checks the topology of the bridge network by sending a new BPDU packet. If the topology is dual-ring, then the algorithm can allocate a SPT (spanning tree) to use a separate ring network via a PVST scheme in order to build the routing table with path cost information from the new BPDU packet sent from each bridge. We assume path cost 1 is equal to one hop count. After all bridges have built their routing tables, the bridge starts data packet transmission based on the routing table.

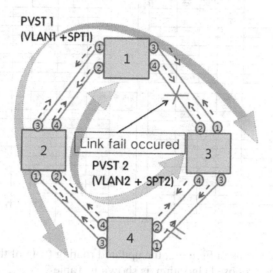

Fig. 2. Change in the spanning tree when link failure occurred

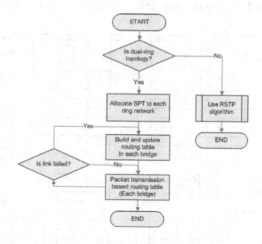

Fig. 3. Procedure for the proposed algorithm

For example, Figure 1 shows the initial routing table for the bridges established by the proposed algorithm.

Table 1. Initial routing table of bridges

Bridge ID	Port ID	Linked Bridge ID	Linked Port ID	Path Cost	Blocked	VLAN ID
1	1	2	3	1	FALSE	1
	1	3	3	3	TRUE	1
	1	4	3	2	FALSE	1
	2	2	4	1	TRUE	2
	2	3	4	3	TRUE	2
	2	4	4	2	TRUE	2
	3	2	1	3	TRUE	1
	3	3	1	1	FALSE	1
	3	4	1	2	TRUE	1
	4	2	2	3	FALSE	2
	4	3	2	1	FALSE	2
	4	4	2	2	FALSE	2

Bridge ID	Port ID	Linked Bridge ID	Linked Port ID	Path Cost	Blocked	VLAN ID
2	1	1	3	3	TRUE	1
	1	3	3	2	TRUE	1
	1	4	3	1	FALSE	1
	2	1	4	3	FALSE	2
	2	3	4	2	FALSE	2
	2	4	4	1	FALSE	2
	3	1	1	1	FALSE	1
	3	3	1	2	FALSE	1
	3	4	1	3	TRUE	1
	4	1	2	1	TRUE	2
	4	3	2	2	TRUE	2
	4	4	2	3	TRUE	2

Bridge ID	Port ID	Linked Bridge ID	Linked Port ID	Path Cost	Blocked	VLAN ID
3	1	1	3	1	FALSE	1
	1	2	3	2	FALSE	1
	1	4	3	3	FALSE	1
	2	1	4	1	FALSE	2
	2	2	4	2	TRUE	2
	2	4	4	3	TRUE	2
	3	1	1	3	TRUE	1
	3	2	1	2	TRUE	1
	3	4	1	1	TRUE	1
	4	1	2	3	TRUE	2
	4	2	2	2	FALSE	2
	4	4	2	1	FALSE	2

Bridge ID	Port ID	Linked Bridge ID	Linked Port ID	Path Cost	Blocked	VLAN ID
4	1	1	3	2	TRUE	1
	1	2	3	3	TRUE	1
	1	3	3	1	TRUE	1
	2	1	4	2	FALSE	2
	2	2	4	3	TRUE	2
	2	3	4	1	FALSE	2
	3	1	1	1	FALSE	1
	3	2	1	1	FALSE	1
	3	3	1	3	FALSE	1
	4	1	2	2	TRUE	2
	4	2	2	1	FALSE	2
	4	3	2	3	TRUE	2

If link failure occurs as in Figure 2, the updated routing table of the bridges, which is established by the proposed algorithm, is shown in Table 2.

Table 2. Updated routing table of bridges after link failure

Bridge ID	Port ID	Linked Bridge ID	Linked Port ID	Path Cost	Blocked	VLAN ID
1	1	2	3	1	FALSE	1
	1	3	3	3	TRUE	1
	1	4	3	2	FALSE	1
	2	2	4	1	FALSE	2
	2	3	4	3	FALSE	2
	2	4	4	2	FALSE	2
	3	2	1	3	TRUE	1
	3	3	1	1	FALSE	1
	3	4	1	2	TRUE	1
	4	2	2	∞	FALSE	2
	4	3	2	∞	FALSE	2
	4	4	2	∞	FALSE	2

Bridge ID	Port ID	Linked Bridge ID	Linked Port ID	Path Cost	Blocked	VLAN ID
2	1	1	3	3	TRUE	1
	1	3	3	2	TRUE	1
	1	4	3	1	FALSE	1
	2	1	4	∞	FALSE	2
	2	3	4	2	FALSE	2
	2	4	4	1	FALSE	2
	3	1	1	1	FALSE	1
	3	3	1	2	FALSE	1
	3	4	1	3	TRUE	1
	4	1	2	1	FALSE	2
	4	3	2	∞	FALSE	2
	4	4	2	∞	FALSE	2

Bridge ID	Port ID	Linked Bridge ID	Linked Port ID	Path Cost	Blocked	VLAN ID
3	1	1	3	1	FALSE	1
	1	2	3	2	FALSE	1
	1	4	3	3	FALSE	1
	2	1	4	∞	FALSE	2
	2	2	4	∞	FALSE	2
	2	4	4	∞	FALSE	2
	3	1	1	3	TRUE	1
	3	2	1	2	TRUE	1
	3	4	1	1	TRUE	1
	4	1	2	3	FALSE	2
	4	2	2	2	FALSE	2
	4	4	2	1	FALSE	2

Bridge ID	Port ID	Linked Bridge ID	Linked Port ID	Path Cost	Blocked	VLAN ID
4	1	1	3	2	TRUE	1
	1	2	3	3	TRUE	1
	1	3	3	1	TRUE	1
	2	1	4	∞	FALSE	2
	2	2	4	∞	FALSE	2
	2	3	4	1	FALSE	2
	3	1	1	2	FALSE	1
	3	2	1	1	FALSE	1
	3	3	1	3	FALSE	1
	4	1	2	2	FALSE	2
	4	2	2	1	FALSE	2
	4	3	2	∞	FALSE	2

3   Performance Evaluation

In this section, describe the performance evaluation of the proposed algorithm through simulation using the OPNET simulator. The algorithm was written in C and then inserted into the bridge node model. Figure 4 shows the network model of the dual-ring bridged network that consists of four bridges. The left figure shows the normal state, and the right figure shows the failed state.

The OPNET simulation parameters for the proposed algorithm are shown in Table 3.

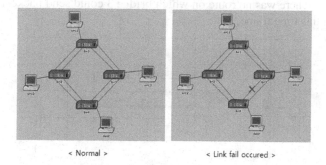

< Normal >   < Link fail occured >

Fig. 4. OPNET network model

Table 3. OPNET simulation parameters

Simulation parameter	Value
Total simulation time	60 sec
Packet send interval of the source node	Constant (1)
Source node distribution (Only one source can send at a time)	Uniform Distribution (about source number)
End-node processing delay	0.5ms
Transmission delay in bridges	0.12ms (1500byte(max in ethernet) /100Mbps)

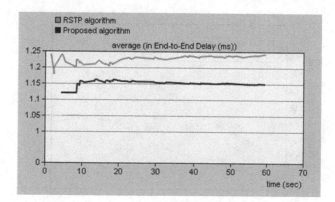

Fig. 5. Average of end-to-end delay between src and dest node

Figure 5 shows the OPNET simulation results based on the parameters in Table 1. The end-to-end delay was calculated using the formula shown below. We assumed that there was no propagation delay.

$$D_{end-to-end} = D_{proc} + D_{prop} + D_{trans} \qquad (2)$$

Figure 6 shows the change in the delay when link failure occurred from 20 - 40 sec in the simulation. Before 20s and after 60s, all end-to-end delays of the proposed algorithm were about 1.2ms. For the 20 - 40s simulation time, there were some peak delays as in RSTP. There was no route on which bridge 3 could send packets to bridge 4 directly during this time frame.

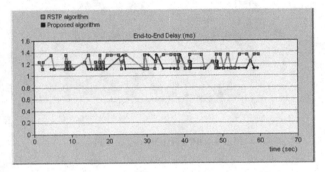

Fig. 6. End-to-end delay when link failure occurred in 20~40s

Finally, Figure 7 shows the average delay with an increasing number of bridges in a dual-ring bridged network.

With the proposed algorithm, the average end-to-end delay increased more slowly than with the RSTP algorithm. The proposed algorithm always selects the shortest path to the destination bridge using the routing table.

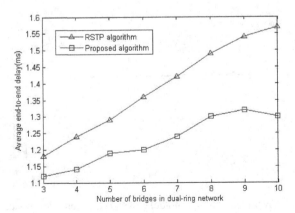

Fig. 7. Average end-to-end delay with number of bridges

4   Conclusions

In this paper, we proposed a routing algorithm that uses two separate spanning trees in a dual-ring bridge network for efficient routing. We demonstrated the performance of the proposed algorithm through simulation using the OPNET simulator. The OPNET simulation results showed lower average end-to-end delay with the proposed algorithm than with the RSTP algorithm in the dual-ring bridged network. In addition, the proposed algorithm was identical to that with the RSTP algorithm because an alternative spanning tree path was used. Therefore, the performance evaluation shows that the proposed algorithm is better than the original RSTP algorithm for a dual-ring bridged network.

Acknowledgments. This work was supported by Basic Science Research Program through the National Research Foundation by Korea (NRF) funded by the Ministry of Education, Science and Technology (2012-0005507).

References

1. IEEE Information Technology, Part 3: Media Access Control (MAC) bridges. ISO/IEC 12802-3, ANSI/IEEE Std 802.1D (1998)
2. IEEE Standard for Local and metropolitan area networks – common specifications. Part 3: Media Access Control (MAC) bridges – Amendment 2 : Rapid Reconfiguration Amendment to IEEE Std 802.1D, 1998 Edition, IEEE Std 802.1w-2001
3. IEEE Standards for Local and Metropolitan area networks Virtual Bridged Local Area Networks – Amendment 3: Multiple Spanning Trees Amendment to IEEE Std802.1QTM , 1998 Edition. IEEE Std 802.1s-2002
4. IEEE Standard for Local and Metropolitan area networks: Virtual Bridged Local Area Networks. IEEE Std 802.1Q-1998
5. CISCO "Per VLAN Spanning Tree (PVST)", http://www.cisco.com/en/US/tech/tk389/tk621/tk846/tsd_technology_support_sub-protocol_home.html
6. IEC 61850 Communication networks and systems in substations-All parts, Reference number IEC 61850-SER
7. International Electrotechnical Commission, Geneva IEC62439 Highly Available Automation Networks, issued (March 2009)
8. International Electrotechnical Commission, Geneva "IEC FDIS 62439-3 Highly Available Automation Networks", PRP & HSR (August 2009)
9. Huynh, M., Goose, S., Mohapatra, P., Liao, R.: RRR: Rapid Ring Recovery Submillisecond Decentralized Recovery for Ethernet Ring. IEEE Transactions on Computers (2011)
10. Marchese, M., Mongelli, M., Portomauro, G.: Simple Protocol Enhancements of Rapid Spanning Tree Protocol over Ring Topologies. In: IEEE Global Telecommunications Conference (2010)

Improving User Throughput
with Interleaved-HARQ in OFDM Systems

Dongwook Kim[1] and Namgi Kim[2],[*]

[1] Div. of EECS, KAIST, Korea
`kimdw@nslab.kaist.c.kr`
[2] Dept. of CS, Kyonggi University, Korea
`ngkim@kyonggi.ac.kr`

Abstract. In this paper, we investigate how to improve user throughput in orthogonal frequency division multiplexing (OFDM)-based cellular systems. We consider an OFDM system which employs the interleaving techniques within hybrid automatic repeat request (HARQ) protocols. To maximize user throughput, we propose an enhanced approach to selecting the modulation and coding scheme (MCS) and interleaving thus this throughput is obtained by considering not only time diversity gain from HARQ operations but also frequency diversity gain from interleaving techniques. Link-level simulation results show that interleaving techniques improve the frame error rate performance of given MCS levels at retransmissions by performing with HARQ operations.

Keywords: MCS, HARQ, interleaving, expected throughput, OFDM.

1 Introduction

Orthogonal frequency division multiplexing (OFDM) has become as a promising physical layer technology in fourth-generation (4G) cellular systems [1] [2] [3]. The essential requirement of the 4G systems is to support high data rate transmissions of 1 Gbps for stationary users and 100 Mbps for mobile users. In the OFDM technology, a high data rate stream is split into a number of lower rate streams that are simultaneously transmitted over a number of sub-carriers. On the other hand, adaptive modulation and coding (AMC) techniques have been considered as an efficient way to provide high data rates in the third-generation (3G) and 4G cellular systems [1] [2] [4] [5]. Since the techniques determine an MCS level with the channel quality which is estimated by MS, errors in the channel estimation may cause a wrong MCS selection. The channel quality may change while the CQI is fed back from MS to BS, which also contributes to a wrong MCS selection. To compensate for these inherent vulnerabilities of AMC techniques, hybrid automatic repeat request (HARQ) techniques which take a retransmission strategy in the physical layer have been proposed [4] [6].

---

[*] Corresponding author.

T.-h. Kim, Y.-h. Lee, and W.-c. Fang (Eds.): FGIT 2012, LNCS 7709, pp. 52–58, 2012.
© Springer-Verlag Berlin Heidelberg 2012

Lastly, in a multi-path propagation environment, a channel perturbed by the frequency-selective fading exhibits mutually dependent signal transmission impairments. These impairments result in a statical dependence among successive transmissions of coded bits so that they may cause bursts of errors, instead of as isolated events. To solve this problem, the interleaving techniques which randomly spread out coded bits of a packet in time or frequency domain before transmission were introduced [7].

In these circumstances, we consider the interleaving techniques are performed with HARQ operations in OFDM systems. Basically, HARQ operations can achieve time diversity gains by retransmitting packets in time-varying channels. In OFDM systems, interleaving techniques can lead to additional frequency diversity gains with HARQ operations by exploiting the frequency-selective characteristics of channel fading.

The design objectives of AMC techniques for the mapping between the channel quality and MCS level depend upon quality-of-service (QoS) requirements for services [8]. Conventional AMC techniques establish a maximum allowable FER which satisfies the required QoS of each service. And they determine an appropriate MCS level which maintains the error rate of transmitted packet within the target FER. However, this mapping design has been only based on the channel quality without considering the performance improvement from HARQ operation. In [9], an MCS selection scheme which exploits both the channel quality and HARQ operation was proposed. However, the authors used the approximated user throughput as the expected throughput. Thus their scheme may select a wrong MCS level which cannot maximize user throughput.

In this paper, we focus on the best-effort type of service which is delay-tolerant up to a predefined maximum delay and we consider an OFDM system which employs both the HARQ protocols and interleaving techniques. We take the view that the QoS of best-effort services is improved by maximizing user throughput and for this, we propose an enhanced MCS selection scheme while taking into account not only the channel quality but also both the HARQ operations and interleaving techniques.

2 Proposed MCS Selection Scheme

In this paper, we consider the CC-based HARQ mechanism to present our proposed MCS selection scheme. We assume that a synchronous HARQ mechanism is employed for slowly varying channels. Thus retransmissions may occur soon after the previous transmission and, during retransmissions, the channel conditions remain constant as that of the initial transmission. If channel conditions vary during retransmissions, the throughput expected before the transmission may be different from the throughput actually achieved. However, our expected throughput based MCS selection scheme is still effective since, as the number of retransmissions increases, the SNR gains increase with HARQ operations and this increases the probability that a packet is successfully decoded.

We consider a random interleaving scheme which follows the uniform distribution to investigate the performance of general interleaving techniques. Thus,

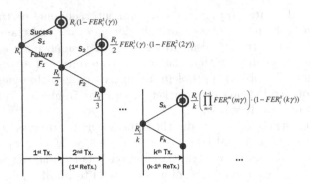

Fig. 1. The throughput estimated at each transmission when the CC-based HARQ mechanism and interleaving techniques are employed

in a frequency selective fading channel, coded bits are uniformly interleaved at each (re)transmission and they may be perturbed by different fading effects at that (re)transmission.

2.1 Expected Throughput with Interleaving-Based HARQ

In this section, we propose a novel method that exactly estimates the expected throughput while taking into account not only the channel quality but also the operation principle of both HARQ and interleaving. Each MS is allowed to transmit its own packet in the transmit time interval (TTI) determined by a scheduling algorithm in BS. For improving the QoS of best-effort services, the MS should choose the MCS level which maximizes user throughput in this TTI. Since it is impossible to recognize the MCS level which maximizes user throughput in advance before actual transmission, we take an enhanced approach to selecting the MCS level which maximizes the expected throughput. In [10], the expected throughput was obtained by considering both the achieved data rate and the decoding success probability obtained at each transmission. If a packet with MCS i whose data rate of R_i is repeatedly sent n times, the achieved data rate is reduced to R_i/n at the n-th transmission. And the throughput at the n-th transmission is estimated by multiplying R_i/n with the probability that a packet is successfully decoded after n transmissions with HARQ operations. Thus, when the maximum number of transmissions is $N_{\max}$, the expected throughput is the summation of each throughput estimated at all $N_{\max}$ transmissions.

As mentioned before, if the interleaving techniques are performed with HARQ operations, the FER curve of a given MCS level changes into more improved ones as the number of retransmission times increases. Thus we extend the expected throughput estimation method proposed in [10] to reflect the FER performance improvement by the interleaving techniques. Figure 1 illustrates the throughput estimated at each transmission when the CC-based HARQ mechanism and interleaving techniques are employed. As shown in Fig. 1, when the data rate of MCS i is R_i and given channel quality is γ, the achieved data rate at the k-th transmission is R_i/k and the achieved SNR at this transmission is $k\gamma$ with the CC-based HARQ mechanism. Moreover, the decoding success probability at the k-th transmission is $\prod_{m=1}^{k-1} FER_i^m(m\gamma)(1 - FER_i^k(k\gamma))$, which implies a packet is successfully decoded at the k-th transmission, conditioned on the previous $k-1$ unsuccessful transmissions. $FER_i^k(\cdot)$ indicates the improved FER curve of MCS i at the k-th transmission, which is caused by additional frequency diversity gains from the interleaving techniques. Therefore the expected throughput obtained after all $N_{\max}$ transmissions is expressed as

$$ET_i(\gamma) = R_i \sum_{k=1}^{N_{\max}} \frac{1}{k} \left(\prod_{m=1}^{k-1} FER_i^m(m\gamma) \right) (1 - FER_i^k(k\gamma)) \tag{1}$$

where $FER_i^k(k\gamma)$ is the associated FER with SNR $k\gamma$ and MCS i at the k-th transmission.

2.2 Enhanced MCS Mapping Design

In this section, we propose an enhanced MCS selection scheme with the expected throughput which maximizes user throughput in OFDM systems. In the conventional AMC techniques, the mapping design is to select the MCS level which maximizes the instantaneous data rate while maintaining a given FER constraint. This scheme is expressed as

$$MCS_{FER_x}(\gamma) = \arg\max_{i \in \Psi} \{R_i | F_i(\gamma) < x\}, \tag{2}$$

where x is the maximum allowable FER and Ψ is the set of MCS levels. A target FER of 1 % can be adopted for real-time services to meet the delay requirement. And, a tareget FER of 10 % which may permit a few number of retransmissions can be adopted for best-effort services.

To fulfill the goal of maximizing user throughput, our proposed MCS selection scheme exploits the expected throughput in (1) and the mapping design is an enhanced approach which selects the MCS level which maximizes (1). Our scheme is expressed as

$$MCS_{ET}^{CC-Int}(\gamma) = \arg\max_{i \in \Psi} R_i \sum_{k=1}^{N_{\max}} \frac{1}{k} \left(\prod_{m=1}^{k-1} FER_i^m(m\gamma) \right) \cdot (1 - FER_i^k(k\gamma)) \tag{3}$$

3 Simulation Results

In this section, we present simulation results for the performance evaluation of our proposed MCS selection scheme. We use 6 MCS levels with bit rates of 0.8 Mbps (1, QPSK, 1/3, 1600), 1.2 Mbps (2, QPSK, 1/2, 2400), 1.6 Mbps (3, 16QAM, 1/3, 3200), 1.8 Mbps (4, QPSK, 3/4, 3600), 2.4 Mbps (5, 16QAM, 1/2, 4800), and 3.6 Mbps (6, 16QAM, 3/4, 7200) where the four elements in the

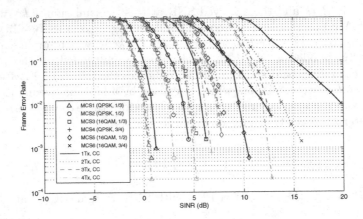

Fig. 2. FER vs. SINR for the 6 MCS levels in the ITU Ped-A 3 km/h channel

parentheses indicate the index, modulation type, code rate, and the size of information bits for each MCS level, respectively. We employ the CC-based HARQ mechanism and the maximum number of transmissions is set to 4. For given 6 MCS levels, to obtain the FER curves improved at retransmissions with the interleaving-based HARQ operations, we implement an HSDPA-OFDM system proposed in [11].

We obtain the FER curves for the 6 MCS levels in the ITU Ped-A 3 km/h and Ped-B 3 km/h channels, respectively, and Fig. 2 representatively shows the results in the ITU Ped-A 3 km/h channel. As shown in this figure, interleaving-based HARQ operations improve the FER performance of given MCS levels at each retransmission. For the MCS level of 6, the SINR which is required to satisfy an FER value of 10 % is lowered by 3.6 dB at the first retransmission. And, the required SINR is lowered by 5.9 dB at the first retransmission to satisfy 1 % FER for the same MCS level.

With the link-level simulation results in both the ITU Ped-A 3 km/h and Ped-B 3 km/h channels, we obtain the hull curves of various MCS selection schemes and Figure 3 shows the results in the Ped-A 3 km/h channel. 'ET, Interleaving' indicates our proposed MCS selection scheme and 'ET' indicates the scheme which is only based on HARQ operations. To compare with these schemes, conventional mapping designs in (2) with the target FERs of both 1 % and 10 % are considered. As shown in Fig. 3, both 'ET' and 'ET, Interleaving' schemes show high throughput, compared to the conventional mapping designs. As the number of transmissions increases, 'ET, Interleaving' scheme achieves higher throughput than 'ET' scheme in a broad SINR region. Especially, in the low SINR regime ranging from −10 dB to −1 dB, 'ET, Interleaving' scheme obtains more improved throughput than 'ET' scheme due to the increased SINR gains from interleaving-based HARQ operations.

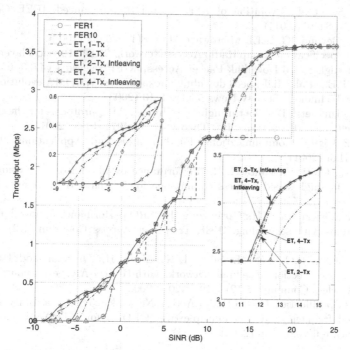

Fig. 3. Throughput vs. SINR in the ITU Ped-A 3 km/h channel

4 Conclusion

In this paper, we have proposed a novel expected throughput estimation method and an enhanced MCS selection scheme which consider the operation principle of both HARQ and interleaving. To show how the interleaving-based HARQ operations improve the FER performance of given MCS levels at retransmissions, we have performed link-level simulations over the implemented HSDPA-OFDM system. With the link-level simulation results, we have obtained the throughput hull curves of our MCS selection scheme and other schemes for slow speed channel models. For the future work, we will evaluate our scheme with fast varying and high speed channel models such as 60km/h and 120km/h.

Acknowledgement. This research was supported by Basic Science Research Program through the National Research Foundation of Korea (NRF) funded by the Ministry of Education, Science and Technology (Grant Number: 2012R1A1A1002133)

References

1. IEEE Standard for Local and metropolitan area networks Part 16: Air Interface for Broadband Wireless Access Systems Amendment 3: Advanced Air Interface, IEEE 802.16 WG (May 2011)

2. Parkvall, S., et al.: Evolution of LTE toward IMT-advanced. IEEE Commun. Mag. 49(2), 84–91 (2011)
3. Steer, M.: Beyond 3G. IEEE Microwave Mag. 8(1), 76–82 (2007)
4. Technical Specification Group Radio Access Network, 25.848 Physical layer aspects of UTRA High Speed Downlink Packet Access, 3GPP release 4 v4.0.0, 03 (2001)
5. Kolding, T.E., et al.: High speed downlink packet access: WCDMA evolution. IEEE Vehicular Technology Society News 50(1), 4–10 (2003)
6. Caire, G., Tuninetti, D.: The throughput of hybrid-ARQ protocols for the Gaussian collision channel. IEEE Trans. Inf. Theory 47(5), 1971–1988 (2001)
7. Sklar, B.: Digital Communications: Fundamentals and Applications, 2nd edn. Prentice-Hall (2001)
8. Caponi, L., Chiti, F., Fantacci, R.: Performance evaluation of a link adaptation technique for high speed wireless communication systems. IEEE Trans. Wireless Commun. 6(12), 4568–4575 (2007)
9. Zheng, H., Viswanathan, H.: Optimizing the ARQ performance in downlink packet data systems with scheduling. IEEE Trans. on Wirelss Commun. 4(2), 495–506 (2005)
10. Kim, D., Jung, B.C., Lee, H., Sung, D.K., Yoon, H.: Optimal modulation and coding scheme selection in cellular networks with Hybrid-ARQ error control. IEEE Trans. Wireless Commun. 7(12), 5195–5201 (2008)
11. Technical Specification Group Radio Access Network, 25.892 Feasibility study for orthogonal frequency division multiplexing (OFDM) for UTRAN enhancement, 3GPP release 6 v6.0.0, 06 (2004)

A Performance Analysis of RESTful Open API Information System

Min Choi[*]

School of Information and Communication Engineering
Chungbuk National University,
52 Naesudong-ro, Heungdeok-gu, Cheongju, Chungbuk 361-763, Republic of Korea
miin.chae@gmail.com

Abstract. RESTful web services easily deploy their web service without physical server through HTTP protocol. This research is to provide a service evaluation, especially in the point of system performance for the Open APIs. Future information systems will be working on smart devices such as smartphones or smart devices. So, this research focuses onto the scalability of RESTful Open API web services by performance evaluation of the RESTful Open APIs. This is because we need to check whether the REST Open API has enough performance as a future mobile cloud platform.

Keywords: RESTful Open API, Web Service, REST Open API performance.

1 Introduction

Mobile computing is the growing trend towards embedding microprocessors in everyday objects so that they can communicate information. Mobile computing devices are completely connected and constantly available.[1] It relies on the convergence of wireless technologies, advanced electronics, and the internet. Today's mobile consumer electronics are not just mobile communication devices, but they change the life style of people and create new cultures. Wherever the place users are, the data exist everywhere that the user wanted. Actually, all the things that people have not ever imagine before are realized by mobile computing.[2, 3, 4]

In this research, we evaluate the performance of RESTful Open APIs for mobile cloud. With the fast development of internet technologies, web based architectures are becoming the major technologies for various fields of mobile computing. Nowadays, we are experiencing a major shift from traditional mobile applications to mobile cloud computing. It improves application performance and efficiency by offloading complex and time consuming tasks onto powerful computing platforms. By running only simple tasks on mobile devices, we can achieve a longer battery lifetime and a greater processing efficiency. This offloading with the use of parallelism is not only faster, but it can also be used to solve problems related to large datasets of non-local resources. With a set of computers connected on a network, there is a vast pool of

---

[*] Corresponding author.

T.-h. Kim, Y.-h. Lee, and W.-c. Fang (Eds.): FGIT 2012, LNCS 7709, pp. 59–64, 2012.

CPUs and resources, and you have the ability to access files on a cloud. Therefore, it is necessary to offload the computation-intensive part by careful partitioning of application functions across the cloud computing. For this purpose, we make use of RESTful Open API web services. So, this research focuses onto the scalability of RESTful Open API web services. We need to check whether the REST Open API has enough performance as a future mobile cloud platform.

The rest of this paper is organized as follows: Section 2 describes related works on this research. Section 3 focuses on the details of REST Open API performance analysis. Finally, we conclude our work and present future research directions in Section 4.

2   Related Work

In the past decade, much research [6] has been put on automated approaches to WSDL/SOAP web service composition. Since WSDL/SOAP web services and REST web service adopt differing styles and view the services from different perspectives, the automated composition problem of these two kinds of web services are very different. WSDL/SOAP web service composition predominately uses AI planning approaches, and these approaches focus on functional composition of individual web services. That is, how to compose a new functionality out of existing component functionalities. However, REST web services model the system from the perspective of resources. The composition of REST web services focuses on the resource composition and state transfer between candidate web services.

As shown in the above, whereas there have been many researched SOAP based web service composition, REST web service composition is untouched field. In Zhao[1]'s paper, it demonstrates automated RESTful web service composition in the context of service-oriented architecture (SOA). The author proposed a formal model for describing individual web services and automating the composition. This paper suggests a method to describe RESTful web service by ontology based conceptual model. This model is used to build the automated composition framework. Zhao[2] proposed a two-stage linear logic based program synthesis approach to automatic RESTful web service composition. The linear logic theorem proof is applied at both resource and service invocation method levels, which greatly improves the searching efficiency and guarantees the correctness and completeness of the service composition. Pautasso[6] identifies a set of requirements for REST web service composition and extends BPEL to accommodate the REST architecture, which aims to enable composition of both traditional web services and REST web service within the same process-oriented service composition language. Alarcon[5] propose a hypermedia-driven approach based on the Resource Linking Language and Petri Nets. Resource Linking Language focuses on the hypermedia characteristics and serves as a description language for RESTful services.

3   System Model and Performance Evaluation

Prior to evaluate the performance in detail, we present a model of system model as a queueing network. The model of our REST Open API Web Service architecture is presented in Figure 1. REST Open API Web Service is composed of 3 components comprising: (1) a web server, (2) a REST web server farms, and (3) internet users. As shown in Figure 1, there are a number of components(nodes) that consist of several queues. A request may receive service at one or more queues before exiting from the system. A model in which jobs departing from Apache Web Server arrive at another queue(i.g., the REST Server Farm from B1 to B4).

Table 1. Configuration parameters

System measure	Apache Web Server	REST Servers
Total arrival rate, λ_i	From 1000/sec to 15000/sec	From 1000/sec to 15000/sec
Service rate, μ_i	15000/sec	15000/sec
Multiple number of servers, s_i	1	From 2 to 11
Traffic intensity, ρ_i	λ/μ	$\lambda/s\mu$

All requests submitted must first pass through the web server for providing HTTP service before moving on to the REST web servers, Jersey. Requests arrive at the web server at an average rate of 1000/sec to 15000/sec, as shown in Table 1. To handle the load, the REST web server components may have several parallel clouded or clustered architecture.

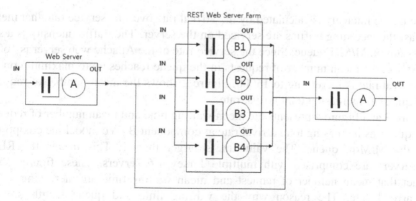

Fig. 1. System evaluation model

Requests arrive at the Apache web server with frequency FreqIn. The initialization process for the request is done at Apache web server. Then, the request proceeds to the component either "REST Web Server Farm" network or depending on the type of the request; if the request is for the REST Web Server, the it goes to the REST Web Server Farm. If the request is for just Web Server, the it goes to the web server. The requests traverses via the internet users and is received by the client's browser, represented by the components at the bottom of Figure 1. Our system model is a sort of open queueing network that has external arrivals and departures. The requests enter the system at "IN" and exit at "OUT". The number of requests in the system varies with time. In analyzing an open system, we assume that the throughput is known (to be equal to the arrival rate), and we also assume that there is no probability of incomplete transfer in this system, so there is no retrial path to go back to node Apache web server. The REST web server farm can have more than one computing servers, especially we present 4 computing servers in Figure 1.

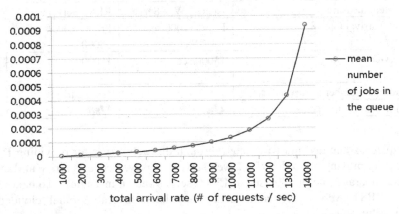

Fig. 2. Mean number of requests in the queue as increasing total arrival rate

The traffic intensity is calculated by the arrival rate over the service rate that means how fast the incoming traffics are serviced on the server. The traffic intensity is a sort of constant on M/M/1 queue. Since the service rate of the Apache web server is 16000 request/sec, the mean number of requests in the queue reaches up to maximum on the total arrival rate is increasing to 15000. Figure 2 shows the mean number of requests in the queue as increasing total arrival rate.

Figure 3 and Figure 4 presents the mean waiting time and mean number of requests in the queue as increasing total arrival rate at component B. We model the component B as the M/M/m queue. The value m is larger than 1. This means the REST web servers are comprised with multiple Jersey 1.6 servers. These figures show the fact that mean number of request and mean waiting time are increasing as the total arrival rate. The reason why the waiting time and queue length are not reaching the maximum even though the total arrival rate is approaches to the maximum value (15000) is due to the multiple REST web servers. Actually, we carried out this experiment with the four multiple servers of Jersey 1.6 REST web service providers.

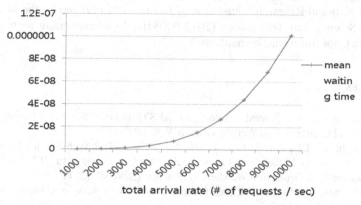

Fig. 3. Mean waiting time as increasing total arrival rate

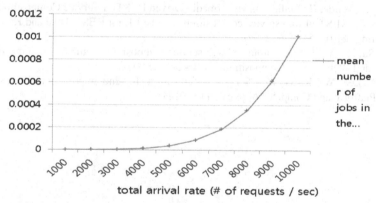

Fig. 4. Mean number of requests in the queue as increasing total arrival rate

4   Conclusion

In this research, we evaluates the performance of RESTful Open APIs for mobile cloud. Recently, we are experiencing a major shift from traditional mobile applications to mobile cloud computing. It improves application performance and efficiency by offloading complex and time consuming tasks onto powerful computing platforms. By running only simple tasks on mobile devices, we can achieve a longer battery lifetime and a greater processing efficiency. This research shows that the scalability of REST Open API web services is satisfiable as a future mobile cloud platform. So, this research shows the scalability of RESTful Open API web services. We checked the REST Open API has enough performance as a future mobile cloud platform.

Acknowledgments. This work is supported by the Basic Science Research Program through the National Research Foundation of Korea (NRF) funded by the Ministry of Education, Science and Technology (2012-0008105). Corresponding author of this paper is Min Choi (miin.chae@gmail.com).

References

1. Zhao, H., Doshi, P.: Towards Automated RESTful Web Service Composition. In: Inteetrnational Conference on Web Services (ICWS) (2008)
2. Zhao, X., Liu, E., Clapworthy, G.J., Ye, N., Lu, Y.: RESTful Web Service Composition: Extracting a Process Model from Linear Logic Theorem Proving. In: IEEE International Conference on Next Generation Web Service Practice (NWeSP) (2011)
3. Li, Z., O'Brien, L.: Towards Effort Estimation for Web Service Compositions using Classification Matrix (2010)
4. Pautasso, C., Zimmermann, O., Leymann, F.: RESTful Web Services vs. Big Web Services: Making the Right Architectural Decision. In: International Conference on WWW 2008 (2008)
5. Alarcon, R., Wilde, E., Bellido, J.: Hypermedia-Driven RESTful Service Composition
6. Pautasso, C.: RESTful web service composition with BPEL for REST. Data and Knowledge Engineering 68(9), 851–866 (2009)
7. Rao, J., Su, X.: A survey of automated web service composition methods. In: Semantic Web Services and Web Process Composition, pp. 43–54 (2004)
8. Choi, M., Lee, W.: REST Web Service Composition. In: 2nd International Workshop of Mobile Platform and Computer Applications (2012)

Genetic Algorithm Based Robot Posture

Dong W. Kim[1], Jong-Wook Park[2], and Sung-Wook Park[2]

[1] Dept. of Digital Electronics, Inha Technical College, Incheon, South Korea
[2] Dept. of Electronics, University of Incheon, Incheon, South Korea
dwnkim@inhatc.ac.kr, jngw@incheon.ac.kr

Abstract. Robot-posture with genetic algorithm is presented in this paper. As a robot platform walking biped robot is used. To cope with the difficulties and explain unknown empirical laws in the robot, practical robot walking on a descending sloped floor is modeled by genetic architecture. These results from the modeling strategy is analyzed and compared.

Keywords: Genetic algorithm, Robot posture, comparison analysis.

1 Introduction

Biped locomotion has been a focus of scientific community for decades. Theoretical studies from various aspects have been accompanied by a lot of simulation work and various practically realized systems from the simplest cases of planar mechanisms to the Honda and Sony humanoid robots, the most advanced biped locomotion robots designed up to now [1][9]-[10]. For a long time already, robots have not been present only in the industrial plants, at a time their traditional work space, but have been increasingly more engaged in the close living and working environment of humans. This fact inevitably leads to the need of working coexistence of man and robot and sharing their common working environment. The walking and living environment, adapted to humans, imposes on robot's mechanical control structure at least two types of tasks related to its motion: motion in a specific environments with the obstacles of the type of staircases, thresholds, multi-level floors, etc., and the motion within a very dynamic scene in which the trajectory of system's motion can be only globally planned and the actual determined on the basis of the instantaneous situation[2]. To achieve walk realization, the foot should be controlled well but generally it cannot be controlled directly but in an indirect way, by ensuring the appropriate dynamics of the mechanism above the foot. Thus the overall indicator of the mechanism behavior is the point where the influence of all forces acting on the mechanism can be replaced by one single force. This point was termed the zero moment point (ZMP). Recognition of the significance and role of the ZMP in the biped artificial walk was a turning point in gait planning and control. As for the indices of biped walking robots

---

[1] Please note that the LNCS Editorial assumes that all authors have used the western naming convention, with given names preceding surnames. This determines the structure of the names in the running heads and the author index.

T.-h. Kim, Y.-h. Lee, and W.-c. Fang (Eds.): FGIT 2012, LNCS 7709, pp. 65–72, 2012.
© Springer-Verlag Berlin Heidelberg 2012

to improve robotic stability, ZMP has been introduced and is commonly used for the gait planning of biped humanoid robots. This is a key point in the control of ASIMO[3], a 26- DOF(Degree Of Freedom) humanoid robot developed by Honda Motor Company in 2000. Vukobratovic et al., [4] investigated the walking dynamics and has proposed ZMP as a good index for walking stability. Kim et al. [5[-[6] employed various computational intelligence methods to design a model of robotic locomotion based on the determination of the ZMP trajectories. Though numbers of existed researches and sophisticated references have been done, some new but essential strategies for the stable robot-moving have still remained for studying and evaluating. Investigating their applicability to the robot is highly demanded since it may exhibit better predictive ability than before, thereby providing more improved insight into human-like walking mechanisms.

In this paper, practical robot walking on a descending sloped floor is employed as robot platform, neuro-fuzzy system, and evolutionary architecture are also used as intelligent modeling strategies. In addition, these results from two methods are shown, analyzed and finally compared.

2   Robot Platform

The identical robot platform employed in [7]-[8] is also used. The robot has 19 joints (three DOFs are assigned to each arm, three and two DOFs are assigned to the hip and the ankles, respectively, and one to each of the two knees). But only 10 dominant joints are used for input candidates. The locations of the joints are shown in Fig. 1.

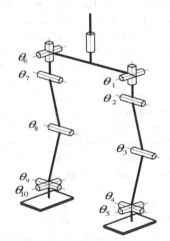

Fig. 1. Joint angle representation of the robot

The height and the total weight are about 445mm and 3Kg, respectively. Each joint is driven by the RC servomotor that consists of a DC motor, gear, and simple controller. Each of the RC servomotors is mounted in the link structure. The motion of walking robot on a descending slope is shown in Fig. 2.

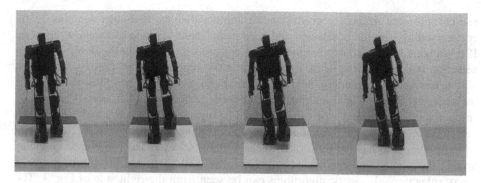

Fig. 2. Walking robot on a descending slope

3   Genetic Algorithm Based Robot Posture

The genetic algorithms (GA) is an efficient tool for searching solutions in a vast search space. By the GA, proper type of MF, number of MF, type of consequent polynomial, set of input variables, and dominant inputs among input candidates are likely to be found in the case where the 10 input candidates have complex correlation.

These parameters stated above in designing a fuzzy system are determined in advance by the trial and error method. But in this paper, the key factors for optimal fuzzy system are specified by GA automatically. When designing a fuzzy system using the GA, the first important consideration is the representation strategy, which is how to encode the fuzzy system into the chromosome. We employ binary coding for the available design specifications. The chromosomes encoded information for fuzzy system are made of 5 sub-chromosomes. The first one has one bit and presents type of membership function. Two types of MF, Triangular and Gaussian MF, are used as the MF candidates. Each is represented by a bit 0 and 1. If the gene in the first sub-chromosome contains 0, the corresponding type of MF is Triangular type. If it contains 1, the MF is Gaussian type. The second sub-chromosome has two bits for number of MF. If many number of MF is selected for certain input variables then fuzzy rules and computational complex can be increased. So we constrain the number of MF to vary only between 2 and 4 for each input variable. The 3rd sub-chromosome has two bits and represents types of polynomial. A total of 4 types of polynomial are used as candidates and each candidate is represented by two bits. Selection of dominant input variables which is greatly contributed to the output and number of these variables is very important. Research of appropriated method for the input selection is still under investigation. In this paper, we handle these problems using the fourth and fifth sub-chromosomes.

To avoid time consuming and heavy structure of fuzzy system, number of input variables to be selected is restricted under four. Input variables as many as the number represented in the sub-chromosome are selected among all input candidates for evolutionary design of fuzzy system. The fifth sub-chromosome is depicted all input candidates. The number of genes in the fifth sub-chromosome is same as the whole candidates of input variables in humanoid robot system. The gene in the fifth sub-chromosome means the corresponding input variables. If a gene contains 1, the corresponding variable is selected and used as an input variable of the fuzzy system. If it contains 0, the variable is ignored and not used. In this way, the dominant input selection is done. For the better understanding the representation strategy, we have a simple example shown in Fig. 3. Using the first and second sub-chromosomes, type of membership function and number of MF are decided as Gaussian type and 2, respectively. Consequent type of polynomial in fuzzy rule is Type 2 and 3 inputs are selected according to the third and fourth sub-chromosomes, respectively. So the type of the polynomial has the form of trilinear. Finally selected and used input variables among the whole input candidates are x2, x7, and x10. Acquired fuzzy model with 8 fuzzy rules through genetic algorithms can be seen from the right side of Fig. 3. The design procedures of evolutionary algorithm are as follows:

(1) All chromosomes in populations are initialized. In the beginning of the process, the initial populations comprise a set of chromosomes that are scattered all over the search space. The populations are all randomly initialized. Thus, the use of heuristic knowledge is minimized

(2) Chromosomes are evaluated. Each chromosome in the population decides a combination of type of MF, number of MF, type of consequent polynomial, number of inputs and corresponding dominant input variables. A model is identified using only the decided parameters through the chromosome. The fitness function is used for the evaluation of the chromosome. We employed commonly used error measurement function which is a mean square error (MSE),

(3) After each chromosome is evaluated and associated with a fitness, the current population undergoes the reproduction process to create the next generation of population. The roulette-wheel selection scheme is used to determine the members of the new generation of population. After the new group of population is built, the mating pool is formed and genetic operators are applied to the chromosomes. The crossover proceeds in three steps. First, two, newly reproduced strings are selected from the mating pool produced by reproduction. Second, a position (one point) along the two strings is selected uniformly at random. The third step is to exchange all characters following the crossing site. We use one-point crossover operator with a crossover probability of Pc (0.85). This is then followed by the mutation operation. The mutation is the occasional alteration of a value at a particular bit position (we flip the states of a bit from 0 to 1 or vice versa). The mutation serves as an insurance policy for recovery of a loss of a particular piece of information (any simple bit). The mutation rate used is fixed at 0.05 (Pm). Generally, after these three operations, the overall fitness of the population improves. Each population generated then goes through a series of evaluation, reproduction, crossover, and mutation.

(4) The design procedure is stopped in the case the termination condition is reached. Else, the above procedure from (2)-(3) is repeated. After the evolution process, the final population generated would consist of highly fit bits that can provide optimal solutions. Finally, the evolutionary Sugeno-type fuzzy model is obtained. Regarding design parameters for evolutionary procedures, 30 chromosomes are generated and evolved gradually according to 0.85 of crossover rate and 0.05 of mutation rate during 25 generations, where each chromosome in the population is

defined. All chromosomes are evaluated by the fitness function based on the mean square error and ranked according to their fitness value. Results of the robot on the decent floor are shown in Figs. 4-6.

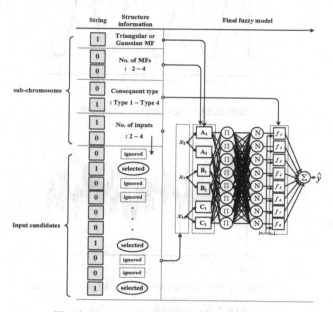

Fig. 3. Genetic Algorithm based architecture

For the best x-coordinate, produced string information is [0, 4, 3, 4: 2, 4, 8, 9]. This string means triangular MF type, 4 MFs, Type 3, and 4 inputs, second, fourth, eighth, ninth, are selected to get good performance. 3.9877 of MSE value is obtained from this string information. For the best y-coordinate, [1, 4, 2, 4: 2, 7, 8, 9] of string information is obtained. So Gaussian MF type, 4 MFs, Type 2, and 4 inputs, second, seventh, eighth, ninth, are selected by evolutionary algorithm and 5.5385 of MSE value is obtained. The corresponding walking trajectory for a descent floor based on the model output is shown in Fig. 6.

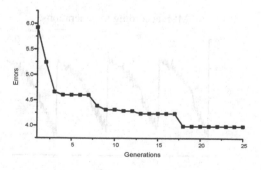

(a) MSE according to generations.

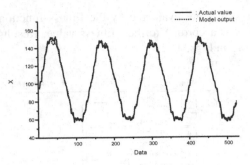

(b) actual values and model output.

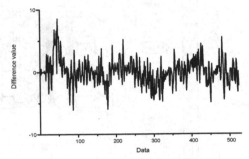

(c) difference between actual values and model output.

Fig. 4. X-coordinate of the robot

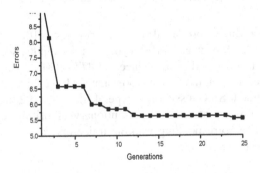

(a) MSE according to generations.

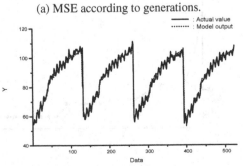

(b) actual values and model output.

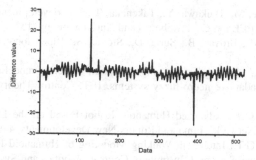

(c) difference between actual values and model output.

Fig. 5. Y-coordinate of the robot

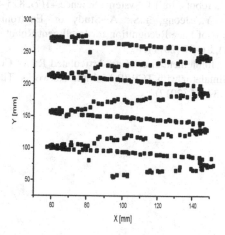

Fig. 6. Walking trajectory on a descent slope

4 Conclusions

Robot posture strategy with genetic algorithm is presented and it results are analyzed in this paper. As a robot platform walking biped robot which has 19 joints is used and trajectory of the zero moment point (ZMP) is employed for the important criterion of the balance. To cope with the difficulties and explain unknown empirical laws in the robot, practical robot walking on a descending sloped floor is modeled by genetic architecture. In this paper, Fig. 6 is finally from the genetic algorithm based model.

References

1. Vukobratovic, M., Brovac, B.: Zero-moment point-thirty five years of its life. Int. J. Humanoid Robotics 1, 157–173 (2004)
2. Vukobratovic, M., Andric, D., Borovac, B.: Humanoid Robot Motion in Unstructured Environment-Generation of Various Gait Patterns from a Single Nominal. In: Kordic, V., Lazinica, A., Merdan, M. (eds.) Cutting Edge Robotics. InTech (2005)

3. Hirai, K., Hirose, M., Haikawa, Y., Takenaka, T.: The development of Honda humanoid robot. In: Proc. IEEE Int. Conf. Robotics and Automation, pp. 1321–1326 (1998)
4. Vukobratovic, M., Brovac, B., Surla, D., Stokic, S.: Biped locomotion. Springer, New York (1990)
5. Kim, D., Seo, S.J., Park, G.T.: Zero-moment point trajectory modeling of a biped walking robot using an adaptive neuro-fuzzy systems. IET. Control Theory Appl. 152, 411–426 (2005)
6. Kim, D., Park, G.T.: Advanced Humanoid Robot Based on the Evolutionary Inductive Self-organizing Network. Humanoid Robots-New Developments, 449–466 (2007)
7. Kim, D., Park, G.T.: Intelligent Walking Modeling of Humanoid Robot Using Learning based Neuro-Fuzzy System. J. Institute of Control, Robotics and Systems 16(10), 963–968 (2010)
8. Kim, D.W., Silva, C.W., Park, G.T.: Evolutionary design of Sugeno-type fuzzy systems for modeling humanoid robots. Int'l J. Systems Science 41(7), 875–888 (2010)
9. Chun, B.T., Cho, M.Y., Jeong, Y.S.: A Study on Environment Construction for Performance Evaluation of Face Recognition for Intelligent Robot. The J. Korean Institute of Inform. Tech. 9(11), 81–87 (2011)
10. Shin, J.H., Park, J.G.: Implementation of an Articulated Robot Control System Using an On/Off-Line Robot Simulator with TCP/IP Multiple Networks. The J. Korean Institute of Inform. Tech. 10(01), 37–45 (2012)

A Reliable QoS Model for Festival Constraint Running on MHAP in Festival Site

Eungnam Ko[1] and Soongohn Kim[2,*]

[1] Division of Information & Communication, Baekseok University,
115, Anseo-Dong, Dongnam-Gu, Cheonan, Chungnam, 330-704, Korea
ssken@bu.ac.kr
[2] Division of Computer and Game Science, Joongbu University,
101 Daehakro, Chubu-Meon, GumsanGun, Chungnam, 312-702, Korea
sgkim@joongbu.ac.kr

Abstract. We propose a RQM_MHAP (Reliable QoS Model of Festival Constraint running on MHAP in Festival Site). RQM_MHAP is a reliable QoS multi-agent model based MHAP with function of an event detection and classification for person's moving line in festival site automatically. It consists of RQM_FEDA and RQM_FECA running on situation-aware ubiquitous computing such as MHAP. RQM_FEDA has a function of event detection running on MHAP for festival sites. This method detects error by inspecting by hooking method. The characteristic of this system is to use the same method to get back again it as it creates a session. RQM_FECA has a function of event classification for festival sites.

Keywords : RQM_MHAP, MHAP, reliable QoS, multi-agent model, person's moving line, festival sites.

1   Introduction

In ubiquitous computing (ubicomp) environments, where computing resources are available everywhere and a great amount of mobile devices play important roles, middleware serves as an essential infrastructure between networks and ubicomp applications [1]. With the advances in resource reservation and scheduling techniques, it is possible to provide end-to-end Quality of Service(QoS) guarantees for distributed applications and services[2]. The smart festival management system is a management system that, for the various festivals that are operated by the local self-governing entities and agencies, enables a direct operation of all the process phases from the advance preparation phase to operation phase and the post management and the administrative tasks, etc. of the planning operational headquarters and agencies [3]. With the rapid development of multimedia and network technology, more and more digital media is generated [4,5,6]. Now it becomes necessary to create an environment where all these resources can be reserved and scheduled in an integrated manner. In

---

* Corresponding author.

T.-h. Kim, Y.-h. Lee, and W.-c. Fang (Eds.): FGIT 2012, LNCS 7709, pp. 73–79, 2012.
© Springer-Verlag Berlin Heidelberg 2012

such an environment, an end-to-end multi-resource reservation will be performed for each client requesting a distributed service, so that it can be guaranteed a certain level of end-to-end QoS [7].

Thus, there is a great need for situation-aware platform to be able to detect and recovery an error whether all QoS requirements of the festival applications are satisfied and analyze tradeoff relationships among the QoS requirements for the festival applications, if all QoS requirements cannot be satisfied to determine a higher priority of QoS requirements for the festival constraints. In this paper, we propose a reliable QoS model for festival constraints running on situation-aware computing such as MHAP.

2   Related Works: MHAP Environment

As shown in figure 1, MHAP has four layered architecture [8]. The physical device and network layer consists of any network and physical device supporting any networking technology. The infrastructure layer introduces infrastructure to provide service management and deployment functions for MHAP services. The MHAP layer consists of MHAP services and provides functionalities constructing HA, which includes event notification, appliance control, HA rule configuration and device management. It uses MOM to support event-driven HA in heterogeneous environment. Facilitating Home Automation needs many different kinds of applications. There are DOORAE agent layer between application layer and MHAP service layer.

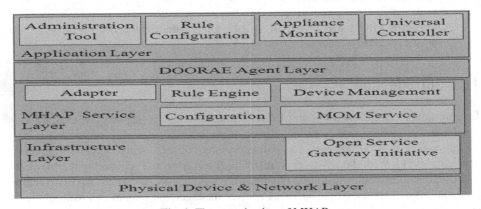

Fig. 1. The organization of MHAP

Nowadays multi-agent systems establish a major research subject in distributed artificial intelligence. In particular, multi-agent modeling makes it possible to cope with natural constraints like the limitation of the processing power of a single agent or the physical distribution of the data to be processed and to profit from inherent properties of distributed system like robustness, fault tolerance parallelism and scalability [9].

3   A Reliable QoS Model for Festival Constraint Running on MHAP in Festival Sites

3.1   The DOORAE for Festival Sites Running on MHAP

DOORAE(Distributed Object Oriented collaboRAtion Environment) is a framework technology for computer collaborative work[10]. It has primitive service functions. Service functions in DOORAE are implemented with object oriented concept for festival sites. We call agent layer. DOORAE provides functions well capable of developing multimedia distance festival system. It includes session management, access control, concurrency control and handling of late comers. As shown in Fig.2, the organization of DOORAE includes 4 layers. The four layers consist of a communication layer, a system layer, a DOORAE agent layer and a multimedia application layer [11]. DOORAE services have many agents for festival sites. They consist of AMA(Application Management Agent), MCA(Media Control Agent), ESA(Event Sharing Agent), SMA(Situation-Aware Session Management Agent), and ACA(Situation-Aware Access and Concurrency Control Agent) for festival sites.

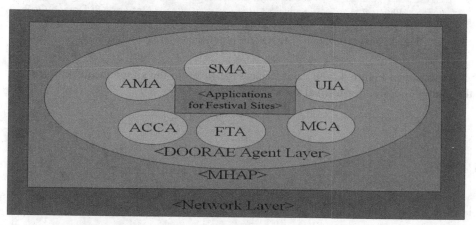

Fig. 2. The organization of DOORAE for Festival Sites running on MHAP

3.2   A Reliable QoS Model for Festival Constraint Running on MHAP in Festival Sites

Our proposed model aims at supporting a reliable QoS model for festival events in situation-aware middleware such as MHAP for festival sites.

This model consists 4 QoS layer such as figure 3: User QoS(including Situation-Aware Application Objects and DOORAE agent), Application QoS(including MHAP service and Other services in MHAP), System QoS(including infrastructure), Network QoS(including Transport Layer Protocols for MHAP Networks) and Device QoS(including Sensors). In this paper, we concentrate in the user QoS layer. There are several constraints which must be satisfied to provide guarantees during multimedia transmission for festival sites. They are time, space, device, frequency, and reliability constraints. Time constraints include delays. Space constraints are such as system buffers. Device constraints are such as frame grabbers allocation. Frequency constraints include network bandwidth and system bandwidth for data transmission. In this paper, we focus on how to represent user QoS during fault tolerance method for festival sites.

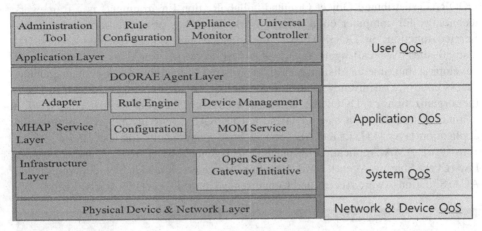

Fig. 3. The organization of DOORAE running on MHAP for festival sites

As shown in Figure 4, you can see message flows in the simultaneous progress of the multiple-session for festival sites.

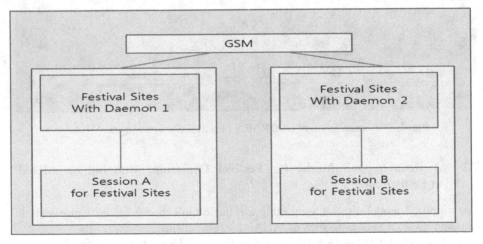

Fig. 4. The Simultaneous Progress of the Multiple-Session for Festival Sites

It consists of GSM, Daemon, Session Manager and FTA for festival sites. FTA must create sequences below if it is decided to be detected and restored for festival sites. First, you can run GSM, run Daemon, FTA and create Session Manager for festival sites. Second, you must register information of creation of service handle and session manager handle by GSM and Daemon for festival sites. Third, you must register information to FTA on Session Manager of creation of Instance handle and application handle by GSM and session manager for festival sites. Forth, You must FTA can receive registration information from GSM for festival sites. To ensure required reliability for situation-aware ubiquitous computing automatically, FTA consists of 2 steps that are an error detection and an error recovery for festival sites. FTA consists of FDA and FRA for festival sites. FDA has a function of error detection for festival sites. FRA has a function of error recovery for festival sites. We are first in need of a method to detect an error for session's recovery. One of the methods detects an error by using "hooking techniques in MS-windows API (Application program Interface)". When an error occurs, a hook is a point in the Microsoft Windows message-handling mechanism where an application can install a subroutine to monitor the message traffic in the system and process certain types of message before they reach the target window procedure for festival sites. Windows contains many different types of hook for festival sites.

4   Simulation Results

To evaluate the performance of the proposed system, an error detection method was used to compare the performance of the proposed model against the conventional model by using DEVS (Discrete Event System Specification) formalism. The DEVS formalism is a theoretical, well grounded means of expressing hierarchical, modular discrete event models. In DEVS, a system has a time base, inputs, states, outputs based on the current states and inputs. The structure of atomic model is as follows [12,13,14].

Before system analysis, the variable that is used in this system. The letter Poll-int stands for "polling interval." The letter App-cnt stands for "The number of application program with relation to FTA session". The letter App_cnt2 stands for "The number of application program without relation to FTA session." The letter Sm-t-a stands for "The accumulated time to register information in SM." We can observe the result value through transducer.

Conventional method for festival site: 2*Poll_int*App_cnt

Proposed method for festival site: 1*Poll_int

Therefore, proposed method is more efficient than conventional method in error detected method in case of App-cnt > 1. We have compared the performance of the proposed method with conventional method for festival site.

The merit of FTA detects an error by using hook techniques for festival site. During process of FTA session, media service instance comes to an end abnormally at times for festival site. In this case, the session's process can come to an end, but it is necessary to protect the user from error by reactivating the media service instance for festival site. We are first in need of a method to detect error for session's recovery for festival site. FTA is a multi-agent system which is implemented with object oriented concept for festival site. This system detects an error by using hook techniques for festival site. The characteristic of this system is to use the same method to get back again it as it creates a session for festival site.

5   Conclusions

The development of multimedia computers and communication techniques has made it possible for a mind to be transmitted from one festival site data to another festival site data in distance environment. This model is a reliable QoS model of DOORAE framework running on situation-aware ubiquitous computing such as MHAP for supporting development on collaborative pervasive computing environment for festival sites. It includes session management, access control, concurrency control and handling errors environment for festival sites. FTA is a system that is suitable for detecting and recovering software error based on pervasive computing environment as MHAP by using software techniques environment for festival sites. One of the methods to detect error for session's recovery inspects process database periodically. But this method has a weak point of inspecting all processes without regard to session environment for festival sites. Therefore, we proposed FTA environment for festival sites. This method detected error by inspecting by hooking method running on pervasive computing environment environment for festival sites. We remain these QoS resolution strategies for error recovery as future work environment for festival sites.

References

[1]   Weiser, M.: Some Computer Science Issues in Ubiquitous Computing. Comm. ACM 36(7), 75–84 (1993)
[2]   Nahrstedt, K., Chu, H., Narayan, S.: QoS-aware resource management for distributed multimedia applications. Journal of High-Speed Networks, Special Issue on Multimedia Networking 7 (1998)
[3]   Lim, B.C., Kim, S.G., Lee, B.C.: Requirements Analysis for Smart Festival Management System. In: Proceedings of the 37th Conference of the KIPS, vol. 19(1), pp. 1004–1006 (2012)
[4]   Zhang, T., Kuo, C.-C.J.: Hierarchical Classification of Audio Data For Archiving and Retrieval. In: ICASSP 1999, Phoenix, vol. 6, pp. 3001–3004 (March 1999)
[5]   Wold, E., Blum, T., Keislar, D., Wheaton, J.: Content-Based Classification, Search, and Retrieval of Audio. IEEE Multimedia 3(3), 27–36 (1996)
[6]   Zhang, H., Kankanhalli, A., Smoliar, S.: Automatic Partitioning of Full-motion Video. In: A Guided Tour of Multimedia Systems and Applications. IEEE Computing Society Press (1995)
[7]   Xu, D., Nahrstedt, K., Viswanathan, A., Wichadakul, D.: QoS and Contention-Aware Multi-Resource Reservation. In: 9th IEEE International Symposium on High Performance Distributed Computing, HPDC 2000 (2000)
[8]   Chen, C.-Y., Chiu, C.-H., Yuan, S.-M.: A MOM-Based Home Automation Platform. In: Szczuka, M.S., Howard, D., Ślęzak, D., Kim, H.-k., Kim, T.-h., Ko, I.-s., Lee, G., Sloot, P.M.A. (eds.) ICHIT 2006. LNCS (LNAI), vol. 4413, pp. 373–384. Springer, Heidelberg (2007)
[9]   Weiβ, G.: Learning to Coordinate Actions in Multi-Agent Systems, pp. 481–486. Morgan Kaufmann Publishers (1998)
[10]   Steinmetz, R., Nahrstedt, K.: Multimedia:computing, Communications & Applications. Prentice Hall PTR

[11]   Hwang, D.J.: Integrated Multimedia Distance Education System for Supporting Various Modes of Student-Professor Collaboration. In: Proceedings of International Conference on SALT, Kissimmee, Fiorida, USA, pp. 19–21 (February 1997)

[12]   Zeigler, B.P.: Object-Oriented Simulation with Hierarchical, Modular Models. Academic Press, San Diego (1990)

[13]   Cho, T.H., Zeigler, B.P.: Simulation of Intelligent Hierarchical Flexible Manufacturing: Batch Job Routing in Operation Overlapping. IEEE Trans. Syst. Man, Cybern. A 27, 116–126 (1997)

[14]   Zeigler, B.P., Cho, T.H., Rozenblit, J.W.: A Knowledge based Environment for Hierarchical Modeling of Flexible Manufacturing System. IEEE Trans. Syst. Man, Cybern. A 26, 81–90 (1996)

An Error Control Agent Running on RCSM
for Smart Festival Management System

Soongohn Kim[1] and Eungnam Ko[2,*]

[1] Department of Computer Science, Joongbu University,
101 Daehakro, Chubu-Meon, GumsanGun, Chungnam, 312-702, Korea
sgkim@joongbu.ac.kr
[2] Division of Information & Communication, Baekseok University,
115, Anseo-Dong, Dongnam-Gu, Cheonan, Chungnam, 330-704, Korea
ssken@bu.ac.kr

Abstract. This paper proposes an error control model running on RCSM (Reconfigurable Context Sensitive Middleware) for smart festival management by analyzing errors of the object data. RCSM provides standardized communication protocols to interoperate an application with others under dynamically changing situations. It describes a hybrid software architecture that is running on situation-aware middleware such as RCSM which has an error or object with a various information for each session and it also supports multicasting with this information for festival management system. (**Keywords** : an error control model, smart festival management, RCSM, hybrid software architecture).

1   Introduction

Advanced information network and multimedia technology are accomplished by combination of educational media through computer, video conference system CSCW(Computer Supported Cooperated Works), environment and interaction between participants of different location with on-screen pictures of each other which are possible to use voice, text and graphic[1]. Context awareness (or context sensitivity) is an application software system's ability to sense and analyze context from various sources; it lets application software take different actions adaptively in different contexts [2]. Currently, the regional local festivals, which are a part of community development projects that utilize the regional cultural resources of the local self-governing entities, contribute in the nurturing of local cultures. And, because of the advantages of festivals -- directly and indirectly -- in terms of their increasing the incomes of the local residents, raising the potential for regional development and being suitable for the acceptance by the dynamic forms of the modern tourism, lately these festivals have been utilized quite a lot. The smart festival management system is a management system that, for the various festivals that are operated by the local self-governing entities and agencies, enables a direct operation

---

[*] Corresponding author.

T.-h. Kim, Y.-h. Lee, and W.-c. Fang (Eds.): FGIT 2012, LNCS 7709, pp. 80–86, 2012.
© Springer-Verlag Berlin Heidelberg 2012

of all the process phases from the advance preparation phase to operation phase and the post management and the administrative tasks, etc. of the planning operational headquarters and agencies [3].

There are two approaches to software architecture on which distributed collaborative applications are based for situation-aware festival sites. Those include CACV (Centralized-Abstraction and Centralized-View) and RARV (Replicated-Abstraction and Replicated-View). We propose an adaptive agent of error or application sharing based on a hybrid software architecture which is adopting the advantage of CACV and RARV for situation-aware festival sites.

Section 2 describes related works. Section 3 denotes an error control model based on RCSM for festival sites data. Section 4 presents simulation results. Section 5 presents conclusions.

2   Related Works

As shown in Table 1, conventional multimedia distance systems are Shastra, MERMAID, MMconf, and CECED. You can see the characteristic function of each system function for multimedia distance system.

Table 1. Analysis of Conventional Multimedia Distance System

Function	Sha-Stra	MER-MAID	MM-conf	CEC-ED
OS	UNIX	UNIX	UNIX	UNIX
Development Location	Purdue Univ. USA	NEC, JAPAN	CamBridge USA	SRI, International
Development Year	1994	1990	1990	1993
Structure	Server /client	Server /client	Centralized or Replicated	Repli-cated
protocol	TCP/IP	TCP/IP	TCP/IP	TCP/IP multicast

A proposed main structure is distributed architecture but for application program sharing, centralized architecture is used. The problem of rapid increase in communication load due to growth in number of participants was solved by letting only one transmission even with presence of many users, using simultaneous broadcasting. Basically, there are two architectures to implement such collaborative applications; the centralized architecture and replicated architecture, which are in the opposite side of performance spectrum. Because the centralized architecture has to transmit huge amount of view traffic over network medium, its performance is reduced to contaminate the benefits of its simple architecture to share a copy of conventional application program. On the other hand, the replicated architecture guarantees better performance in virtue of its reduced communication costs. However, because the replicated architecture is based on the replication of a copy of application program, it is not suit to use for application sharing realization [4-9]. However, it did not include error control or application sharing agent in the conventional architecture.

3   An Adaptive Collaboration Platform with Error Control Agent Running on RCSM for Festival Sites Data

3.1   An Adaptive Collaboration Platform Running on RCSM

Figure 1 shows how all of RCSM's components are layered inside a device. All of RCSM's components are layered inside a device. The Object Request Broker of RCSM (R-ORB) assumes the availability of reliable transport protocols; one R-ORB per device is sufficient. The number of ADaptive object Containers (ADC)s depends on the number of context-sensitive objects in the device. ADCs periodically collect the necessary "raw context data" through the R-ORB, which in turn collects the data from sensors and the operating system. Initially, each ADC registers with the R-ORB to express its needs for contexts and to publish the corresponding context-sensitive interface. RCSM is called reconfigurable because it allows addition or deletion of individual ADCs during runtime (to manage new or existing context-sensitive application objects) without affecting other runtime operations inside RCSM [2].

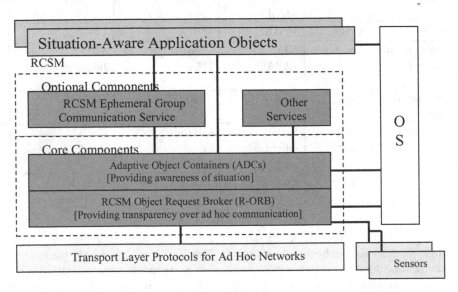

Fig. 1. Integrated Components of RCSM

DOORAE is made up of a distributed architecture for a collaborative multimedia distance education system and forms several levels according to service functions for festival data. DOORAE is a foundation technology for computer collaborative work that allows development of required application by combining many agents composed of units of functional module, provided by DOORAE, when user wishes to develop new application field. As it can be seen on Figure 2, DOORAE's basic structure consists of DOORAE application program, DOORAE agents, operating system and communication subsystem. DOORAE agents are composed of SEMA and APMA. SEMA is a session management agent that appropriately control and manages session and opening / closing of sessions, even in the case of several sessions being generated at the same instant. APMA is an application management agent that handles request of application. SEMA consist of GSM, LSM, AMA, CRPA, ACCA, and COPA. APMA consist of MECA, INA, UIA, and APSA. AMA is an agent that has functions of application management. CRPA is an agent that has functions of managing formation control of DOORAE communication protocol for festival data. ACCA is an agent that has functions of managing floor control and concurrency control for festival data. COPA is an agent that has functions of providing participants same view for festival data.

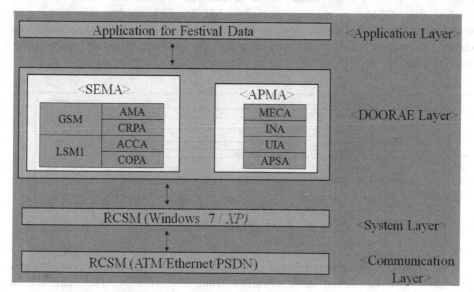

Fig. 2. DOORAE Platform based on RCSM Architecture for Festival Data

3.2 An Adaptive Collaboration Platform Running on RCSM for Festival Sites Data

For a festival, based on the characteristics of the festival and in accordance with separation into a preparation phase, operation phase, post management and reporting phase, the requirements for each of the phases are defined and a management system is developed for -- in a logical order -- planning, design and development.
For the requirements of the festival operation phase, what is needed are the assessment data needed for operation such as punctuality check, smoothness check, surveys, etc. and the management side requirements such as schedule reporting, visitor feedback, event management, risk management, visitor traffic flow trace, etc.

During the festival operation, systems for the design and construction of festival site facilities and festival risk management are important requirements as well. For smooth feedback during the festival operation phase, the interoperability between the management that applied QRCode (Quick Response Code) and automatic visitor processing system is essential.

3.3   An Adaptive Collaboration Platform with Error Control Agent Running on RCSM for Festival Sites Data

SMA consists of GSM(Global Session Manager), Daemon, LSM(Local Session Manager) and PSM(Participant Session Manager). GSM has the function of controlling whole session when a number of sessions are open simultaneously for festival data. LSM manages only own session for festival data. For example, LSM is a local session manager in distributed multimedia environment for festival data. GSM can manage multiple LSM for festival data. Daemon is an object with services to create session for festival data. Session management can create the sequence below and you can see the message flow in Figure 3 for festival data.

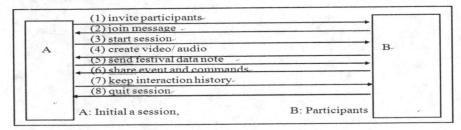

Fig. 3. Session Management for festival sites

This approach is based on the idea of comparing the expected error type which is generated with the actual error occurred from festival sites. The sequence of recovery's message flow for festival sites can be shown in Figure 4. If an error is to be recovered, you can create sequences below with ECA(Error Control Agent) for festival sites. It creates a session with initial configuration information. It requests port ids for audio/video servers to build-up a Local Session Manager. It assigns port ids for audio/video servers of an application. It invites to the session and build-up a session instance monitor. It sends invited messages to start build-up of session instance monitor. It builds up Session Instance Monitor using the configuration information from LSM. It sends joint message to the Local Session Manager. It sends session information to Global Session Manager for set-up of GSM table. It begins a session for festival sites. It exchanges message or command between LSM and PSM and media data between media server based on interpretation of message handler for festival sites.

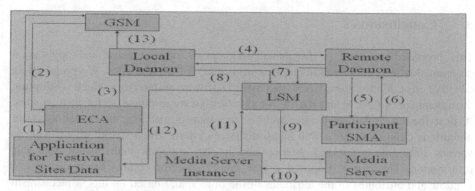

Fig. 4. The relationship between GSM, Daemon and LSM with Error Control Agent for Festival Sites Data

4   Simulation Results

There are two approaches to software architecture on which distributed collaborative applications are based for situation-aware festival sites. Those include CACV (Centralized-Abstraction and Centralized-View) and RARV (Replicated-Abstraction and Replicated-View). We proposed an adaptive agent of error or application sharing based on a hybrid software architecture which is adopting the advantage of CACV and RARV for situation-aware festival sites. For the structure of software implementation, the CACV(Centralized-Abstraction and Centralized-View) and the RARV(Replicated-Abstraction and Replicated-View) are extreme approaches to design software architecture on which distributed, collaborative applications are based. The CARV(Centralized-Abstraction and Replicated-View) architecture is also comparable with those architecture in terms of performance [10]. Overview of the command serialization overhead is.

Table 2. Comparison for Software Architecture in situation-aware environment

	Centralized	Replicated	Hybrid(Proposed)
Set initial State	Easy	Hard	Medium
Allow Late Comer	Easy	Hard	Easy
Command Serialization	Easy	Hard	Easy
Communication Overhead	High	Low	Low
Probability	Good	Bad	Good
Performance	Bad	Good	Good
Application Copy	One	More than one	More than one
Control Complexity	Low	High	High
Error Control	No	No	Yes
Festival Sites	No	No	Yes

5   Conclusions

This proposed structure is distributed architecture but for error and application program sharing, centralization architecture is used for festival sites. We proposed an adaptive error control agent based on a hybrid software architecture which is adopting the advantage of CACV and RARV for situation-aware middleware for festival sites. It described a hybrid software architecture that is running on situation-aware ubiquitous computing for a web based distance system which has an object with an various information for each session and it also supports multicasting with this information. This paper proposed a new model of error control by analyzing the window and attributes of the attributes of the object, and based on this, a mechanism that offers a seamless view without interfering with error and application program sharing is also suggested for festival sites. We remain an adaptive agent of error and application program sharing with error elimination function for domino effect running on a hybrid software architecture which is adopting the advantage of CACV and RARV based on situation-aware for festival sites.

References

1. Park, G.C., Hwang, D.J.: Design of a multimedia distance learning system: MIDAS. In: Proceedings of the IASTED International Conference, Ptiisburgh, USA (April 1995)
2. Yau, S., Karim, F., Wang, Y., Wang, B., Gupta, S.: Reconfigurable Context-Sensitive Middleware for Pervasive Computing. IEEE Pervasive Computing 1(3), 33–40 (2002)
3. Lim, B.C., Kim, S.G., Lee, B.C.: Requirements Analysis for Smart Festival Management System. In: Proceedings of the 37th Conference of the KIPS, vol. 19(1), pp. 1004–1006 (April 2012)
4. Ko, E.-N.: A Web Based Multimedia Distance Education System With An URL and Error Synchronization Function. WSEAS Transactions on Computers 3(4), 1142–1146 (2004)
5. Barreto, A.B., Zhai, J.: Physiologic Instrumentation for Rea-time Monitoring of Affective State of Computer Users. In: Proceedings of WSEAS USA Miami Conference, pp. 484–220 (April 2004)
6. Anupam, A., Bajai, C.L.: Collaborative Multimedia Scientific Design in Shastra. In: Proceeding of the ACM Multimedia 1993, pp. 447–456 (August 1993)
7. Ohmori, T., Watabe, K.: Distributed Cooperative Control for Application Sharing Based on Multiparty and Multimedia Desktop Conferencing Systems: MERMAID. In: 4th IEEE ComSoc International Workshop on Multimedia Communications, April 1- 4 (1992)
8. Crowley, T., Tomlinson, R.: MMConf: An Infrastructure for Building Shared Multimedia Applications. In: CSCW 1990 Proceedings (October 1990)
9. Craighill, E., Skinner, K.: CECED: A System For Informal Multimedia Collaboration. In: Proceedings ACM Multimedia 1993, August 1-6 (1993)
10. Lauwers, J.C., Lantz, K.A.: Collaboration Awareness in Support of Collaboration Transparency: Requirements for the Next generation of Shared Window Systems. In: Proc. of ACM CHI 1990, pp. 302–312 (April 1990)

The Decomposed K-Nearest Neighbor Algorithm for Imbalanced Text Classification

Hyung-Seok Kang[1], Kihyo Nam[2], and Seong-in Kim[1]

[1] Division of Industrial Management Engineering, Korea University, 5-1 Anam-dong, Seongbuk-gu, Seoul 136-701, Republic of Korea
{hyoungsuk1,tennis}@korea.ac.kr
[2] UMLogics Co., Ltd., E-420 Pangyo Inovalley, 622 Sampyung-dong, Bundang-gu, Seongnam-city, Kyungki-do 463-400, Republic of Korea
nkh@umlogics.com

Abstract. As textual data have exponentially increased, it is focused that a need for automatic classification of relevant data to one of pre-defined classes. In many practical applications, they assume that training data are evenly distributed among all classes, but they are suffered from an imbalanced problem. Several algorithms and re-sampling methods have been proposed to overcome an imbalanced problem, but they are still facing the overfitting and information missing. This paper proposes the Decomposed K-Nearest Neighbor (DCM-KNN). In training step, the DCM-KNN decomposes training data into misclassified and correctly-classified data set based on the result of traditional KNN, and finds the appropriate KNN for each set. In test step, the DCM-KNN estimates whether test data is similar to misclassified and correctly-classified data set, and applies the appropriate KNNs. Experimental results show that proposed algorithm can achieve more accurate results in an imbalanced condition.

Keywords: Text classification, K-Nearest Neighbor, Imbalanced problem, Overfitting.

1 Introduction

Since textual data have increased dramatically, a need for classify textual data based on their contents is increased. Text classification (categorization) is the process of assigning pre-defined class to textual data [9]. Recently, text classification has been applied in a variety of domains, such as spam filtering [6] and sentiment classification [21]. Machine learning techniques such as the Naive Bayesian Filter [2, 5, 12], the K-Nearest Neighbor (KNN) [3, 14, 16, 17, 19, 20], and hybrid techniques [1, 18] have been applied in text classification. Especially, the KNN is widely used because of its simplicity and efficiency [17]. In spite of its merits, the KNN has problem of inductive biases or model misfits, since the uneven distribution in training data will affect the KNN classified result negatively [15]. It is quite often that the class distribution is imbalanced [4]. Several novel KNN algorithms [3, 16, 17, 20] and

T.-h. Kim, Y.-h. Lee, and W.-c. Fang (Eds.): FGIT 2012, LNCS 7709, pp. 87–94, 2012.

re-sampling methods [7, 8] to overcome an imbalanced problem have been proposed. However, these algorithms and methods are still facing the problem of overfitting and data missing [4].

We propose the Decomposed K-Nearest Neighbor (DCM-KNN), which avoids overfitting and information missing. The DCM-KNN consisted of training step and test step. In training step, the DCM-KNN decomposes training data into misclassified and correctly-classified training data set based on the result of traditional KNN, and finds the appropriate KNN and parameters for each set. In test step, the DCM-KNN estimates whether test data belong to misclassified or correctly-classified data set. Finally, DCM-KNN optionally applies the appropriate KNNs which are found in training step.

2   Related Works

Several KNNs to overcome an imbalanced problem have been proposed. Yang et al. [20] proposed the average of similarity-KNN (AS-KNN), which divides the sum of similarity of each class by the number of the data of each class in the nearest neighbors. Baoli et al. [3] proposed the adaptive-KNN (ADPT-KNN), which uses the different number of training data and different K values for each class. For larger classes, the ADPT-KNN assigns the larger K than smaller classes. Tan [16] proposed the neighbor weighted-KNN (NW-KNN), which allocates larger weight to the smaller classes and smaller weight to the larger classes. Tan [17] proposed the drag pushing-KNN (DP-KNN), which increases or decreases the weights of features of classes in order to induce right decision for misclassified training data.

Several re-sampling methods for adjusting the size of training data have been proposed. Japkowicz [7] and Japkowicz & Stephen [8] proposed over-sampling method increasing the number of data in small class and under-sampling method reducing the number of data in large class. Although both over-sampling and under-sampling can alleviate the problem, there are some side effects, such as overfitting and information missing [4].

3   DCM-KNN

The main concepts of the DCM-KNN are decomposing data into misclassified and correctly-classified data set, and applying the appropriate KNNs for each set. In training step, training data are classified by traditional KNN into misclassified and correctly-classified data set. Additionally, we assume that the nearest neighbors of misclassified data have the potential of misclassification. In spite of nearest neighbors of misclassified data are classified correctly, they might be classified into misclassified data set if the number of nearest neighbors with the same class is less then threshold (*Acceptable*). Finally, the DCM-KNN finds the appropriate KNN and parameters for each set. Fig. 1(a) represents a brief example, having 2 classes (C_{Black}, C_{White}), 2 features (f_1, f_2), and 45 training data (30, 15) for understanding a concept of the DCM-KNN.

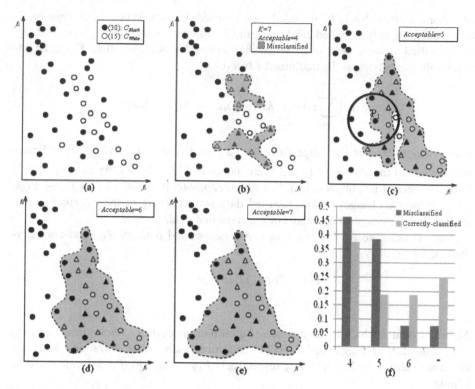

Fig. 1. Comparison of misclassified and correctly-classified data set according to the *Acceptable*

3.1   Training Step

(Step 1) Compose set T_{MTD} that are misclassified by traditional KNN from training data,

$$T_{MTD} = \{t_e \mid C_{TRA}(t_e) \neq C(t_e), e = 1, 2, ..., m\}, \tag{1}$$

$C_{TRA}(t_e)$ is the result of traditional KNN and $C(t_e)$ is the real class label of training data t_e. In fig. 1, Triangle points represent the misclassified and are the elements of T_{MTD}.

(Step 2) Compose set $T_{candidate}$ that are the K nearest neighbors of T_{MTD}.

$$T_{candidate} = \{t_c \mid t_c \in KNN(t_e)\}, t_e \in T_{MTD}, \tag{2}$$

t_c which is classified correctly are closed to t_e, so we assume that t_c has the possibility of misclassification. For example, the P_1 in Fig. 1(c) has 4 black and 3 white neighbors and is correctly classified as C_{Black}. But it is the nearest neighbor of misclassified data. As a result, P_1 is the element of $T_{candidate}$.

(Step 3) Compose set T_{PMTD} that is likely to be chosen from $T_{candidate}$. In this step, we judge misclassified possibility of t_c using the nonnegative integer parameter *Acceptable*. The *Acceptable* is threshold for judging t_c may remain to misclassified data set. When the *Acceptable* is greater than the number of dominant nearest neighbors, a point should be included misclassified data set. When the *Acceptable* is equal to K, it is only excluded condition from T_{PMTD} that all nearest neighbors of t_c, t_{cj}, are classified as same class of t_c. When the *Acceptable* is greater than K, the DCM-KNN will also behave as the traditional KNN do.

$$T_{PMTD} = \{t_c \mid \sum_{j=1}^{K} y_1(t_{cj} \in KNN(t_c), t_c) < Acceptable\}, \tag{3}$$

where *Acceptable* has the range from $\lceil K/2 \rceil$ to K and $y_1(t_{cj}, t_c) \in \{1, 0\}$ indicates whether or not the classes of t_{cj} and t_c are same. In Fig. 1(c), As the number of P_1's dominant nearest neighbors is less than the *Acceptable*, P_1 is included in T_{PMTD}. Figs. 1(b-e) show the changes of misclassified data set according to the *Acceptable*, and gradual including nearest neighbors of misclassified data.

(Step 4) Separate all training data into misclassified data set T_{MD} and correctly-classified data set T_{CD}.

$$T_{MD} = T_{MTD} \cup T_{PMTD}, \tag{4}$$

$$T_{CD} = T \cap T_{MD}^c.$$

(Step 5) Count x which is the number of dominant nearest neighbors for all training data, and calculate $F_{MD}(x)$ and $F_{CD}(x)$ by summing the number of training data with the same value x in T_{MD} and T_{CD}, respectively. $F_{MD}(x)$ and $F_{CD}(x)$ are calculated as follows,

$$F_{MD}(x) = \sum_{i=1}^{v} y_2(t_i), t_i \in T_{MD}, \tag{5}$$

$$F_{CD}(x) = \sum_{j=1}^{u} y_2(t_j), t_j \in T_{CD},$$

$$\text{where} \quad y_2(t) = \begin{cases} 1, if \max_q\{ \sum_{x_r \in KNN(t)} y(x_r, c_q)\} = x \\ 0, otherwise \end{cases}, \lceil K/2 \rceil \le x \le K,$$

$y(x_r, c_q) \in \{1, 0\}$, indicates whether or not a nearest neighbor x_r belongs to class c_q, v is the number of training data in misclassified data set, and u is the number of training data in correctly-classified data set.

(Step 6) Calculate $P_{MD}(x)$ and $P_{CD}(x)$ that is the proportion of $F_{MD}(x)$ and $F_{CD}(x)$. $P_{MD}(x)$ is formulated as $F_{MD}(x)/v$ and $P_{CD}(x)$ is formulated as $F_{CD}(x)/u$. For example, in Fig. 1(f), the number of misclassified training data is 32 and the data with the 5 dominant nearest neighbors are 15, and the proportion, $P_{MD}(5)$, is 0.47.

(Step 7) Find the appropriate KNN for misclassified and correctly-classified data set. In this paper, we use the NW-KNN and traditional KNN. The NW-KNN is applied to misclassified data set, and the traditional KNN is applied to correctly-classified data set. For the sake of choosing parameter K and λ, each data set is recursively separated by KNNs. Then, we find near optimal K and λ that maximizes classification accuracy.

3.2   Test Step

(Step 1) Find the nearest neighbors of d_s that we are willing to classify, and calculates x_s which is the number of dominant nearest neighbors.

(Step 2) Compare $P_{MD}(x_s)$ with $P_{CD}(x_s)$. If $P_{MD}(x_s)$ is greater than $P_{CD}(x_s)$, then the DCM-KNN applies the NW-KNN. Otherwise, the DCM-KNN applies the traditional KNN. For example, we assume that a certain test datum with the nearest neighbors composed of 5 black points and 2 white points has 5 dominant nearest neighbors. We compare $P_{MD}(5)$ with $P_{CD}(5)$ in Fig. 1(f), and choose the proportion of misclassified ($P_{MD}(5)$) because that proportion is bigger than correctly-classified ($P_{CD}(5)$). As a result, this datum is regarded as misclassified data set and the NW-KNN is applied.

4   Experimental Results

4.1   Experiment Design

We used open example[1] to evaluate the accuracy of the DCM-KNN. The example is Reuters articles (Reuters-21578) which represents corporate acquisitions. There are 1000 positives, 1000 negatives, and 600 test data. Each of data consists of 9947 features. In this paper, the entire training data sets were selected randomly. Using the DCM-KNN and other KNNs mentioned in section 2, we compared the performances of four cases having the different numbers of training data in each class: (1,000, 100), (1,000, 200), (1,000, 300), and (1,000, 1000).

4.2   Comparison and Analysis

Fig. 2, representing the accuracy of algorithms, shows that the DCM-KNN achieves better accuracy in many cases. In the case of extremely imbalanced condition, the DCM-KNN shows a decided difference in Fig. 2(a). Also, in the case of balanced condition, the DCM-KNN maintains the higher level of accuracy as shown in Fig. 2(d). In conclusion, the DCM-KNN shows small degradation of accuracy in imbalanced condition and compared to that of balanced condition.

We also show precision, recall, and F-measure. We select the best K and parameters according to accuracy and Table 1 shows these measures from imbalanced condition (1000, 100) to balanced condition (1000, 1000). The DCM-KNN shows better performance in imbalanced condition.

---

[1] Downloadable at `http://download.joachims.org/svm_light/examples/example1.tar.gz`

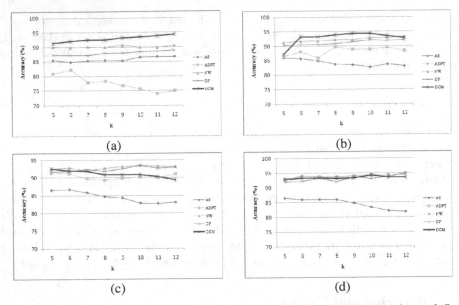

Fig. 2. Comparison of accuracy between four cases. (a) shows the comparison of five algorithms for the (1000, 100), (b) (1000, 200), (c) (1000, 300), and (d) (1000, 1,000).

Table 1. Comparison of precision, recall and F-measure between KNNs

Case	KNN (*K*)	Positive			Negative		
		Precision	Recall	F-measure	Precision	Recall	F-measure
1000: 100	AS (11)	0.82	0.94	0.88	0.93	0.79	0.86
	ADPT (6)	0.75	0.98	0.85	0.97	0.66	0.79
	NW (9)	0.85	0.99	0.91	0.98	0.83	0.90
	DP (12)	0.82	0.99	0.90	0.99	0.78	0.87
	DCM (12)	0.92	0.97	0.94	0.97	0.92	0.94
1000: 200	AS (5)	0.82	0.92	0.87	0.91	0.80	0.85
	ADPT (8)	0.84	0.97	0.90	0.97	0.82	0.89
	NW (12)	0.89	0.98	0.93	0.98	0.88	0.93
	DP (10)	0.89	0.96	0.92	0.95	0.88	0.92
	DCM (9)	0.96	0.92	0.94	0.93	0.96	0.94
1000: 300	AS (6)	0.86	0.88	0.87	0.88	0.85	0.86
	ADPT (5)	0.87	0.97	0.92	0.96	0.86	0.91
	NW (11)	0.91	0.96	0.94	0.96	0.90	0.93
	DP (10)	0.91	0.96	0.94	0.96	0.91	0.93
	DCM (5)	0.93	0.92	0.92	0.92	0.93	0.92
1000: 1000	AS (5)	0.91	0.81	0.86	0.83	0.92	0.87
	ADPT (12)	0.97	0.92	0.95	0.93	0.97	0.95
	NW (12)	0.97	0.92	0.95	0.93	0.97	0.95
	DP (12)	0.98	0.92	0.95	0.92	0.98	0.95
	DCM (10)	0.97	0.91	0.94	0.92	0.97	0.94

5   Conclusion

In this paper, we suggested an algorithm for imbalanced condition that increases the performance of text classification. Training data were separated into misclassified and correctly-classified data set, and different KNNs were applied to each set.

We compared the results of the DCM-KNN with the other KNNs, in cases of having the different numbers of training data in each class: (1,000, 100), (1,000, 200), (1,000, 300), and (1,000, 1000). For the experimental result, we used Reuters articles. There are 1000 positives, 1000 negatives, and 600 test data. We used the entire training data sets that were selected randomly. The experimental result showed that the DCM-KNN achieves excellent performance when it comes to extremely imbalanced condition.

We note that though in training step, the DCM-KNN required dense calculations due to its parameters, in test step, the DCM-KNN needed similar complexity as contrasted with other KNNs. We considered simple example with two separated data sets that are misclassified and correctly-classified. The DCM-KNN can be expanded to use various sets, and hybridized the diverse machine learning techniques.

References

1. Aci, M., Inan, C., Avci, M.: A hybrid classification method of K-Nearest Neighbor, Bayesian methods and genetic algorithm. Expert Systems with Applications 37(7), 5061–5067 (2010)
2. Androutsopoulos, I., Koutsias, J., Chandrinos, K., Paliouras, G., Spyropoulos, C.: An experimental comparison of Naïve Bayesian and keyword-based anti-spam filtering with personal e-mail messages. In: Proceedings of the 23rd Annual International ACM SIGIR Conference on Research and Development in Information Retrieval, pp. 160–167 (2000)
3. Baoli, L., Qin, L., Shiwen, Y.: An adaptive K-Nearest Neighbor text categorization strategy. ACM Transactions on Asian Language Information Processing 3(4), 215–226 (2004)
4. Chen, E., Lin, Y., Xiong, H., Luo, Q., Ma, H.: Exploiting probabilistic topic models to improve text categorization under class imbalance. Information Processing & Management 47(2), 202–214 (2011)
5. Chen, J.N., Huang, H.K., Tian, S.F., Qu, Y.L.: Feature selection for text classification with Naïve Bayes. Expert Systems with Applications 36(3), 5432–5435 (2009)
6. Carpinter, J., Hunt, R.: Tightening the net: A review of current and next generation spam filtering tools. Computers & Security 25(8), 566–578 (2006)
7. Japkowicz, N.: The class imbalance problem: Significance and strategies. In: Proceedings of the International Conference on Artificial Intelligence (IC-AI), pp. 111–117 (2000)
8. Japkowicz, N., Stephen, S.: The class imbalance problem: A systematic study. Intelligent Data Analysis 6(5), 429–449 (2002)
9. Jiang, S., Pang, G., Wu, M., Kuang, L.: An improved K-Nearest Neighbor algorithm for text categorization. Expert Systems with Applications 39(1), 1503–1509 (2012)
10. Joachims, T.: Text Categorization with Support Vector Machines: Learning with Many Relevant Features. In: Nédellec, C., Rouveirol, C. (eds.) ECML 1998. LNCS, vol. 1398, pp. 137–142. Springer, Heidelberg (1998)

11. Joachims, T.: Learning to classify text using support vector machines. Kluwer Academic Publishers, Norwell (2002)
12. Lee, L.H., Isa, D., Choo, W.O., Chue, W.Y.: High relevance keyword extraction facility for Bayesian text classification on different domains of varying characteristic. Expert Systems with Applications 39(1), 1147–1155 (2012)
13. Lee, L.H., Wan, C.H., Rajkumar, R., Isa, D.: An enhanced support vector machine classification framework by using Euclidean distance function for text document categorization. Applied Intelligence 37(1), 80–99 (2012)
14. Manne, S., Kotha, S.K., Fatima, S.S.: Text categorization with K-Nearest Neighbor approach. In: Proceedings of the International Conference on Information Systems Design and Intelligent Applications, vol. 132, pp. 413–420 (2012)
15. Shi, K., Li, L., Liu, H., He, J., Zhang, N., Song, W.: An improved KNN text classification algorithm based on density. In: IEEE International Conference on Cloud Computing and Intelligence Systems (CCIS), pp. 113–117 (2011)
16. Tan, S.: Neighbor-weighted K-Nearest Neighbor for unbalanced text corpus. Expert Systems with Applications 28(4), 667–671 (2005)
17. Tan, S.: An effective refinement strategy for K-Nearest Neighbor text classifier. Expert Systems with Applications 30(2), 290–298 (2006)
18. Wan, C.H., Lee, H.L., Rajkurmar, R., Isa, D.: A hybrid text classification approach with low dependency on parameter by integrating K-Nearest Neighbor and support vector machine. Expert Systems with Applications 39(15), 11880–11888 (2012)
19. Yang, Y.: An evaluation of statistical approaches to text categorization. Information Retrieval 1(1-2), 76–88 (1999)
20. Yang, Y., Ault, T., Peirce, T., Lattimer, C.W.: Improving text categorization methods for event tracking. In: Proceedings of the 23rd Annual International ACM SIGIR Conference on Research and Development in Information Retrieval, pp. 65–72 (2000)
21. Ye, Q., Zhang, Z., Law, R.: Sentiment classification of online reviews to travel destinations by supervised machine learning approaches. Expert Systems with Applications 36(3), 6527–6535 (2009)

A Novel Packet Transmission Scheme
with Different Periods According to the HSR Ring
Direction in Smart Grid

Seokjoon Hong and Inwhee Joe

[1] Department of Electronics and Computer Engineering, Hanyang University,
Seoul, 133-791 South Korea
daniel379@hanyang.ac.kr
[2] Division of Computer Science and Engineering, Hanyang University,
Seoul, 133-791 South Korea
iwjoe@hanyang.ac.kr

Abstract. High-availability Seamless Redundancy (HSR) is a redundancy protocol that provides duplicated frames for separate physical paths with zero recovery time. HSR is suitable for time critical applications in Industrial Ethernet
Networks. However, the existing HSR scheme makes the unnecessary traffic by
redundant frame copies. This drawback will degrade the network performance
and may cause network congestion or delays. Thus, we propose a packet transmission scheme with different periods based on HSR ring topology for reducing
network traffic load. Since it uses different transmission period by IEC 61850
traffic types, it can be adaptive for smart grid automation network technology.
The main idea of the proposed scheme is using a different packet transmission
period on each port of the HSR node. On one port near to destination, the node
sends packets with the default transmission period, which is the same with the
existing HSR scheme. On the other port, the node sends packets with an extended transmission period according to the delay requirement of IEC 61850
traffic types. By using the extended transmission period, the proposed scheme
can reduce the network traffic and retain HSR network's availability. Also, we
evaluate the proposed scheme by using OPNET simulation tool. The performance evaluation results show that the proposed scheme is better than the existing HSR scheme.

Keywords: Different transmission periods, extend transmission period,
IEC61850 traffic type, network traffic load, smart grids.

1   Introduction

An important characteristic of Ethernet is its resilience, i.e., the capability to sustain
user traffic in the presence of network faults.

The legacy 802.1d Spanning Tree Protocol (STP) [1] is the first algorithm to prevent data looping and recovery when a link failure occurs.. Because of poor convergence speed, the 801.w Rapid Spanning Tree Protocol (RSTP) has been introduced [2].

T.-h. Kim, Y.-h. Lee, and W.-c. Fang (Eds.): FGIT 2012, LNCS 7709, pp. 95–102, 2012.

Network resilience is also critical for Industrial Ethernet networks such as smart grid networks. There are International Electrotechnical Commission (IEC) standards for smart grid implementation. IEC 61850 [3] is an international standard for station-bus application, which lets IEDs (intelligent electronic devices) communicate with each other and with a substation controller. The IEC 62439 standard [4] defines redundancy methods applicable to most industrial networks, which differ in topology and recovery time.

Parcvallel Redundancy Protocol (PRP) and High Availability Seamless Redundancy (HSR) [5] are the latest additions to the IEC 62439 standard. Designed for mission critical and time sensitive applications such as those found in electric utility protection and control applications, PRP and HSR provide guaranteed behavior under failure conditions and increased network reliability. Higher network uptime translates to reduced outages and maintenance resulting in overall cost savings.

The HSR protocol is especially adaptive for ring topologies. However, redundant connections to other networks such as coupled rings or mesh topologies are also possible. As a redundancy protocol for the Ethernet network, the HSR provides duplicated frames on separate physical paths with zero recovery time.

The main drawback of HSR is the unnecessary traffic due to the redundant frame copies that are generated and circulated inside the network. This downside will degrade the network performance and may cause network congestion and delay.

Improvement of HSR Traffic Performance [6] proposed two approaches to reduce the unnecessary traffic in HSR. The first approach is Quick Removing (QR) that is to remove the redundant frame copies from the network when all the nodes have received one copy from the sent frame and began to receive a redundant copy. The second approach is Virtual Ring (VRing) which is to divide an HSR network into several VRings.

In this paper, we introduce a packet transmission scheme with different periods based on HSR ring topology for reducing network traffic load. In Section 2, we describe a packet transmission scheme with different periods based on HSR ring topology. In Section 3, we evaluate the performance of the proposed scheme in terms of traffic load using OPNET simulation tool. Finally, we conclude in Section 4.

2   A Packet Transmission Scheme with Different Periods

In this section, we propose a packet transmission scheme with different periods based on HSR ring topology. In the existing HSR algorithm, DANH (Doubly Attached Node implementing HSR), send packets with same transmission periods on both ports for zero recovery time.

However, this feature of the existing HSR algorithm always makes many unnecessary packets in normal state.

So, we propose a packet transmission scheme with different periods on each port. On one port which is near to destination, the node sends packets with default transmission period which is the same with existing HSR scheme. And on the other port which is far from destination. The node sends packets with extended transmission period according to communication requirement of IEC 61850 traffic types [7].

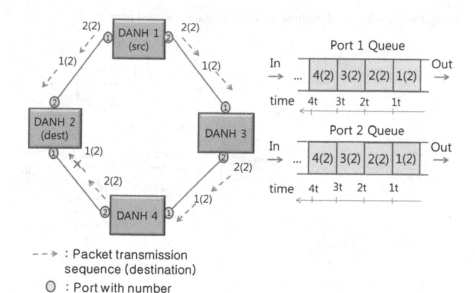

--→ : Packet transmission sequence (destination)

O : Port with number

Fig. 1. Packet transmission of the existing HSR algorithm

Type 1		Type 2	Type 3	Type 4	Type 5	Type 6
1A	1B					
3~10 ms	20~100 ms	<100ms	<500ms	3~10ms	≥1000ms	Not defined

Fig. 2. IEC 61850 Substation Message Type and communication requirement

The scheme uses following pseudocode algorithm for calculating transmission period t to extend.

> Whenever the node sends packet in normal state,
>
> IF (t < 0.9 * $L_{max}(Tr(f))$) THEN (t = t + 1dt)
>
> (At first, t = 1dt, 1dt is time for transmitting one packet.)
>
> IF (t > 0.9 * $L_{max}(Tr(f))$) THEN (t = t - 1dt)
>
> When link failure occurs, t = ldt

Fig. 3. Pseudo code algorithm for extending transmission period

Here, is max latency value of traffic f which is specified in communication requirement of IEC 61850 traffic types. For example, if node send Type1(1A) packet to destination, the is 10ms. And we multiply it by 0.9 for providing an error tolerance of 10%.

Using this pseudocode algorithm, we can calculate extended period.

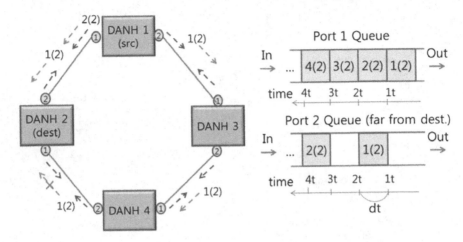

--→ : Link cost calculation, routing table building through BPDU packet

--→ : Packet transmission sequence (destination)

Fig. 4. Packet transmission of the proposed scheme

Figure 4 shows the main idea of the proposed scheme. The source node is DANH 1 and the destination node is DANH 2. If the DANH 1 send packet to DANH 2, it send packets with default transmission period which is same with existing HSR algorithm on port 2 which is near to DANH2. And it sends packets with extended transmission period on port1 which is far from destination.

Figure 5 shows the change of packet transmission period when link fail occurs. If the link failure occurs on one side of the node in the ring network, the node send packet with default transmission period on the other side.

The procedure for our algorithm is shown in Figure 6. First, the proposed algorithm makes their layer 2 routing table with the path cost information from new type BPDU packet sent from each node. We assume path cost 1 is equal to one hop count. After all nodes have built their routing table, the node starts data packet transmission on each port based on the routing table.

And Table 1 shows a routing table for the DANH 1 (of Figure 4) established by the proposed algorithm. The "near to dest" column of table means whether the port of the node is near to destination.

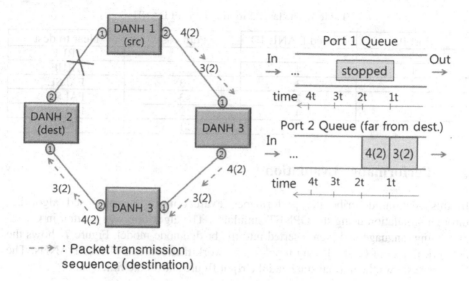

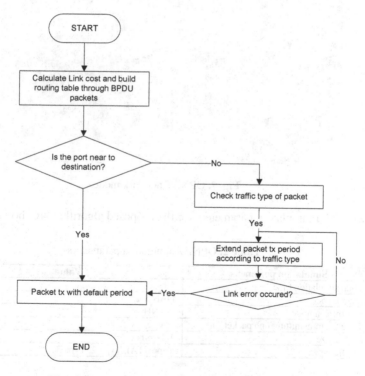

Fig. 5. Change transmission period when link failure occurred

Fig. 6. The procedure for proposed algorithm

Table 1. The layer 2 routing table of DANH

Port ID	Linked DANH ID	Path cost	Near to dest
1	2	1	TRUE
1	4	2	TRUE
1	3	3	FALSE
2	2	3	FALSE
2	4	2	FALSE
2	3	1	TRUE

3   Performance Evaluation

In this section, describe the performance evaluation of the proposed algorithm through simulation using the OPNET simulator. The algorithm was written in C programming language and then inserted into the bridge node model. Figure 7 shows the network model of the HSR ring topology network that consists of four DANHs. The left figure shows the normal state and the right figure shows the failed state.

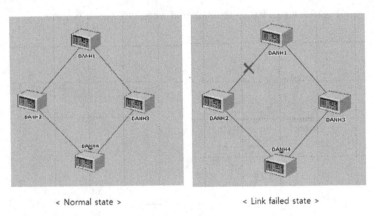

< Normal state >   < Link failed state >

Fig. 7. OPNET network model

The OPNET simulation parameters for the proposed algorithm are shown in Table 2.

Table 2. OPNET simulation parameters

Simulation parameter	Value
Total simulation time	60 sec
Source node	DANH 1
Destination node	DANH 2
Time for transmitting one packet (dt)	1ms
Packet size	1000bits
Traffic types	Type1(1A), Type 2, Type 3

Figure 8 shows total traffic load of the network according to increase source traffic. Because of duplicated packets, the existing HSR algorithm makes doubled traffic load of source traffic.

But, with the proposed scheme, traffic load of network is slightly more than half of those with the existing HSR algorithm by using extended transmission period according to traffic types.

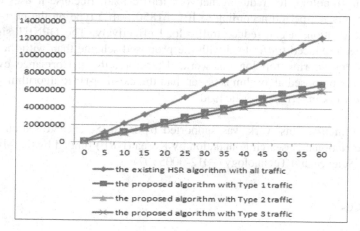

Fig. 8. Total traffic load (bps) of the network according to increase source traffic (Mbps)

Figure 9 shows the change of traffic load when link failure occurs in 20~40s in the simulation. Before 20s and after 40s, traffic load of network with the proposed scheme is slightly more than half of those with the existing HSR algorithm. For the 20~40s simulation time, the result shows that the proposed scheme makes same traffic load with the existing algorithm.

The reason is that the propose scheme use same transmission period on the other port when link failure occurs.

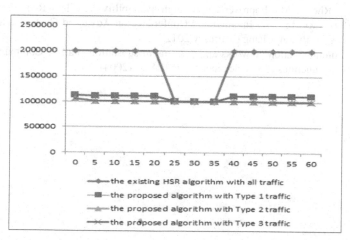

Fig. 9. Total traffic load (bps) changes when link failure occurred in 20~40s simulation time (sec)

4   Conclusions

In this paper, we proposed a packet transmission scheme with different periods based on HSR ring topology for reducing network traffic load. Because it uses extended packet transmission period according to IEC 61850 traffic type on the port which is far from destination, it can reduce traffic load effectively. The OPNET simulation results showed reduced traffic load with the proposed scheme than with the existing HSR algorithm in ring topology network. Therefore, the performance evaluation shows that the proposed algorithm is better than the existing HSR algorithm for a ring topology network in terms of traffic load.

Acknowledgments. This work was supported by Basic Science Research Program through the National Research Foundation by Korea (NRF) funded by the Ministry of Education, Science and Technology (2012-0005507).

References

1. IEEE Information Technology, Part 3: Media Access Control (MAC) bridges. ISO/IEC 12802-3, ANSI/IEEE Std 802.1D (1998)
2. IEEE Standard for Local and metropolitan area networks – common specifications. Part 3: Media Access Control (MAC) bridges – Amendment 2: Rapid Reconfiguration Amendment to IEEE Std 802.1D, 1998 Edition, IEEE Std 802.1w-2001 (1998)
3. IEC 61850 Communication networks and systems in substations-All parts, Reference number IEC 61850-SER
4. International Electrotechnical Commission, Geneva IEC62439 Highly Available Automation Networks, issued (March 2009)
5. International Electrotechnical Commission, Geneva IEC FDIS 62439-3 Highly Available Automation Networks, PRP & HSR (August 2009)
6. Nsaif, S.A., Rhee, J.M.: Improvement of high-availability Seamless Redundancy (HSR) traffic performance. In: 14th International Conference on Advanced Communication Technology (ICACT), PyeongChang (February 2012)
7. DL/T 20. Communication networks and systems in substations Part 5: Communication requirements for functions and device models, [S] 18(4) (2004)

Automated Classification of Galaxies
Using Invariant Moments

Mohamed Abd Elfattah[1,5], Mohamed A. Abu ELsoud[2],
Aboul Ella Hassanien[3,5], and Tai-hoon Kim[4]

[1,2] Computer Science Dept. Mansoura University
m_abdelfatah@ymail.com, moh_soud@mans.edu.eg
[3] Faculty of Computers and Information, Cairo Univesrity, Egypt
[4] School of Information Science, University of Tasmania, Australia
[5] Scientific Research Group in Egypt (SRGE)
http://www.egyptscience.net

Abstract. Classification and identification of galaxy shape is an important issue for astronauts since it provides valuable information about the origin and the evolution of the universe. Statistical invariant features that are functions of moments have been used as global features of galaxy images in their pattern recognition. In this paper, an automated training based recognition system that can compute the statistical invariant features for different galaxy shapes is investigated. The proposed algorithm is robust, regardless of orientation, size and position of the galaxy inside the image. Feature vectors are computed via nonlinear moment invariant functions for each galaxy shape. After feature extraction, the recognition performance of classifier in conjunction with these moment–based features is introduced. Computer simulations show that Galaxy images are classified with an accuracy of about 90% compared to the human visual classification system.

Keywords: Invarinat Moments, Mean Squared Error (MSE), Fisher Score.

1 Introduction

Galaxies are gravitationally bounded gaseous mass composed mostly of dust, and aggregates of billions of bright stars. Galaxies with their morphological structure, essentially their shape and general visual appearance, gives astronomers much information about their content of matter and their evolution. Morphological galaxy classification is a system used by astronomers to classify galaxies based on their structure and appearance [1], [2]. It is becoming an important issue because astrophysicists frequently make use of large database of information either to test existing theories, or to form new conclusions to explain the physical processes governing galaxies, star-formation, and the nature of the universe.

However old, the most common and still used classification scheme is the system devised by Sir Edwin Hubble in 1936. The Hubble's classification scheme classifies galaxy photographs into four main categories as follows: Elliptical, Spiral, Barred

T.-h. Kim, Y.-h. Lee, and W.-c. Fang (Eds.): FGIT 2012, LNCS 7709, pp. 103–111, 2012.

spiral, Irregular. Currently, astronomers manually classify galaxies from galaxies' photographs based on the human visual recognition system. This method is slow, and is certainly not a worthy activity for an astronomer to be engaged in. This method is also subject to human error especially when dealing with noisy or unclear images, and thus leads to some undesired misclassifications. Moreover, astronomy has recently seen an explosion of data, as programs like the Sloan Digital Sky Survey (SDSS) will generate nearly 50 million images of galaxies alone.

Fortunately, access to this amount of data has become possible in the past decade; in conjunction with the development of computer aided classification algorithms in the area of image processing and hence; it is the promising solution with much scope for machine learning. Computer aided classification is also known as automated classification with partial engagement by the human factor or even the absolute independence of the human factor at all.

Recently, many machine learning based algorithms were applied to automatic classification of galaxy images [3], [4] and demonstrated considerable success in several experiments. Automated methods for galaxy image analysis are also based on the classification of galaxy image datasets into the four known morphological classes [5]. The Gini coefficient method [6] and the CAS method [7] are examples of these attempts .Some of these attempts were developed to classify galaxies by analyzing their internal structure.

Other attempts have been made to apply neural networks that use features extracted from the images as well as raw pixel data as inputs to the neural networks. For example, locally weighted regression using principal component analysis used by Calleja and Fuentes [8] has achieved a 90% success rate for two classifications (spiral and elliptical) using about 310 training examples. Naïve Bayes based classification techniques [6], [9] follows the same approach to this problem with varying success. Another class of image classification techniques is those dependent on the transform methods such as the Discrete Cosine Transform (DCT) and the Discrete Wavelet Transform (DWT) compared with the artificial neural networks techniques [10]. In 2012, Shamir [11] propose an image analysis unsupervised learning algorithm that can detect peculiar galaxies in datasets of galaxy images.

The images used in this paper were obtained from the Zsolt Frei Catalogue provided by the department of Astrophysical Sciences at Princeton University [12]. This catalogue contains approximately 113 different galaxy images and is often used as a benchmark for astronomical study as the images are carefully calibrated. Taking into account the occurrence of galaxies and charged coupled device (CCD) camera multiple images stacking and supported by Sloan Digital Sky Survey (SDSS).

In this paper, our goal is to apply an automated classification algorithm that is suitable for massive data set. This will fasten the process of classification, while decreasing the classification error. We explore the effectiveness of invariant moments as useful features extracted from galaxy image data, and the performance of an automated training based algorithm. We have selected the Hu seven invariant moments to reduce the dimensionality of the feature space this was the main reason behind a lengthy algorithms operating on a large set of features. A common way to resolve this problem was feature selection [13], which reduces the dimensionality by selecting a subset of features from the input feature set.

The rest of the paper is structured in the following way: In Section (2) we describe the image analysis, Denoising. In Section (3) we describe with the aid of mathematical formulation the proposed algorithm and the features that are used to classify the test set of images. Experimental results and finally in Section (4) while conclusions and future work are presented in section (5).

2   Galaxies Image Analysis and Denosing

After the traditional operation of transforming the color image into a gray scale image and for the invariant moments to be calculated the image must contain only the desired galaxy, thus, the image must be denoised. Since the type of noise that is dominating the image is the spike noise, the Denoising algorithm must be able to remove this spike noise. Simply edge detection is the only Denoising process that is required as the spikes has a sharp edge distinguishing it from local intensity variation in the image. As we can seen from Figure (1), the edge detection has successfully detected. This is true for any image whether is belongs to the training set or the test set, for the features calculated are strongly affected by the noise content in the image.

Fig. 1. Image Denoising results

Fortunately the area of the image that contains the galaxy is characterized by slow variation in intensity such that there is no a sharp boundary between the area of the galaxy and its neighborhood. This helped a lot in the process of separating the desired content from undesired objects such as distant stars, comets or any other astronautical objects that is observed in the same image.

3   The Proposed Classification Algorithm

The following algorithm is proposed to develop the classification of galaxy images using of invariant moments features. The galaxy images must be first de-noised before feature extraction. The images are minimized to 313×313 pixel dimensions in order to ease the computational burden.

Step1: Create a 7x1 feature vector through the process of feature extraction that is performed by computing the Hu seven invariant moments for all of the training and test galaxy images.

Step2: Select one of the test images and calculate the Mean Squared Error (MSE) which is weighted according to the Fisher score vector. The MSE is measured between the desired image that is a test image and the images constituting the set of the training images.

Step 3: Decide on the class of the test image according to the class of the corresponding image that produces the minimum MSE through one of the four galaxy types, that is, the spiral, barred spiral, Elliptical and the Irregular galaxy types.

3.1   Feature Extraction

Traditionally, moment invariants are computed based on the information provided by both the shape boundary and its interior region (Hu, 1962, Prokop and Reeves, 1992).Given a continuous function $f(x, y)$ defined on a region D in the x-y plane, these regular moments are defined as:

$$m_{pq} = \iint_D x^p y^q f(x, y) dx dy \tag{1}$$

Although the moments used to construct the moment invariants are defined for continuous space two dimensional functions f(x, y), however practical images are defined on discrete two dimensional space in the form of pixels and hence they are computed in discrete form as:

$$m_{pq} = \sum_{j=0}^{N-1} \sum_{i=0}^{M-1} (i \Delta x)^p (j \Delta y)^q f(i \Delta x, j \Delta y) \tag{2}$$

Where i, j are pixel indices in the **x** and **y** directions respectively, $\Delta x, \Delta y$ are the corresponding space sampling intervals and M, N are the number of pixels in the **x** and **y** directions respectively. Strictly speaking, the seven moments defined by Hu are computed by the normalized central moments defined as:

$$\eta_{pq} = \frac{\mu_{pq}}{\mu_{00}^\gamma} \tag{3}$$

$$\mu_{pq} = \sum_{j=0}^{N-1} \sum_{i=0}^{M-1} (i \Delta x - \bar{x})^p (j \Delta y - \bar{y})^q f(i \Delta x, j \Delta y) \tag{4}$$

Where $\bar{x}$ and $\bar{y}$ are the image centroids defined as $\bar{x} = \dfrac{m_{10}}{m_{00}}$ and $\bar{y} = \dfrac{m_{01}}{m_{00}}$, μ_{00}^γ is

the normalization constant and . .. ... [. . . . . 2] . . 1.

In terms of the central moments, the seven moments are given as shown in Eq. (5).

$$M_1 = \eta_{20} + \eta_{02}$$

$$M_2 = (\eta_{20} - \eta_{02})^2 + 4\eta_{11}^2$$

$$M_3 = (\eta_{30} - 3\eta_{12})^2 + (3\eta_{21} - \eta_{03})^2 \qquad (5)$$

$$M_4 = (\eta_{30} + \eta_{12})^2 + (\eta_{21} + \eta_{03})^2$$

$$M_7 = (3\eta_{21} - \eta_{03})(\eta_{30} + \eta_{12})[(\eta_{30} + \eta_{12})^2 - 3(\eta_{21} + \eta_{03})^2]$$

$$- (\eta_{30} + 3\eta_{12})(\eta_{21} + \eta_{03})[3(\eta_{30} + \eta_{12})^2 - (\eta_{21} + \eta_{03})^2]$$

The most interesting property of this type of features is that all of the above seven moments are invariant to galaxy scale, position, and orientation. The feature vector of the input image to the procedure is thus defined as:

$$X = [\ M_1\ M_2 \ldots \ldots M_7\ ]^T \qquad (6)$$

Where $(.)^T$ denotes the matrix transpose operation.

3.2   Classification Technique

The distance between two image feature vectors X and Y can then be computed by using a simple Weighted Nearest Neighbor rule, as described by: the following form:

$$d_{MSE} = \sqrt{(X_f - Y_f^i)W_f(X_f - Y_f^i)^T}, i \in \{1,2,3,4\} \qquad (7)$$

Where W_f the assigned Fisher weight is score of feature f, i is the class number and d_{MSE} is the computed weighted distance between the two feature vectors.

The predicted class of a given test image is simply determined by the class number corresponding to the shortest weighted distance between a source image and the test image. It given in the following equation:

$$d_{MSE} = \underset{i}{\arg\min}\{\sqrt{(X_f - Y_f^i)W_f(X_f - Y_f^i)^T}\}, i \in \{1,2,3,4\} \qquad (8)$$

With W_f is The Fisher score matrix.

3.3   A Brief Review of Fisher Score

In this section, we briefly review Fisher score for feature selection, and discuss its shortcomings. The key idea of Fisher score is to find a subset of features. Features, such that in the data space spanned by the selected features, the distances between data points in different classes are as large as possible, while the distances between data points in the same class are as small as possible. In particular, given the selected features and the *Fisher Score* is computed using the following equation:

$$F(X_j) = \frac{\sum_{k=1}^{C} n_k (\mu(j,k) - \mu(j))^2}{\sigma_j^2} \qquad (9)$$

Where

$$\sigma_j^2 = \sum_{k=1}^{C} n_k (\sigma(j,k))^2$$

$$\mu(j) = \sum_{k=1}^{C} n_k (\mu(j,k))^2$$

With C is the number of classes, n_k is the size of the dataset in each class and $\mu(j,k)$ and n_k are the mean vector and size of the kth class respectively in the data space, i.e., $k = 1,2,....n_k$ and $\mu(j)$ is the overall mean vector of the reduced data. Then the Fisher score of the jth feature is easily computed.

4   Experimental Results and Analysis

The method was tested using a dataset of spiral, barred spiral, elliptical and irregular galaxy images representing the most common types of galaxies and firstly classified manually by the author. The author classification is assumed to be 100% perfect as the human recognition system is supposed to be an absolute reference for classification. The galaxies in the dataset are divided into two groups, that is, the training set consisting of only 6 images for each galaxy type and 68 test images that were all selected randomly by the MATLAB simulation program from an overall set of 108 image dataset.

This study has the advantage of being independent of the image whether being monochromatic or color as the image is firstly transformed to a monochromatic black and white image, the galaxy position, orientation and size inside the image, in opposite to the Galaxy Zoo monochrome images, which were introduced by the Galaxy Zoo bias study (Lintott et al. 2008). However, the proposed algorithm is highly sensitive to the noise as the number of tested features is very small, that is, only seven invariant moments. Hence, an image Denoising technique is required to remove noisy pixels that do not belong to the galaxy pixels. This noise appears in the form of spikes, scattered at different positions in the image as a large scale salt and pepper noise .Another advantage of the used algorithm is the dependence on a very small dataset for each class, that is, only six training images were used for the training phase and a small number of features was tested without the need to select the most top ranked features from the Fisher score matrix. Although color images were used, no color features were used in this study as the images are transformed to the gray scale. The results of simulation over the whole available data set show that about

~90% of the galaxy images were classified correctly to the assumed classes of galaxies, as can be seen from Table(I). Some of the classifications results are shown in Table (I) .In simulations the classes are assigned a number as follows:

1- Number "1" is assigned for Spiral galaxies
2- Number"2" is assigned for barred spiral galaxies
3- Number"3" is assigned for Elliptical galaxies
4- Number"4" is assigned for galaxies of irregular shape.

Table 1. Some of the classifications results

Galaxy Image	Author Class.	Auto. Class.	Mse
1	Spiral	Spiral	2.2922
2	Spiral	Spiral	0.7546
3	Spiral	Irregular	2.3686
4	Spiral	ELLIPTICAL	1.1197
5	Barred Spiral	Barred Spiral	0
6	BARRED SPIRAL	Spiral	1.8826
7	ELLIPTICAL	ELLIPTICAL	0.6741
8	IRREGULAR	IRREGULAR	0

The Fisher score of all features that are used for classification are arranged in a descending order in Figure (2). As can be seen from this figure that the top ranked feature is the first central moment and there is a clear distinction between the value of the Fisher score for the first feature and the remaining six features. This implies that the MSE classification may depend only on one feature and ignoring the remaining features will not strongly affect the decision of the predicted class. It is expected that for larger datasets that may be larger than 2000 images in some algorithms, the proposed classification algorithm is promising to show excellent results that are competitive to those algorithms that use too large dataset and excessive number of features that may overcome 2500 features as well . It can be assumed that the classification accuracy can be improved when using datasets of nearby, large or bright galaxies. It can be correctly concluded that the proposed algorithm is sensitive to the superimposed noise in the image, hence; if better Denoising techniques were used, the features of central moments are less affected by this noise.

The error calculated in Table (I) is the weighted MSE not the error in the common sense that ranges from 0 to 1.This error can be divided by the number of used features so that it doest not exceed 1 however, we did not do so in order to emphasize the idea of the weighted MSE. It is possible to increase the probability of correct decision, the is, the fraction of images that is correctly classified from the whole test set, while reducing the probability of misclassification by investigating the sources of error .Intuitively speaking, as the size of the training set increases. As said before, a powerful advantage of this algorithm is its dependence on a small number of features tested without the need to select the most top ranked features from the Fisher score.

However; the features are ranked according to their Fisher score and shown in Fig. (2). As is clear the first two moments are observably the top ranked and it may be attractive to operate on these two features only while ignoring the remaining five, however it is not recommended to do so as the used features are extracted from very noisy images and the final decision of the classifier will be more subject to error as the decision lies on a smaller number of features. In addition these seven features all together are known to distinguish the object on interest and reducing the number of distinguished features may lead to an overlap in the features of different classed and hence wrong decisions.

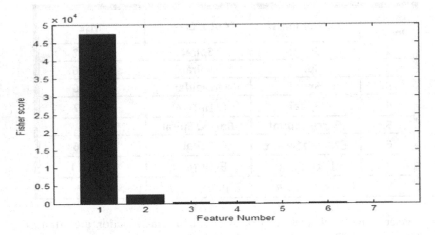

Fig. 2. The Fisher score of the used features

5   Conclusions and Future Works

As a shape descriptor technique, the evidence to date is that moment invariants are very good features to use when dealing with particular types of shapes such as alphanumeric characters (Hu, 1962). The aim of this paper was to investigate the usefulness of moment invariants for the automatic identification of common galaxy shapes. When tested for the more generalized cartographic shapes, moment invariants seem to work. There is good distinction between classes although overlap occurs but within classes the discrimination is not as strong. This indicates that moment invariants alone will not be sufficient. To find an optimal result the moment invariants technique will be compared with other techniques currently being investigated. These include Fourier descriptors, scalar descriptors and boundary chain coding. Moreover, all the techniques are looking at the object shapes in isolation. Future work will be to combine some or all the methods mentioned using data fusion techniques to produce a more reliable object recognition system. A millions of galaxy images will be processed in classification algorithm. The complexity of proposed algorithm and classification efficiency will be computed.

References

1. Young, M.: The Technical Writer's Handbook. University Science, Mill Valley (1989)
2. Pettini, M., Christensen, L., D'Odorico, S., Belokurov, V., Evans, N.W., Hewett, P.C., Koposov, S., Mason, E., Vernet, J.: CASSOWARY20: a wide separation Einstein Cross identified with the X-shooter spectrograph. Monthly Notices of the Royal Astronomical Society 402, 2335–2343 (2010)
3. Shamir, L.: Automatic morphological classification of galaxy images. Monthly Notices of the Royal Astronomical Society 399, 1367–1372 (2009)
4. Banerji, M., Lahav, O., Lintott, C.J., Abdala, F., Schawinski, K., Bamford, S., Andreescu, D., Raddick, M., Murray, P., Jordan, M., Slosar, A., Szalay, A., Thomas, D., Vandenberg, J.: Galaxy Zoo: reproducing galaxy morphologies via machine learning. Monthly Notices of the Royal Astronomical Society 406, 342–353 (2010)
5. Kormendy, J., Bender, R.: A proposed revision of the Hubble sequence for elliptical galaxies. The Astrophysical Journal 464, 119–122 (1996)
6. Abraham, R.G., Van Den Bergh, S., Nair, P.: A new approach to galaxy morphology. The Astrophysical Journal 588, 218–229 (2003)
7. Conselice, C.J.: The relationship between stellar light distributions of galaxies and their formation histories. The Astrophysical Journal Supplement 147, 1–28 (2003)
8. Calleja, J., Fuentes, O.: Machine Learning and Image Analysis for Morphological Galaxy Classification. Monthly Notices of the Royal Astronomical Society 24, 87–93 (2004)
9. Mohamed, M.A., Atta, M.M.: Automated Classification of Galaxies Using Transformed Domain Features. IJCSNS International Journal of Computer Science and Network Security 10(2) (February 2010) 86
10. Liang, Y., Kelemen, A.: Time lagged recurrent neural network for temporal gene expression classification. International Journal of Computational Intelligence in Bioinformatics and Systems Biology 1(1) (2009)
11. Shamir, L.: Automatic detection of peculiar galaxies in large datasets of galaxy images. Journal of Computational Science 1, 1–23 (2012)
12. Frei, Z.: Zsolt Frei Galaxy Catalog (1999), http://www.astro.princeton.edu/frei/catalog.htm (retrieved 2002 from Princeton University, Department of Astrophysical Sciences)
13. Banerji, M., Lahav, O., Lintott, C.J., Abdala, F., Schawinski, K., Bamford, S., Andreescu, D., Raddick, M., Murray, P., Jordan, M., Slosar, A., Szalay, A., Thomas, D., Vandenberg, J.: Galaxy Zoo: reproducing galaxy morphologies via machine learning. Monthly Notices of the Royal Astronomical Society 406, 342–353 (2010)

The Quality Control of Software Reliability Based on Functionality, Reliability and Usability

Hye-Jung Jung and Suck-Joo Hong

Department of Digital Information and Statistics, PyeongTaek University,
PyeongTaek, 450-701, Korea
jhjung@ptu.ac.kr

Abstract. Software quality control is very important. We have concern about software reliability deeply. Many research workers study about software reliability. We want to evaluate software quality as quantity. Especially, we worry about software failure data. We have to find the method software reliability by using software failure data. We propose that software test cases for evaluating of software functionality and usability. We propose that the evaluating of software reliability. We introduce the international standards of software quality control. Also, in this paper, we propose the quality testing metric for those criteria. Our evaluation method of software quality is based on the international standards ISO/IEC 9126-2 and ISO/IEC 25000 series.

Keywords: Quality Evaluation, ISO/IEC 25000, ISO/IEC 9126-2, Functionality, Usability, Reliability, International Standards.

1 Introduction

Software systems have been used in variety of fields. Software technology has been growing rapidly and software has become an essential part of many applications including industrial, military, financial, healthcare, educational areas.

Usually, software development model consists of following phases: requirement, specification, design, coding, testing, operation, and maintenance. Nowadays, we think that software testing is very important. We emphasis the software testing. So, we study about software testing for control of software quality. For example, six sigma is a measurement of software quality. Finding software errors in the early stage through software testing is very important because the cost of correcting an error is very high if an error is found after the system is released [2], [3]. Especially, we concern about safety of software. Nowadays, users have many kinds of requirements. So, we have to consider user's requirement before development of software. So, we have to start software testing early. We know CMM for software quality control. CMM is a specialized the control of software quality. Usually, developer manages the software development project by development cost and schedule. The Software Engineering Institute(SEI) at Carnegie Mellon University make the Capability Maturity Model(CMM). CMM is a method to improve the development and delivery

T.-h. Kim, Y.-h. Lee, and W.-c. Fang (Eds.): FGIT 2012, LNCS 7709, pp. 112–118, 2012.

of software. CMM consists of 5 levels: level 1 is Ad hoc, level2 is Repeatable, Level 3 is Defined, Level 4 is Managed, and Level 5 is Optimizing.

CMM supports 4 areas: Process Management, Project Management, Engineering, Support. The Process Management of CMM is organization process focus, organization process definition, organization training, organizational process performance and organizational innovation and deployment. Project management consists of Project Planning, Project Monitoring and Control, Supplier Agreement Management, Integrated Project Management, Risk Management, Integrated Teaming, Quantitative Project Management. Engineering consists of Requirements Development, Requirements Management, Technical Solution, Product Integration, Verification, Validation. Support consists of Configuration Management, Process and Product Quality Assurance, Measurement and Analysis, Organizational Environment for Integration, Decision Analysis and Resolution, Causal Analysis and Resolution. So, CMM consists of 5 levels, that is initial, managed, defined, quantitatively managed, optimizing.

Initial is that results are unpredictable because they are dependent on individuals' skills and efforts. Repeatable is that basic process have been established on a project level, making it possible to replicate performance on similar projects. Defined is that standard processes have been integrated across the IT organization and used consistency on all projects. Managed is that detailed measurements and quantitative.

In this paper, we introduce the international standards of software quality testing in chapter 2. And, we proposed the software test cases of software quality evaluation in chapter 3. We introduce the result in chapter 4.

2   International Standards of Software Testing

II.   Currently, there are three quality models in ISO/IEC 25000 series(we called SQuaRE(Software Quality Requirement and Evaluation)), that is the quality in use model and the product quality model and data quality model. We can apply these models to evaluate software quality and data quality. For example, we express the use model: Efficiency, Effectiveness, Satisfaction, Freedom from risk, Context coverage. The product quality model consists of system/software product quality properties into eight characteristics: functionality, efficiency, compatibility, usability, reliability, security, maintainability, and portability.   We evaluate the product or system provided functions that meet stated and implied needs when used under specified condition in functionality . We evaluate the product or system can be used by specified users to achieve specified goals with effectiveness, efficiency and satisfaction in a specified context of use.

Characteristics   consist of   the subcharacteristics. For example, functionality consists of the functional completeness, functional correctness, functional appropriateness. Also, usability consists of the appropriateness recognizability, learnability, operability, user error protection, user interface aesthetics, accessibility. The reliability consists of maturity, availability, fault tolerance and recoverability. The product quality are useful for specifying requirements, establishing measures and performing quality evaluations.

The quality life cycle model divide the three principal phases. First, the product under development phase is the subject of external measures of software quality. Second, the product testing phase is the subject of external measures of software quality. Third, the product in use phase is the subject of quality in use.

SQuaRE series of standards consists of the following divisions under the general title Systems and software product Quality Requirements and Evaluation:

ISO/IEC 2500n - Quality Management Division,
ISO/IEC 2501n - Quality Model Division,
ISO/IEC 2502n - Quality Measurement Division,
ISO/IEC 2503n - Quality Requirements Division, and
ISO/IEC 2504n - Quality Evaluation Division.

Figure 1 illustrates the organisation of the SQuaRE series representing families of standards, further called Divisions.

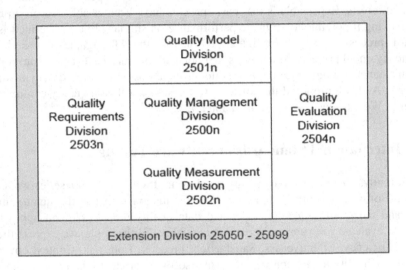

Fig. 1. Organization of SQuaRE series of International Standards

This International Standard is part of the 2502n – Quality Measurement Division that currently consists of the following International Standards:

ISO/IEC 25020 – Measurement Reference Model and Guide: provides a reference model and guide for measuring the quality characteristics defined in ISO/IEC 2501n Quality Model Division. The associated standards within the Quality Measurement Division provide suggested measures of quality throughout the product life-cycle.

ISO/IEC 25021 – Quality Measure Elements: offers quality measure elements that can be used to construct software quality measures.

ISO/IEC 25022 – Measurement of Quality in Use: provides measures for the characteristics in the quality in use model.

ISO/IEC 25023 – Measurement of System and Software Product Quality: provides measures for the characteristics in the product quality model.

ISO/IEC 25024 – Measurement of Data Quality: provides measures for the characteristics in the data quality model.

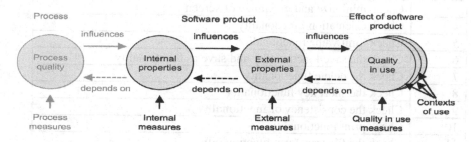

ID	Name	Description	Measurement Function & QMEs
FCP-G-1	Functional implementatio n coverage	How complete is the implementation according to requirement specifications?	$X = 1 - A/B$ A = Number of missing or unsatisfying functions detected in evaluation. B = Number of functions stated in requirement specification.
NOTE A missing or unsatisfying function/operation may be: a) Function and operation that do not perform as specified in user manuals or requirement specification. b) Function and operation that do not provide a reasonable and acceptable outcome to achieve the intended specific objective of the user task.			

3   Test Cases of Software Testing

In ISO/IEC 25000 series, stakeholder defined the following types of users. Primary user is the person who interacts with the system to achieve the primary goals, secondary users defined the person who provide support, for example content provider, system manager, security manager. Indirect user defined the person who receives output, but does not interact with the system. The product quality model divided product quality properties into eight characteristics (functionality, efficiency, compatibility, usability, reliability, security, maintainability and portability). In this paper, we propose the evaluation test cases of functionality and usability. We study the experimental data for finding common factor. We have studied the test cases of software quality evaluation. So, we select common factor among test cases of many type of software. We propose the test cases of functionality of software quality evaluation.

Table 1. Functionality Test Cases

number	Test case of functionality
1	Check login functionality
2	Check undo functionality
3	Check minimize and maximize of screen
4	Check calculation functionality
5	Check limit value functionality
6	Check the save functionality and save as functionality
7	Check the delete functionality
8	Check the short key functionality
9	Check the consistency of functionality
10	Check print functionality
11	Check the file transform functionality
...	etc

We have to check that help functionality, open functionality, so on.

Usability characteristics are very important. Especially, the end user satisfaction of software is very important. Sometimes we survey the questionnaire for finding satisfaction of software. We propose the test cases of usability quality testing.

Table 2. Usability Test Cases

number	Test case of usability
1	Check the adviser usability
2	Check the providing of error messages
3	Check the unknown message
4	Check the button problem
5	Check the essential article input
6	Check the consistency of vocabulary
7	Check the error of information display
8	Check the adjust of interface
9	Check the consistency of field name
10	Check the learnability
11	Check the user error protection
...	etc

Software reliability is very important. Many scholars study about software reliability. As a comparison to hardware development, we are very difficult to estimate the software reliability. We propose the estimation of software reliability. So, we have studied the software reliability growth model to estimate the software reliability. Software life cycle consists of the requirement and specification, design, coding, testing and maintenance. During the software testing, we test the software program and we detect software failure. The software reliability is very important because of the high maintenance cost associated with it. Software reliability models are very useful in analyzing collected failure data and they are important tools to assess the reliability level reached at the current time. We propose the test cases of reliability quality evaluation.

Table 3. Reliability Test Cases

number	Test case of reliability
1	When we save the files, does the program down?
2	We want to open the file, is it working?
3	We want to use short key, is it working?
4	When we update is it working?
5	When we use special font, does the program down?
6	When we modify the file, does the program down?
7	To the protect error, can we provide the message?
8	To use the program, does the program manage in license?
9	For using the program, does the program down?
10	When we use the elimination, is it working?
11	Does the message provide?
...	etc

We propose the test cases for evaluating the software reliability. We are very difficult the estimating the software reliability. So, we need the software failure data for analyzing software quality. We can measure the software reliability when we have a failure data. We need the common test cases for software testing. We admit the difference testing result according to the tester. If we have a common factor for software testing, we can reduce the difference of testing result. We have to study test cases for software testing.   We have to study more for finding test cases.

4   Conclusion

It is generally not sufficient to determine the reliability of the software only by using software testing metric. Software has to be tested in order to meet the measurement of the software quality, which is one of the most important goals of software testing. In this paper, we suggest the test cases of software testing metric evaluation to evaluate the functionality, usability and reliability. We have to find the more test cases in common factor for software testing. Also, we are going to apply international standard test cases for evaluating of software quality. If it is possible, we use the graphical analysis techniques such as quality control charts and probability plot. We are going to study estimation and prediction for reliability of software using the test cases.

References

[1] Dirk, M., Laibarra, B., Kraan, R.P., Wallet, A.: Software Quality and Software Testing in Internet Times. Springer (2002)

[2] Jelinski, Z., Moranda, P.B.: Software reliability research. In: Freiberger, W. (ed.) Statistical Computer Performance Evaluation, pp. 465–497. Academic Press, New York (1972)

[3] Jung, H.J.: Software Reliability Growth Modeling and Estimation for Multiple Errors Debugging. Ph.D. Dissertation, Kyungpook National University (1994)

[4] Littlewood, B., Verrall, J.L.: A Bayesian reliability growth model for computer software. Applied Statistics 22, 332–346 (1973)

[5] ISO/IEC 9126, Information Technology - Software Quality Characteristics and Metric - Part 1, 2, and 3

[6] ISO/IEC 12119, Information Technology - Software Package - Quality requirement and testing

[7] ISO/IEC 14598, Information Technology Software Product Evaluation - Part 1 - 6

[8] ISO/IEC 25000, Software engineering - Software product Quality Requirements and Evaluation (SQuaRE) - Guide to SQuaRE (2005)

[9] ISO/IEC 25010, Software engineering - Software product Quality Requirements and Evaluation (SQuaRE) - Quality Model and guide (2009)

[10] ISO/IEC 25021, Software engineering - Software product Quality Requirements and Evaluation (SQuaRE) – Quality measure elements (2007)

[11] ISO/IEC 18000-6, Information Technology – Radio Frequency Identification for Item Management-Part 6: Parameters for air interface communications at 860MHz to 960MHz (2004)

[12] Moskowitz, P.A., Lauris, A., Morris, S.S.: Privacy – Enhancing Radio Frequency Identification Tag: Implementation of the Clipped Tag. IBM White Paper (May 2006)

[13] Goel, A.L., Okumoto, K.: A Time-dependent error detection rate model for software reliability and other performance measures. IEEE Trans. Reliability R-28(3), 206–211 (1979)

[14] Goel, A.L.: Software reliability models: assumptions, limitations, and applicability. IEEE Trans. Software Eng. SE-11(12), 1411–1423 (1985)

[15] Okumoto, K., Goel, A.L.: Optimum release time for software systems based on reliability and cost criteria. Journal of Systems and Software 1, 315–318 (1980)

[16] Langberg, N., Singpurwalla, N.D.: A Unification of some software reliability models. SIAM Journal of Scientific and Statistical Computation 6(3), 781–790 (1985)

[17] Nayak, T.K.: Software Reliability: Statistical Modeling and Estimation. IEEE Transactions on Reliability 35(5), 566–570 (1986)

Topic Map Based Management System
for Social Network Service

HwaYoung Jeong[1] and BongHwa Hong[2,*]

[1] Humanitas College of Kyunghee University, Hoegi-dong, Seoul, 130-701, Korea
[2] Dept. of Information and Communication, Kyunghee Cyber University,
Hoegi-dong, Seoul, 130-701, Korea
hyjeong@khu.ac.kr,
bhhong@khcu.ac.kr

Abstract. Social network service (SNS) has become in a powerful diffusion media and technique in several fields such as communication, e-commerce and business marketing. And, nowadays, the relationship between the people in our society is also very important role to keep their concern or interest. In this environment, the people use SNS such as Twitter, Me2Day, Facebook, Linknow and so on. In this paper, we propose relationship management system using topic map for SNS. In order to make this system architecture, topic map that is to analyze and design the relation of human factor as a topic was used.

Keywords: SNS, management system, topic map, cloud computing.

1   Introduction

Nowadays, Internet is one of the most used diffusion media in the world, this is largely due in part to social networks, such as Facebook©, Twitter©, Youtube©, among others. However, there are few applications that combine the functionality of different social networks. For example, although there are different social networks to share photos and images such as Flickr©, Photobucket© and Picasa©; it is necessary an application that combine the functionality of these social networks, providing faster results in comparison with doing these tasks in a separately way in each social network [1]. As a component of their business models, SNS companies sell digital decorative products with which customers can adorn their online avatars and online game companies offer game users a broad range of virtual weapons to use in online games. Each individual customer not only consumes these digital products, but also exchanges them as gifts within his/her local neighborhood. Online customers give these digital products to others in order both to acquire social status and to build relationships. Gift-giving behavior in consumer networks, which occurs frequently and effortlessly in the online environment, is a symbolic means for relationship-building and self-expression. Customer's social networks play a vital role in explaining customer value for SNS companies. Companies constantly attempt to identify and upgrade profitable customers by evaluating customer behavior patterns.

---

* Corresponding Author.

T.-h. Kim, Y.-h. Lee, and W.-c. Fang (Eds.): FGIT 2012, LNCS 7709, pp. 119–126, 2012.
© Springer-Verlag Berlin Heidelberg 2012

Companies in the business field use the well-known and convenient RFM (recency, frequency, and monetary value) method. This method helps researchers and marketers to formulate differentiated offers for each customer, and to upgrade customer segments based on customer value [2].

A topic map is a document conforming to a model used to improve information retrieval and navigation using topics as hubs in an information network. Topic maps are created and used to help people find the information they need quickly and easily. Topic maps can be formatted as a wide variety of finding aids, including printed indexes, glossaries, and many kinds of high-performance online finding aids [3].

In this paper, we propose management system to keep and control human relationship in the cyber space. In order to make the system model, topic map that is to design and evaluate the relation with the topics (human factors). The rest of this paper is structured as follows. Section 2 describes related works. In Section 3, we propose the management system model in SNS. Section 4 shows the design of topic map based relationship's management system. Section 5 provides concluding remarks, practical implications of our research, and future work.

2   Related Works

2.1   SNS

"Social network services (SNS)" has become a recent buzzword as the personal media market is emerging as a top web-based business. Social network services can be defined as an individual web page which enables online, human-relationship building by collecting useful information and sharing it with specific or unspecific people. Many social network service sites such as MySpace, Facebook, Hi5 and Cyworld allow their users to join or create groups so that they can interact with others who have similar interests. According to comScore, several major social networking sites have experienced dramatic growth in 2007 [7]. Example is, Facebook members can create self-descriptive profiles that include links to the profiles of their "friends", who may or may not be offline friends. Facebook requires that anybody who wants to be added as a friend have the relationship confirmed, so Facebook friendships define a network (graph) of reciprocated ties (undirected edges) that connect individual users. (In this article, we use the words "edge" and "link" interchangeably.) Amanda et al., showed the relation of Facebook network as shown in Fig 1 [9].

Most of the modern Social Network Services (SNSs) are based on a collaborative paradigm, where content that is published and shared between participants is produced by the users themselves. Such aggregation of personal and possibly sensitive information belonging to several million of users is the real wealth owned by today's major OSN providers (e.g., Facebook, MySpace), that offer free registration to their social platform in exchange for a free access to user data [8]. In traditional social network theory, a social network is defined as a set of social entities that includes people and organizations that are connected by a set of socially meaningful relationships and who interact with each other in sharing the value. The traditional form of a social network service focuses on relationship types such as friends and face-to-face relationships, but social network services are recently bringing more focus to online virtual community and computer mediated communication.

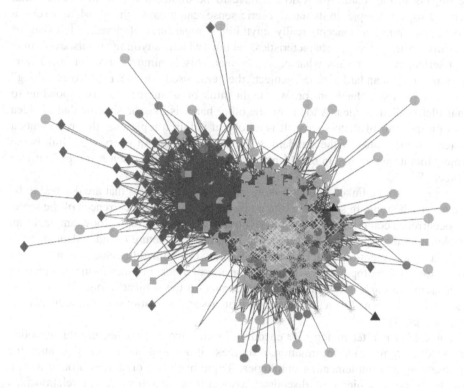

Fig. 1. (Color online) Largest connected component of the student-only subset of the Reed College Facebook network. Different node shapes and colors indicate different class years (gray circles denote users who did not identify an affiliation), and the edges are randomly shaded for easy viewing. Clusters of nodes with the same color/shape suggest that common class year has an important effect on the aggregate structure.

Online social network services build and verify social networks for the individuals and communities who share interests and activities with one another, or who are interested in exploring the interests and activities of others. Social network services can be regarded as web-based services that allow individuals to construct a public or semi-public profile within a bounded system, articulate a list of other users with those who share a connection, and view their list of connections and also those made by others within the system [7].

2.2   Topic Map

Topic maps is a fairly new ISO certified standard (ISO 13250, 2002) for organizing digital content. Its main implementation area has been the World Wide Web where it is used for structuring subject portals and similar document types. However, in theory a topic map can be used to model any real world-relationship, and the objects in the relationships do not have to be digitized [5]. In this point, what then is a topic? A topic, in its most generic sense, can be any "thing" whatsoever – a person, an entity, a concept, really anything – regardless of whether it exists or has any other specific characteristics, about which anything whatsoever may be asserted by any means whatsoever. In fact, this is almost word for word how the topic map standard defines subject, the term used for the real world "thing" that the topic itself stands in for. We might think of a "subject" as corresponding to what Plato called an idea. A topic, on the other hand, is like the shadow that the idea casts on the wall of Plato's cave: It is an object within a topic map that represents a subject. In the words of the standard: "The invisible heart of every topic link is the subject that its author had in mind when it was created. In some sense, a topic reifies a subject..."

A topic may be linked to one or more information resources that are deemed to be relevant to the topic in some way. Such resources are called occurrences of the topic. An occurrence could be a monograph devoted to a particular topic, for example, or an article about the topic in an encyclopedia; it could be a picture or video depicting the topic, a simple mention of the topic in the context of something else, a commentary on the topic (if the topic were a law, say), or any of a host of other forms in which an information resource might have some relevance to the subject in question. A topic association is (formally) a link element that asserts a relationship between two or more topics [4].

Topic Map is a technology for encoding knowledge and connecting this encoded knowledge to relevant information resources, it is used as a formal syntax for representing and implementing ontologies. Topic maps are organized around topics, which represent subjects of discourse; associations, which represent relationships between the subjects; and occurrences, which connect the subjects to pertinent information resources.

Definition 1. We define a Topic Map model as following seven tuples:
$$TM := (T_C, T_O, T_A, T_R, T_I, R_H, R_A)$$

- T_C denotes a set of topic types
- T_O denotes a set of occurrence types
- T_A denotes a set of association types
- T_R denotes a set of role types
- T_I denotes a set of instance topics
- R_H denotes a set of subsumption hierarchy relations
- R_A denotes a set of associative relations

These entities have different meaning and usage, and so we measure the similarity between same entity types only [6].

3   Management System for SNS

In this paper, we propose topic map based management system in SNS environment. Fig 2 shows the management system structure considering the relation between person and person with their activity.

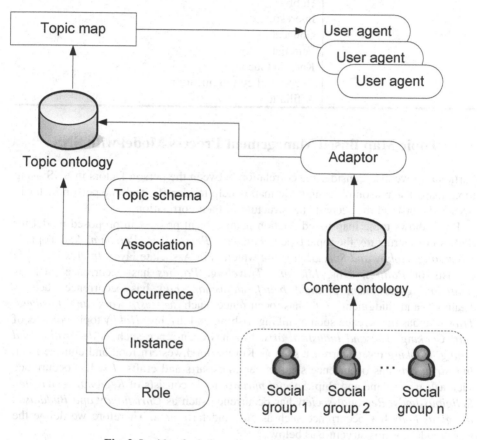

Fig. 2. In side of relation-management system for SNS

The proposed system has topic ontology that is consists of topic schema, association, occurrence, instance and role. The topic schema deals with perform the construction of the topic and their relation for SNS. Also content ontology that is to collect the information of each social group was used. Adaptor process handles between content ontology and topic ontology. User agent performs to search social topic with only person factor which is in topic ontology. Because the relation of person's correlation between them with their activity in SNS.

Table 1 shows person's factor for SNS. The factor means the real item of social community in social groups.

Table 1. The person's factor for SNS

Subject	Attribute
Personality	Name
	Gender
	Address
	Hobby
	Interesting
Activity	Connect to
	Familiar
	Keep in touch
	Account of communication
	Affiliation

4   Topic Map Based Management Process Model with SNS

Particularly we also consider the correlation between the person factors in SNS using topic map. The reason of using topic map is help to identify each the person factor in SNS and construct the accurate the structure of their correlation.

Fig 2 shows topic map based relation management process in proposed model for SNS. In this structure, the topic type is *Person 1, Person 2,..., Person n*. And Topic is *Interesting, Hobby and Special purpose* which is in Associate layer. *Interesting topic* consists of *Polities, Law, Life and Traveling. Polities* has occurrence such as *politician, government, political belief, statesman. Law* has occurrence such as retaining and judgment. *Life* has occurrence such as *rest, work and business. Traveling* has occurrence such as hiking, fishing and driving. *Hobby* topic consists of *Car, Cooking, Toy and Industrial arts. Car* has occurrence such as *decoration and tuning. Cooking* has occurrence such as Korean food,western food and chinese food. *Industrial arts* has occurrence such as ceramics, arts and crafts. *Toy* has occurrence such as car, airplane and ship. *Special purpose* topic consists of *Regional society and Religious body. Regional society* has occurrence such as *Christianity and Buddhism. Religious body* has occurrence such as city and farm area. Therefore we define the topic model for this structure as below.

Definition 2. We define a SNS Topic Map model as following seven tuples:
$$TM := (T_C, T_T, T_O, T_A, T_R, T_I, R_H, R_A)$$

- T_C denotes a set of topic types
- T_T denotes a set of topic
- T_O denotes a set of occurrence
- T_A denotes a set of association
- T_R denotes a set of role
- R_A denotes a set of associative relations

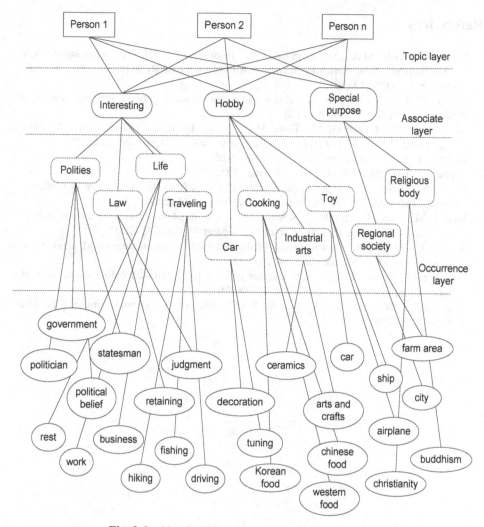

Fig. 3. In side of relation-management system for SNS

5   Conclusion

In SNS environment, it is very important work to identify the relation with person to person and know how to construct their relation between their activity and correlation.

In this paper, we propose management system to keep and control human relationship in the SNS environment. In order to make the system model, topic map was used to design and evaluate person's relation. In the topic model, it has topic ontology that is consists of topic schema, association, occurrence, instance and role. The topic schema deals with perform the construction of the topic and their relation for SNS. In this structure, the topic type is *Person 1, Person 2,..., Person n*. And Topic is *Interesting, Hobby and Special purpose* which is in Associate layer.

References

1. Paredes-Valverde, M.A., Alor-Hernández, G., Rodríguez-González, A., Hernández-Chan, G.: Developing Social Networks Mashups: An Overview of RESTBased APIs. Procedia Technology 3, 205–213 (2012)
2. Joo, Y.-H., Kim, Y., Yang, S.-J.: Valuing customers for social network services. Journal of Business Research 64, 1239–1244 (2011)
3. Newcomb, S.R., Biezunski, M.: Topic Maps go XML, http://148.226.12.104/bitstream/123456789/10350/2/Steven%20R.%20Newcomb%20-%20Topic%20maps%20go%20to%20XML.pdf
4. Pepper, S.: The TAO of Topic Maps, Ontopia (2002)
5. Pharo, N.: Topic maps – knowledge organisation seen from the perspective of computer scientists. In: ELAG 2004, Trondheim, Norway, June 9 - 11 (2004)
6. Kim, J.-M., Shin, H., Kim, H.-J.: Schema and constraints-based matching and merging of Topic Maps. Information Processing and Management 43, 930–945 (2007)
7. Kwon, O., Wen, Y.: An empirical study of the factors affecting social network service use. Computers in Human Behavior 26, 254–263 (2010)
8. Aiello, L.M., Ruffo, G.: LotusNet: Tunable privacy for distributed online social network services. Computer Communications 35, 75–88 (2012)
9. Traud, A.L., Muchaa, P.J., Porter, M.A.: Social structure of Facebook networks. Physica A 391, 4165–4180 (2012)

Starfish Recognition Using Adaptive Filter[*]

Jong-Ik Kim[1], Si-Byung Nam[2], Sung-Rak Kim[3], and Do-Hong Jeon[3]

[1] Dept. of Computer Science, Kwandong University
KangNumg, South Korea
dyhjclub@kd.ac.kr
[2] Dept. of Electronics, Kangwon National University
Samcheok, South Korea
sbnam@kangwon.ac.kr
[3] Dept. of Computer Engineering, Kwandong University
KangNung, South Korea
dhjeon@kd.ac.kr

Abstract. The image capture method used for starfish recognition technology currently studied has limitations in capturing color images by using the area of visible ray in the poor underwater environment. This paper uses the infrared ray image which has a strong penetrating power underwater and is less sensitive to the noise of floating matter to settle the issue. The captured infrared ray underwater images are classified by the proposed adaptive filter. The adaptive filter is divided into the all pass filter, low pass filter and high pass filter by the decision function from the histogram distribution curve. Each of the classified image groups came to obtain a satisfactory result with the recognition of 87.5% as a result of recognition of starfish by using the number of concave and convex feature points.

Keywords: Adaptive Filter, Starfish, Asterias Amurensis, Recognition.

1 Introduction

The number of individuals of Asterias amurensis, which recently has been causing much damage to the shellfish farming fishermen, is rapidly increasing due to the increase of coastal pollution and water temperature.

The methods of rescue of Asterias amurensis with vigorous rate of reproduction and excellent reproductivity are divided into the physical method to control the density of individuals by using a dredge net or a fish trap and the biological method to use Triton shell, which is the natural enemy of starfish. However, there are questions being raised about the efficiency and effectiveness. The rescue of Asterias amurensis with no clear natural enemy in the polluted environment and excellent reproductivity is the most effective to capture them during the breeding season[1,2]. Currently, the

---

[*] This research was financially supported by the Ministry of Education, Science Technology (MEST) and National Research Foundation of Korea(NRF) through the Human Resource Training Project for Regional Innovation.

T.-h. Kim, Y.-h. Lee, and W.-c. Fang (Eds.): FGIT 2012, LNCS 7709, pp. 127–134, 2012.
© Springer-Verlag Berlin Heidelberg 2012

studies related to Asterias amurensis are divided into the studies for effective capture of starfish and the studies for creation of new values of captured starfish. For the effective capture of starfish, the studies on the recognition of Asterias amurensis using the image processing must be conducted, but they are very insufficient due to the lack of infrastructure[3,4].

This paper focuses on the image processing of underwater individuals for recognition of starfish as a method of rescue of starfish. The image capture method used for the starfish recognition technology currently studied has limitations in capturing color image from the dark sea bottom by using the area of visible ray in the poor underwater environment. In order to settle the issue, this paper suggests the method to use the infrared ray image which has an excellent penetrating power underwater and is less sensitive to the noise of underwater floating matter and to thereby increase the recognition of starfish by using the adaptive filter from the captured infrared ray image.

2   Starfish Image

2.1   Infrared Ray Image

Infrared rays are an electromagnetic wave with the wavelength which is longer than that of visible ray and shorter than that of radio waves, and are used in various fields. Infrared rays are a form of energy transfer and a kind of electromagnetic waves with the wavelength ranging from about 0.8 through 1000μm As the wavelength of infrared rays occupies a very broad area, it is explained by dividing into several areas[5].

Infrared rays are as in Table 1 according to the terminology of IEC.

Table 1. IBC of standard (IEC usage St 841)

Designation	wavelength
Short Wave Infrared Radiation	0.8 ~ 3.0 μm
Medium Wave Infrared Radiation	3.0 ~ 6.0 μm
Long Wave Infrared Radiation	6.0 ~ 1000 μm

This paper captures the image by using the wavelength of area of infrared rays in order to capture the image in the poor underwater environment.

2.2   Image Spatial Filter

Among the linear spatial filter techniques showing the relationship with adjacent pixels, there is the convolution processing technique, which is the most general method. This technique defines the convolution of the two signals of x(n) and h(n) with Formula 1.

$$x(n) \times h(n) = \sum_{k=0}^{N} x(n-k)h(k)$$

$$(1)$$

This method can be said to add the value of multiplying each adjacent pixel by weighted value about the raw pixels, and x(n) is the raw pixel, and h(n) is determined with the small matrix called the convolution mask[6].

In the method of execution of convolution, the input image I_0 through I_8 are 3 x 3 raw input images, and M_0 through M_8 are the values of convolution mask. For the output image, the value of result of adding all the values of multiplying each of I_0 through I_8 and M_0 through M_8 by the paired value is inputted. When conducting convolution, for the outermost image edge, the coefficient of empty cells is supposed to be 0 and the operation is conducted with the first method. The method of execution of convolution is as in Figure 1[7].

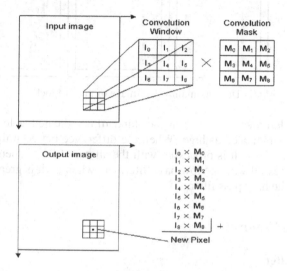

Fig. 1. Processing method convolution

3   Pattern Classification Using Histogram

This paper proposes the adaptive filter in the process of preprocessing to increase the starfish recognition. As the adaptive filter, the optimum processing adaptive filter is applied by the histogram decision function. The adaptive filter is classified into the all pass filter, the low pass filter and the high pass filter by the decision function. The classified images are binary-coded after conducting each processing process.

The inputted infrared ray image is changed into the gray level image in which one pixel has the intensity value of 0 through 255. The histogram of image expresses the properties of each of the light image, dark image, image with low dynamic range and image with high dynamic range well. In the histogram image, the X-axis shows the value of gray scale, and the Y-axis shows the number of pixels for each of the value of gray scale.

In the histogram distribution, the block integration is conducted for 51 blocks in total by dividing the value of gray scale of 0 through 255 into 5 pixels each. Then the maximum value among the 51 blocks is found, and the maximum value is called max. The maximum value image of the 51 blocks for each image is as in Figure 2.

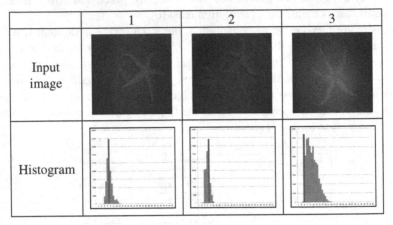

Fig. 2. The maximum value image of the 51 blocks

The sum of the left areas with max as the standard is indicated as low, and the sum of the right areas is indicated as high. When the difference between the areas of low and high is less than 10%, it is processed with the all pass filter. When low is greater than high, it is processed with the low pass filter, and when high is greater than low, it is processed with the high pass filter.

4   Adaptive Filter

4.1   All Pass Filter

When the difference between the areas of low and high of decision function is less than 10%, the original image is immediately binary-coded to protect the image from loss. The dilation operation is conducted to show the scarfskin of starfish as an area in the Input Image 1, which is binary-coded. As the dilation operation expands the small white points, the scarfskin of starfish is indicated as an area. The image of result of all pass is as in Figure 3.

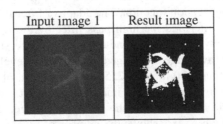

Fig. 3. All pass image of input image 1

4.2   Low Pass Filter

When low is greater than high in decision function, it is processed with the low pass filter. Though it has a clear area, the biggest weak point is that as there is color in the scarfskin of starfish itself, even the scarfskin of starfish is included in the edge detection. To solve this problem, the low pass filter is used. The low pass filter has the effect to make the parts with high edge dull and to make the entire image softer.

There are cases where the edge is made vague by several noises even though the edge of starfish is clear. These noises can be recognized as starfish at the time of edge detection. The noises are removed by using the median filter. The median filter is a filter that sorts the values of surrounding pixels in the ascending or descending order and then uses the value of pixel in the center.

The method of binary-coding is used in many image processing processes such as separating the object from the background and simplifying the overall information of image by extracting only the pixels with a certain value of concentration or greater. The image of result of low pass is as in Figure 4.

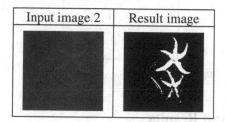

Fig. 4. Low pass image of input image 2

4.3   High Pass Filter

When high is low in the decision function, it is processed with the high pass filter. The high pass filter is a high pass mask proposed with the central point with high picture and the adjacent value of low negative number to make the low edge higher. The high pass image has the effect to express the area of starfish clearer than the gray image. Binary-coding is conducted to separate the object from the backgrounds after high pass.

As the scarfskin of starfish has several colors, only the shape of starfish looking like a star is not shown. To solve this problem, the dilation operation is conducted. The image of result of high pass is as in Figure 5.

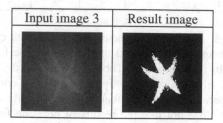

Fig. 5. High pass image of input image 3

5   Starfish Recognition

Each image uses the area labeling. It is a method of area division conducted in binary images, and several objects can exist in one binary image. It is a process to give a unique number to every pixel belonging to the same object, and when an object has the number of pixels which is a certain number or less, it is removed, and the edge detection is conducted. The features of starfish are extracted with the image created through the process for the recognition of Asterias amurensis. Asterias amurensis has 5 arms in the shape of a star or a pentagon as in Figure 6. The apex of the arm of starfish is called the convex feature point, and the apex of the inner edge between arms is called the concave feature point.

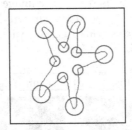

Fig. 6. Structural features for a starfish

6   Experiment and Results

This study obtained the number of convex and concave feature points extracted with the feature extraction technique for the evaluation of performance of recognition of Asterias amurensis processed from the proposed adaptive filter. The results of extraction of concave and convex feature points of starfish are as in Table 2.

Table 2. The convex and concave point of input image

Image	Goal		All pass image		Low pass image		High pass image		Decision
	Convex number	Concave number	Convex number	Concave number	Convex number	Concave number	Convex number	Concave number	
1	7	7	7	3	7	5	7	3	low=high
2	7	7	6	4	7	6	6	4	low>high
3	5	5	5	5	5	4	5	5	low<high

The numbers of target convex and concave feature points counted directly by a person in the sample image are compared to analyze the performance of proposed adaptive filter. The results of judgment of Table 3 are analyzed as follows.

In Image 1, in all the filter processes, only the number of convex feature points is equal to the target number, and for the number of concave feature points, only the low pass filter image comes close not like the results of decision function, and it can be said to be an exception of the study results. In Image 2, the low pass filter decided by the decision function is the nearest to the target number, and it is a good result of decision function. In Image 3, the all pass filter and the high pass filter were equal to the target number, and it is a good result of decision function as the high pass filter decided by the decision function is included.

The result of judgment of the 50 starfish images in total by the histogram decision function proposed by this study, which is the result method of Table 2, is as in Table 3.

Table 3. The recognition result of input image

Classification \ Filter	Classification number	low=high	low>high	low<high	Recognition	Recognition
low=high	36	30	4	2	30/6	83.3%
low>high	48	4	40	4	40/8	83.3%
low<high	116	4	7	105	105/11	90.5%
					Result of recognition	87.5%

In the adaptive filter, in the 200 images in total, the all pass filter was judged to be 36 images, and showed the recognition of 83.3%, which are 30 out of 36 images. The low pass filter was judged to be 48 images, and showed the recognition of 83.3%, which are 40 out of 48 images. The high pass filter was judged to be 116 images, and showed the recognition of 90.5%, which are 105 out of 116 images. The entire result of recognition by classified images showed a high recognition of 87.5% as the result of the study.

7   Conclusion

The image processing method for starfish recognition comes to extract the features of the image captured with camera through the preprocessing process and to recognize the individuals from the extracted features. The image capture method used for the starfish recognition technology currently studied has limitations in capturing the image from dark sea bottom in case of color image using the area of visible ray in the poor underwater environment.

This paper captured and used the infrared ray underwater image with strong penetrating power to settle the issue. The captured images were divided into the all pass filter, the low pass filter and the high pass filter by the proposed adaptive filter, and were used as the input image for recognition of underwater individuals. The recognition was conducted by obtaining the number of convex and concave feature points with the feature extraction technique for the evaluation of performance of the image processed from the proposed adaptive filter.

Among the 200 images in total at the adaptive filter, 30 images out of 36 images were recognized with the all pass filter. The low pass filter recognized 40 images out of 48 images, and the high pass filter recognized 104 images out of 116 images. The result of study showed a high recognition of 87.5% entirely.

It can be known that for the parts where the edge detection was difficult due to underwater floating matter and complicated backgrounds, the preprocessing process classifying the images and conducting the processes needed for each of them is effective for starfish recognition as it can increase the recognition of edge detection.

References

1. Yun, D.-S.: Technology Trends for the use of the Starfish. EBN Co., Ltd., (August 5, 2009) 09:30:03
2. Jang, S.-H.: Starfish Role of Stock in the Farm Environment. College of Marine Science. Gyeongsang National Univ. (2000)
3. MBC, War of Starfish, MBC SPECIAL (September 24, 2010)
4. Shin, Y.-T., Lee, S.-M.: Systematic Promotion Plan of Aquafarm Purifying Project. Korea Maritime Institute
5. Maldague, X.P.V.: Infrared methodology and technology. Gordon and Breach Science Publishers, Amsterdam (1994)
6. Samsung SDI homepage, http://www.samsungsdi.com
7. Yang, D.-J.: A Study on the Image Noise Reduction of Flat Panel TV using LoG Bilateral Spatial filter, School of Electrical & Computer Engineering, Graduate School of Univ. of Seoul (2009)

A Study on the Multi-location Recognition System Based on CCS

Seongsoo Cho[1], BongHwa Hong[2], and Hae-Gill Choi[3,*]

[1] Dept. of Electronic Engineering, Kwangwoon University, 20 Kwangwoon–ro,
Nowon-gu, Seoul, 139-701, Korea
[2] Dept. of Information and Communication, Kyunghee Cyber University,
Hoegi-dong, Seoul, 130-701, Korea
[3] Dept. of Information and Communication, Kyunghee Cyber University,
Hoegi-dong, Seoul, 130-701, Korea
css@kw.ac.kr, {bhhong,hgchoi}@khcu.ac.kr

Abstract. As invisible technology in ubiquitous generation, location recognition technology has been understood as rudimentary technology for various service provisions in field of transportation, military, distribution, home network, and more. Although location recognition system in traffic information is widely provided based on the GPS system which is a core basis technology for provision of traffic information, it has drawbacks of low accuracy, and shaded zone occurs due to secure of communication visibility. In this study, energy efficient and data-centric protocol of multiple location recognition systems that can recognize locations in shaded zone such as parking lot or tunnel is proposed and demonstrated. It bases on the Chirp Spread Spectrum (CSS) method which applies ISM Band of IEEE 802.15.4 so as detailed location recognition is possible only by the wireless RF (Radio Frequency). As the result of multi-network environment, it was likely to compose a network with less than 6% of data error ratio and less than 18 centimeters of error range of Tag node. Moreover, it can guarantee 13.5 days from 0.7 days in life span of tag node through applying 20 seconds low-power algorithm and minimum frequency of power consumption in 3V, 1500mAh battery condition.

Keywords: CSS, TOA, WPAN, Location, Protocol.

1 Introduction

Location recognition technology has been understood as 'invisible technology' which is a core basis technology for various service provisions in transportation, military, Home Network, distribution, medical treatment, construction site and more. Especially in transportation, location recognition technology is used as foundation technology for traffic and vehicle management as well as its navigation. Currently, location recognition technology through GPS (Global Positioning System) is widely used, however without confirmed LoS (Line of Sight), GPS service is unattainable and the accuracy is low.

---

* Corresponding author.

T.-h. Kim, Y.-h. Lee, and W.-c. Fang (Eds.): FGIT 2012, LNCS 7709, pp. 135–143, 2012.
© Springer-Verlag Berlin Heidelberg 2012

To overcome this problem, lots of technologies using Wireless Personal Area Network (WPAN) to recognize the location have been developing indoors and in shaded zone where they are impossible to use satellite communication. Even though network technology of Zigbee, location estimation technology using ultra sonic wave sensor, and location recognition technology through signal amplitude of Zigbee have been studied, these have drawbacks of accuracy, expensive cost, and securement of communication visibility [1,2]. Therefore, in order to procure recognition technology with high accuracy and low power, IEEE 802.15. 4a Tasking Group has enacted standard of new technology that is possible to measure high accuracy distance with low power and low cost.

In this study, energy efficient and data-centric network protocol which it can presume location in wide area and compose broaden network is demonstrated. It bases on the ISM Band CSS method of IEEE 802. 15. 4a which it enables to measure distance by wireless RF in WPAN.

2   The Characteristics of DBO-CSS

2.1   Frequency and Transmission Speed

IEEE 802.15. 4a that is suggested for low-power location recognition is a standard including Impluse Radio-Ultra Wide Band (IR-UWB) and CSS as ISM Band. Thus, it contains 2.45 GHz frequency bandwidth for CSS, from 3.1 GHz to 10.6 GHz frequency bandwidth for UWB, and from 250 MHz to 750 MHz frequency bandwidth. Also, it provides transmission speed ranging from 250 kb/s to 2 Mb/s as maximum in CSS application and 842 kb/s in IR_UWB application[3].

2.2   Chirp Pulses

Chirp pulse is a signal in which the carrier signal increases or decrease with constant slope depends on the characteristic of linear frequency in certain bandwidth. The following equation is written in terms of Rectangular Linear Chirp:

$$S_{chirp}(t) = Re[exp[j\left(\omega_s + \frac{\omega_{BW}}{2T_{chirp}}t\right)t + \theta_0] \times [u(t) - u(t - T_{chirp})]] \quad (1)$$

T_{chirt}: signal duration of Linear Chirp
ω_s : Start frequency for sweeping of Linear Chirp
ω_{BW}: Bandwidth of sweeping
u_t : Unit Step function

Fig. 1 shows chirp signal as time function. The phase is increasingly changed because frequency increasing rate is constant.

Differential Bi-Orthogonal Shift Keying (DBO-CSK) method is used as modulation of CSS. It can transmit data through phase modulation with certain linear chirp. Phase modulation methods are composed of: Binary Phase modulation and Quadrature Phase modulation [3,4].

Symmetric Double Sided Two-Way Ranging (SDS-TWR) Protocol is distance measuring method which it depends on the time difference between two equipments. The distance is calculated by measuring time of arrival and response time [6-9].

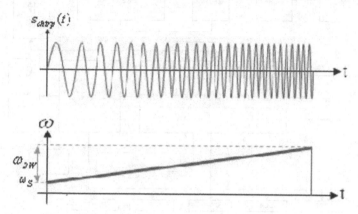

Fig. 1. Change in pulse and frequency with chirp signal

2.3   Organization of WPAN

Sensor network technology is a kind of ad-hoc networks because nodes can compose of network by themselves and they take roles in router and data source. However, sensor network technology has differential characteristics such as limited node resource, dependence of battery, mobility, data transmission model, data concentration, real-time data character and sensor data base. Therefore, network technologies with various architectures are developed, and the representative network technologies are classified according to data-centric, clustering and hierarchical architecture, flat structure and low power, QoS and real-time, location-based, and more[10]. Nodes are distinguished based on the data they can provide themselves with a method of differentiating particular node within broaden sensor network through designed concept. This is due to the fact that it is hard to give m value of each node to all nodes having limited resource and arranged in quantity. With this, users have to write interest using properties-based naming, and have to transmit it to nodes. A representative networking technology is called Directed diffusion, in which node could only response when the received data are equal to their own data.

3   Demonstration and Performance Results

3.1   Developing Environment

The equipment used in this research is node of Nanotron company applying standard CSS of the first IEEE 802. 15. 4a [11]. The following Fig. 2 is its composition:

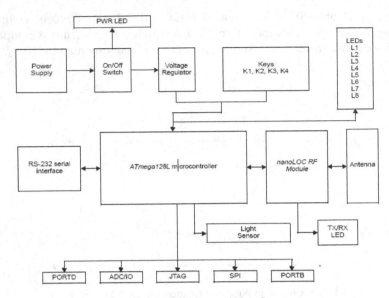

Fig. 2. Block diagram of NanoLocc

3.2   Information Value Collected by Tag Node

Tag node collects distance between anchors and transmits to base station. Fig. 3 shows collected information value before sending.

In Cell 1, when tag nodes of 11, I2, and 14 were operated, it shows the output of measured value of each node in base station and frame is composed that number of FID is 4, it shows transmission value to base station that frame is generated by the order of transmission RF power and distance, tag node number, power state of cell number.

3.3   Multi-network Organization

Each cell organizes network every 30 seconds, and cell number is applied according to ID value of base station. Base station is located at the center, and distance between embodied network and the base station is is 4.3m.

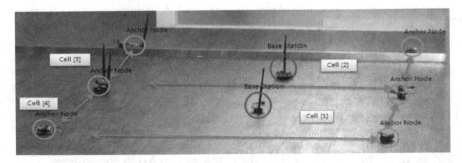

Fig. 3. Multi-network oranization diagram

3.4   Monitoring Program

Borland C++ tool is used to design application program for measurement. (Fig. 4) Application program received and modified frame from main base station through serial communication. Application program is composed of monitoring part for displaying location that is based on converting coordinate value of tag node into pixel; and it indicated error rate of distance, occurance rate of data error, cell recognition error rate, and data collection error for measuring performance of proposed protocol, with real-time frame data.

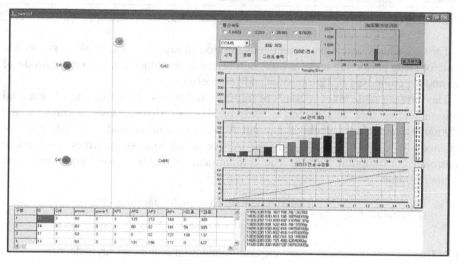

Fig. 4. Program for verification

4   Experiment Results

4.1   Measured Results of Power Consumption in Tag Node

Proposed low power algorithm is designed to cut power off throughout unnecessary communication time by giving tag node period in order to reduce power consumption and guarantee maximum deactivate time. Table 1 shows current consumption of each node at the following condition.

Table 1. NanoLoc Device current consumption

RF Module	
Current Consumption when transmitting	30 mA
Current consumption when receiving	33 mA
Current consumption in seep mode	2μA
Micro Controller	
Current consumption in actine mode	100 mA
Current consumption in sleep mode	0.07 mA

Table 2. Opreation current consumption of tag node

Frame		Transmit	receive	Time[m/s]
Cell recognition	Ranging Frame	6	3×BS(3)	120+90
Cell Information Request	Cell Information	1		20
Cell Information Receive	Cell Information	-	1	10
Distance measure	Ranging	2×An(2)	3×An(2)	80+60
Collection Data Transmission	Collection Data		-	20
Almega 128 Consumption Current	Active Mode	100mA		150
Total		12	16	560

Table. 2 shows opreation current consumption of tag node and Table. 3 shows life cycle of sleep period tag node. a total number of communication in Active Mode of tag node is composed of 12 transmits and 16 receives.

The time tag node takes is 20m/s of transmit and 10m/s of receive, therefore a total communicative time that tag node takes is 560m/s. Also, 240m/s of transmit and 120m/s of receive are calculated through Active times in tag node. The life cycle of tag node is calculated with sums of Active operation, sleep times, and micro controller consumption 100mA. The communication number shows communication number of time.

$$\text{life-cycle[day]} = \frac{\text{Battery Capacity } (1500\text{mA} \times 3600\text{sec} \times 1000)}{\text{Cmmunication Number(1 day)} \times \text{Active} \times \text{Consumption}} \quad (2)$$

$$((3600\text{sec} \times 24 \times 1000 \times \text{sleep}) - (\text{Active} \times \text{Communication Number(1day)} \times \text{sleep}))$$

Table 3. Life cycle of sleep period Tag Node

Period (sec)	Battery Capacity (mA/h)	Consumption Current Active(mA)			Sleep (mA)	Active Time(m/s)		Total Time	Operation Number (1day)	Day
		Transmission	Receive	AVR		Transmission	Receive			
20	1500	30	33	100	0.072	240	120	550	4320	13.7
15	1500	30	33	100	0.072	240	120	550	5670	10.3
10	1500	30	33	100	0.072	240	120	550	8640	6.9
5	1500	30	33	100	0.072	240	120	550	17280	3.5
1	1500	30	33	100	0.072	240	120	550	86400	0.7

For the result of measurment, when the sleep period is set up in 20 seconds, 3 V, 1500mA/h volume of battery was used, and maximum of 163 mA within 550m/s, the life cycle of tag node was calculated as 13.7 days.

Fig. 5 shows life cycle of tag node. a stable power supply is required in order to measure the distance only with RF signal in case of used node. In effect, we were able to verify the raise of data error and distance as consumption of the battery increases.

In such environment, the outcome of applying low power algorithm in order to maximize the life of moving tag node was extension of its life from 0.6 to 13.7 days when capacity of 1500mA/h battery was used.

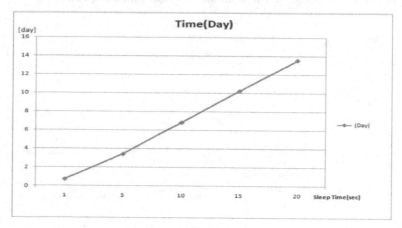

Fig. 5. Life cycle of tag node

However, delay of the data occurs and more currents are consumed compared to those nodes of the original sensor network environment. Therefore, securing hardware for minimizing the current consumption of RF module is required, and a further study of communication algorithm that can minimize the number of transmit and receive is needed.

4.2   Experiment Result

Fig. 6 shows data collection delay of BS for tag node count. a condition of the experiment was to run 8 of the tag nodes, 11, 12, 13, 14, 15, 16, 17, and 18 in cell.

A speed of collecting information of node 11 was measured as 200 of average data, and sleep period was increasing from 1 to 10seconds. Because active time of tag node is 0.55 seconds, in order to prevent signal interference, tag node gets extra 1 second of sleep time in case it does not receive cell information. We have proved that 1 second delay occurs when sleep period is set for 10seconds and it take actions with 8 of the various tag node conditions.

Based on the result above, a possibility of delay with a collision of each node in a 10 seconds period can be explained as x=Tea/It; It represents time period of tag node, and Tea represents tag node counts. When there were more than 7 tag node counts, a delay of the operation occurred, and when there was a movement in 2 nodes with 1 second period a delay also occurred. Therefore, a further study on the algorithm that can schedule an operation of Tag node which is concentrated in multiples of node condition in areas such as airport or park is needed.

A data collecting error occurs according to signal interference and power supply of the node during the process of measuring the distance of Anchor node. This occurs when a tag node reaches the time overlapped with a different tag node during the process of collecting its data. This overlapping phenomenon occurs severely as tag node increases; we have found that more than 90% of data measurement error occurs when 10 tag nodes operate in 3 seconds sleep period within one cell.

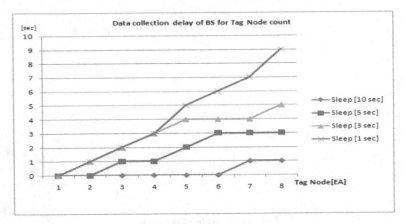

Fig. 6. Data collection delay of BS for Tag Node count

In order to reduce an error ratio, we have verified less than 6% of data collecting error is possible when operation of tag node is scheduled in 5 second period according to the base station as well as Active Mode period, and Sleep of tag node for low power as this study proposed.

5   Conclusion

In this study, protocol of multiple location recognition using 2.45 GHz CSS of IEEE 802.15.4a standard is proposed and demonstrated. This sensor network technology is receiving attention for next generation, which we have proposed an agent for managing efficient network.

As a result, we have reduced an error ratio to 6% for signal interference in each tag node occurring in multiple network condition, and as we applied 29 second period in order to minimize power consumption, we have delayed life of tag node to 13.7 days. Moreover, cell recognition of tag node in multiple network condition has shown more than 95% of accuracy and location recognition has shown less than 18 centimeters of an error.

CSS based location recognition system was implemented to be possible to trace the movement with just a RF signal distinct from previous sensor network equipment such as ultrasonic waves, infrared light, and PAR. It also showed a high accuracy on the location recognition. Therefore, we expect it to be the core basis technology with WPAN condition for various service applications in distribution, medical treatment, Home Network, military. However, further study on RF module which it could minimize the energy consumption and battery skills in order to delay life of the network and output of stabled transmit RF. Moreover, advanced study on the coordinate measurement algorithm for accurate location measurement in various cell structures need to be performed.

References

[1] Yong, K.H., Duk, K.S., Gil, S.D.: A tendency Local Location Awareness Technolog. Institute for Information Technology Advancement (November 2007)
[2] Shinyoung, Y., Hojung, C.: IEEE 802.15.4/Ultrasound-based Tracking Technique in Wireless Sensor Networks 33(1B) (2006)
[3] International Standards Research, Proposal Based UWB, Orthotron (August 2005)
[4] PART 15.4: Wireless Medium Access Control (MAC) and Physical Layer (PHY) Specifications for Personal Low-Rate Wireless Personal Area Networks (LRWPANs)
[5] Hach, R.: Symmetric Double Sided Two-Way Ranging, IEEE P802.15 Working Group for Wireless Personal Networks (WPAN), Doc. IEEEP.802. 15-05-0334-00-004a (June 2005)
[6] Qi, Y., Kobayashi, H., Suda, H.: On time-of-arrival positioning in a multipath environment. IEEE Trans. on Vehicular Technology (2006) (to appear)
[7] Guvenc, I., Sahinoglu, Z.: Threshold-Based TOA Estimation for Impulse Radio UWB System. In: IEEE International Conference on Ultra Wideband Systems and Technologies, pp. 420–425 (September 2005)
[8] Jeong, H., Lee, J.O., Lee, J.Y., Park, N.S., Jin, G.J., Kim, B.S.: Technical Trends of Sensor Networking. ETRI 22(3) (June 2007)
[9] Nanotron Technologes Gmbh, NanoLoc Raging Demonstrator: User Guide, Version 1. 01, NA-cx-0721-0377-1,01

Extracting Pilot Preferred Display from Data Transfer and Recording System

Ki-Il Kim[1], SeokYoon Kang[1], and Kyoung Choon Park[2]

[1] Department of Informatics, Engineering Research Institute
Gyeongsang National University, Jinju, Korea
[2] Aero Master Corp. Sacheon, Korea
kikim@gnu.ac.kr

Abstract. As the recording system such as DTRS (Data Transfer and Recording System)[1] on aircraft becomes available, amount of information during the flight can be obtained and utlilized efficiently. In this paper, we address how to extract pilot preferred display information over dyniamc layout system on an aircaft. To acheive this, display configuration for specific events are recorded in DTRS whenerver they occur. And then, through developed software, we can recognize the pilot's perference of diplay for corresponding event. Furthermore, this function can be extened to extract other useful information for the flight and mission information by modifying software in a flexbile way.

Keywords: DTRS, Viewer, Software Development.

1   Introduction

In the aircraft, the cockpit of it contains flight instruments on an instrument panel, and the controls which enable the pilot to fly the aircraft. Recently, the noticeable current development trend for cockpit is known as glass cockpit[2-3] that features electronic instrument displays, typically large LCD screens, as opposed to the traditional style of analog dials and gauges[4]. This means that previous analog and stand-alone instruments are replaced by digital and integrated one. For example, navigation system through the GPS system is introduced in glass cockpit nowadays. This trend is led by software that is regarded to play a great role in aircraft system. Moreover, the software plays a great role in many research works such as Enhanced Vision System, Synthetic Vision System, Combined Vision System, and Automatic Dependent Surveillance-Broadcast. More detailed functions in glass cockpit, more convenient and flexible display method is introduced in new aircraft system. One of them is flexible layout system. While previous display is regarded as the fixed layout system where the replacement of each instrument on the cockpit is not allowed, current glass cockpit supports movement of instruments according to the pilot's control. This system is become popular because it is implemented in F-35 made by Lockheed Martin.

In parallel with display system, recording system such as DTRS for mission and flight plays a great role in training pilot. DTRS consists of two respective units,

T.-h. Kim, Y.-h. Lee, and W.-c. Fang (Eds.): FGIT 2012, LNCS 7709, pp. 144–147, 2012.

DTRU (Data Transfer and Recording Unit) and RMM (Removable Memory Module). For the normal operation, first, steering points, communication information, initialization data for primary operation, data for satellite navigation are recorded into the RMM that is coupled with DTRU in the aircraft. And then, the data is loaded by MC (Mission Computer). Upon loading, corresponding data is used for the pilot to recognize the given mission as well as accomplish it in a right way through MFD (Multi Function Display), IUFCP (Integrated Up-Front Control Panel). In addition, for the analysis in a mission on the ground, fault information of aircraft, mark point, threat and geographic information during the flight, identification information for OFP (Operational Flight Program), GPS time, and pilot aviation are recorded consecutively. This operation helps us to identify how much missions are certainly accomplished as to the predetermined plan through ground system.

In this paper, we propose how to extract specific information from the DTRS. Among lots of information, we focus on how to figure out pilot preference for dynamic layout display system that is designed to change cockpit configuration according to pilot preference. To achieve this, we design new software to extract information and database system. Furthermore, we explain the implementation issues.

The rest of paper is organized as follows. Background of the research work is explained in the section 1. We describe the conceptual design model in following section. Finally, we present implementation issues.

2   Software Architecture

The component of new software is illustrated in Fig. 1. The main task of each component is as follows.

- Data Acquisition: This component is designed to read data recorded in the DTRS. In order to read data correctly, corresponding component should have information for format and type of each field.
- Data Parsing: This component includes the processing task which converts the reading data into the raw data of the user software, for example, Flight Simulator[4]. Since each simulator uses different data format, the component is essential for reformatting. Also, if a simulator cannot use the value directly, a value should be replaced by new one according to equation for data conversion. Otherwise, a value is used by the simulator software without any change.
- Graphic Display: This component shows the user preference for display. According to the configuration, corresponding event and matching display are identified by this component. We use the commercial flight simulator for display.

The components describe above are connected through several interface. The details for them are as follows.

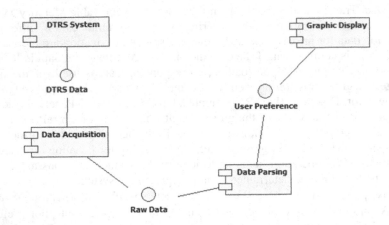

Fig. 1. Component diagram

- DTRS Data: This interface indicates the data file recorded in DTRS.
- Raw Data: It is the same as file in DTRS but copied for further processing. It means that original file is kept without any change.
- User Preference: After parsing, only defined information from raw data is collected.

By using mention components and interface, DTRS and user display software are collaborated by exchanging related data.

3   Implementation Issues

For the predetermined Event_ID representing unique event on aircraft, we search the database to check which layout is the most preferred with it. For the matching pattern, two different policies are concerned in this section.

3.1   Window Based

In this method, the entries with same Event_ID are first extracted from the database. And then, the total number for each layout is counted. After this task is done, we count Instrument_ID for identifying how many times each instrument appears in each window. Upon completing this job, a system shows the candidate for layout at corresponding event.

3.2   Layout Based

Unlike the window based that is dependent on respective appearance in layout, this scheme records the layout as string, for example, "13452876" is for the first layout from up to down, left to right placement. After corresponding layer is selected, the counting is conducted with the whole string. And then, the layout with the largest number of recording is recommended to the pilot.

In addition to above two methods searching the most preferred display, we can add useful functions to proposed scheme. First, we can make use of time information to suggest the layout in a principle of time locality. According to configuration, a recent layout during defined duration will be concerned for selection. This is very useful when each pilot has tendency to change his preference. Also, we can modify the current system to suggest multiple preferences according to the order. That is, a pilot can have multiple recommendations for the event from the proposed system.

4   Conclusion

In this paper, we propose conceptual design for analyzing data in DTRS. Specially, we focused on collecting user preference for display at the predetermined event. To achieve this, DTRS should be capable of recording display layout whenever events happen. Also, new software is designed to identify and recognize the user preference. Furthermore, this software will be extended to get other information by enhance algorithms.

Acknowledgments. This research was supported by the Ministry of Education, Science Technology (MEST) and National Research Foundation of Korea(NRF) through the Human Resource Training Project for Regional Innovation and the MKE(The Ministry of Knowledge Economy), Korea, under the ITRC(Information Technology Research Center) support program (NIPA-2012-H0301-12-3003) supervised by the NIPA(National IT Industry Promotion Agency).

References

1. Data Transfer System, http://heasarc.gsfc.nasa.gov/dts/
2. Knight, J.: The Glass Cockpit. IEEE Computer, 92–95 (2007)
3. Read, B.C.: Developing the Next Generation Cockpit Display System. Proceedings of IEEE AES System Magazine, 25–28 (1996)
4. Flight Simulator, http://www.microsoft.com/games/flightsimulatorx/

Dynamic Race Detection Techniques
for Interrupt-Driven Programs*

Guy Martin Tchamgoue, Kyong Hoon Kim, and Yong-Kee Jun**

Department of Informatics, Gyeongsang National University,
Jinju 660-701, South Korea
guymt@ymail.com, {khkim,jun}@gnu.ac.kr

Abstract. Data races are notorious concurrency bugs that are difficult
to be reproduced and may lead programs into unintended nondetermin-
istic executions. Asynchronous interrupts introduce fine-grained parallelism into interrupt-driven programs making them prone to data races
and hard to be thoroughly tested and debugged. Unfortunately, only few
tools and techniques have been proposed for dynamic data race detection
in interrupt-driven programs that are however widely used in embedded
systems. This paper surveys the existing dynamic race detection techniques for interrupt-driven programs, analyzes them to circumscribes
the problems they face in reporting data races, and finally highlights the
challenges that a dynamic race detection for interrupt-driven program
needs to overcome.

Keywords: Data races, interrupt, interrupt handlers, dynamic race
detection.

1 Introduction

Data races [1,8] represent one of the most notorious class of concurrency bugs
in shared-memory parallel programs including interrupt-driven programs. Data
races occur when two accesses to a shared memory location are performed without proper synchronization, and at least one of the accesses is a write. Interrupt-
driven programs are prone to data races as they have to deal with external asynchronous interrupts that seriously increase the number of their execution paths.
Asynchronous interrupts introduce fine-grained parallelism into these programs
making them difficult to be thoroughly tested and debugged. Interrupt-driven
programs are commonly used in device drivers, operating systems, or in real-time
embedded applications. Data races in interrupt-driven programs often remain

* This research was supported by the MKE (The Ministry of Knowledge Economy),
Korea, under the ITRC (Information Technology Research Center) support program
supervised by the NIPA (National IT Industry Promotion Agency), NIPA-2012-
H0301-12-3003.
** Corresponding Author: In Gyeongsang National University, he is also involved in
the Engineering Research Institute (ERI).

T.-h. Kim, Y.-h. Lee, and W.-c. Fang (Eds.): FGIT 2012, LNCS 7709, pp. 148–153, 2012.

undetectable until the exploitation phase leading the application into unpredictable executions and results sometimes with severe consequences. A typical example is the well-known accident of the Therac-25 [7] where, as the result of a data race caused by the keyboard interrupt handler, many people received fatal radiation doses.

An increasing attention has recently been given to dynamic race detection techniques [2,3,6,9] for interrupt-driven programs. Regehr [9] proposed a method to random test interrupt-driven programs by randomly fire interrupts at random time intervals. Higashi et al. [3] proposed to test for all data races in a program by generating an interrupt after every instruction that accesses a shared variable. The work done by Erickson et al. [2] aims to detect data races in low-level operating system kernel code by randomly samples parts of the program to be used as race candidates for the race detection and uses data and code breakpoints to detect conflicting accesses to shared variables. Lee et al. [6] proposed to convert an interrupt-driven program into a corresponding multithreaded program and to use an existing dynamic race detection tool to detect data races into the newly generated programs. Unfortunately, all these techniques are still inefficient because they either fail to accurately detect conflicting accesses to shared variables or report huge amount of false positives.

This paper presents a survey of existing dynamic data race detection techniques targeting interrupt-driven programs. The paper then analyzes those solutions to circumscribe the problems they face in reporting data races. We also highlight some of the challenges to be overcome for an efficient data race detection in such programs.

For the remainder of this paper, Section 2 gives an overview of interrupt-driven programs and data races. Section 3 presents a survey of existing data race detection techniques and highlights their challenges and problems. Section 4 gives the conclusion of this work.

2   Interrupt-Driven Programs and Data Races

A system is interrupt-driven when a significant amount of its processing is initiated and influenced by external concurrent interrupts [9]. Interrupts are defined as *hardware signals* as they are generated by the hardware in response to an external operation to indicate an environment change. To service each interrupt, an asynchronous callback subroutine called *interrupt handler* is required. For many operating systems, interrupts are managed inside the kernel. However, for many constrained embedded systems with a thin kernel layer like TinyOS [5], applications have to provide and manage their own interrupt handlers.

Contrarily to threads, interrupt handlers cannot block: they run to completion except when preempted by another interrupt handler [4,9]. Interrupts have an asymmetric preemption relation with the non-interrupt code: interrupt handlers can preempt non-interrupt code but not the contrary. Interrupts are nested when they preempt each other. Nesting interrupts are used to allow time-sensitive

```
1:  void interrupt_handler(int data){
2:      if(packetNumber<BufferSize){
3:          packet[packetNumber++]=data;
4:      }
5:  }
6:  void main_task(){
7:  ...
8:      if(packetNumber==BufferSize){
9:          packetNumber=0;
10:         send(packet);
11:     }
12: ...
13: }
```

(a) An Example Program

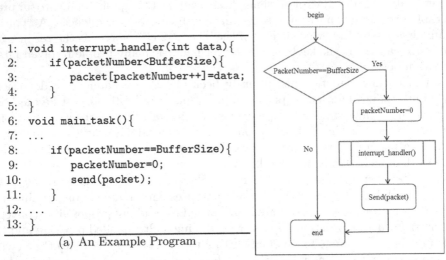

(b) A Racy Execution Instance of the Program in Fig.1(a)

Fig. 1. An Example Program with Data Races

operations to be handled with low latency [9]. An interrupt is said to be reentrant when it directly or indirectly preempts itself. In order to minimize the impact of interrupt handlers on non-interrupt code, all long-latency operations must run in split-phase [4]. With this mechanism, interrupt handlers immediately return after servicing critical operations and *post* heavy computations for later execution as a new task or process.

Asynchronous interrupts are signaled by external devices such as network interfaces and can fire at any time that the corresponding device is enabled [9,10]. Interrupt-driven programs present a very simple concurrency model which however allows high and complex interleaving at runtime with an exponentially increasing number of execution paths. Since the only way to share data between a program and its interrupt handlers is through global variables, these programs are prone to data races. To protect sensitive parts of the program, interrupts must be *disabled* before and *enabled* only after critical sections. Interrupts handlers must therefore be written efficiently not to monopolize the processor since they can also preempt each other. In interrupt-driven programs, data races may happen when a shared variable is uncoordinately accessed with at least one write by both an interrupt handler and a non-interrupt code or by multiple interrupt handlers. An example can be seen in the synthetic program in Fig.1(a) if an interrupt is received in between instructions 9 and 10 as represented in the flow chart of Fig.1(b). In this case, the first entry of the shared array `packet` will be overwritten and a wrong packet processed. To remove this data race, the given interrupt must be disabled at line 7 and enabled again only at line 12.

Table 1. Comparison of Race Detection Tools

Tools	Accuracy	Scalability	Coverage	False Positives	Overhead
Regehr [9]	No	Yes	High	Yes	Low
Higashi et al. [3]	No	Yes	High	Yes	High
Erickson et al. [2]	No	Yes	Low	Yes	Low
Lee et al. [6]	Yes	Yes	Low	No	High

3 Dynamic Race Detection

In this section, we present a survey of existing dynamic techniques and tools to detect data races in interrupt-driven programs. We also discuss some of the challenges and problems to be handled for an efficient data race detection in such programs.

3.1 Detection Techniques

Data races are an important issue in interrupt-driven programs which are getting pervasive with the popularization of embedded systems. Therefore, there is an urgent need to explore more effective techniques to detect them ahead of the exploitation phase of programs. However, only few works have recently focused on dynamic data race detection in interrupt-driven programs as summarized in Table 1.

Regehr [9] proposed a method to random test event-driven applications by randomly fire interrupts at random time intervals. The main challenge in this work is to obtain adequate interrupt schedules by solving a tradeoff between generating a dense or a sparse interrupt schedule. With a dense interrupt schedule, there are always many pending interrupts, making the processor busy in interrupt mode and starving non interrupt code. On the other hand, a sparse schedule provokes less preemption among interrupts, then no or only few bugs might be detected. To be able to test for all data races in a program, Higashi et al. [3] proposed to generate one interrupt after every instruction that accesses a shared variable and to substitute a corrupted memory with a value provided by the developer. However, generating an interrupt at each access will seriously impact the detection overhead. These two techniques however do not basically focus on race detection. As testing tools, they are not sufficient for debugging interrupt-driven programs since they can only reveal the presence of data races, but fail to accurately detect their source or root causes and therefore require important manual inspection for real data race detection.

The work done by Erickson et al. [2] aims to detect data races in low-level operating system kernel code by randomly samples parts of the program to be used as race candidates for the race detection and uses data and code breakpoints to detect conflicting accesses to shared variables. This work does not primarily target interrupt-driven programs, but can still report some data races due to asynchronous interrupts at kernel level. However, this paper also has difficulties to accurately detect conflicting accesses to shared variables. Lee et al. [6] proposed to convert an interrupt-driven program into a corresponding multithreaded program and to use an existing dynamic race detection tool to detect data races into the newly generated programs. However, this technique eliminates the asynchronous character of interrupts and therefore, may miss data races. Also, the size and complexity of existing race detector for multithreaded make it difficult to be directly applied to interrupt-driven programs.

3.2 Detection Challenges

Detecting data races in interrupt-driven programs is quite challenging and generally requires complex and sophisticated tools. However, it is primordial for an efficient race detection tool to be able to accurately detect conflicting accesses to shared variables. Unfortunately, as presented in Table 1, this problem seems to be the most challenging for all existing solutions [2,3,6,9] targeting interrupt-driven programs. As a result, except for the one in [6], these tools tend to produce many false positives.

Most interrupt-driven programs may have to deal with a huge number of interrupts, therefore the race detection tool should be scalable enough to handle the exponentially increasing number of paths at runtime due to asynchronous interrupts. Since embedded software generally run in constrained environments, a dynamic data race detection technique should also consider the space and time overhead problem and be as light as possible. By converting interrupt handlers into threads, the work presented in [6] maybe scalable, but certainly misses some properties of interrupts like being non-preemptive or asynchronous. For a better coverage of the program, a dynamic data race detection technique may be coupled with other testing tools [3,9] that stimulate the program by sending it external interrupts. Given that all existing solutions [2,3,6,9] fail to meet these requirements together, there is still an urgent need for an efficient dynamic race detection tool for interrupt-driven programs.

4 Conclusion

Handling asynchronous interrupts introduce fine-grained parallelism into interrupt-driven programs making them prone to data races and other concurrency bugs that may lead them into unexpected non deterministic executions with uncertain output. In this paper, we presented a survey of existing solutions for dynamically detecting data races in interrupt-driven programs and also analyzed the challenges and problems to be considered for an effective dynamic data race detection in such programs. Our analysis revealed that there is still a great need for an efficient and accurate dynamic race detection tool for interrupt-driven progams. In our future work, we will investigate new approaches to provide such a tool for interrupt-driven programs.

References

1. Banerjee, U., Bliss, B., Ma, Z., Petersen, P.: A Theory of Data Race Detection. In: Parallel and Distributed Systems: Testing and Debugging, pp. 69–78. ACM (July 2006)
2. Erickson, J., Musuvathi, M., Burckhardt, S., Olynyk, K.: Effective Data-Race Detection for the Kernel. In: Operating Systems Design and Implementation. USENIX (2010)
3. Higashi, M., Yamamoto, T., Hayase, Y., Ishio, T., Inoue, K.: An Effective Method to Control Interrupt Handler for Data Race Detection. In: Workshop on Automation of Software Test, pp. 79–86. ACM (2010)
4. Gay, D., Levis, P., Behren, R.V., Welsh, M., Brewer, E., Culler, D.: The nesC Language: A holistic Approach to Networked Embedded Systems. In: Programming Language Design and Implementation, pp. 1–11. ACM (2003)
5. Hill, J., Szewczyk, R., Woo, A., Hollar, S., Culler, D.E., Pister, K.S.J.: System Architecture Directions for Networked Sensors. In: Architectural Support for Programming Languages and Operating Systems, pp. 93–104. ACM (2000)
6. Lee, B.-K., Kang, M.-H., Park, K.C., Yi, J.S., Yang, S.W., Jun, Y.-K.: Program Conversion for Detecting Data Races in Concurrent Interrupt Handlers. In: Kim, T.-h., Adeli, H., Kim, H.-k., Kang, H.-j., Kim, K.J., Kiumi, A., Kang, B.-H. (eds.) ASEA 2011. CCIS, vol. 257, pp. 407–415. Springer, Heidelberg (2011)
7. Leveson, N.G., Turner, C.S.: An Investigation of the Therac-25 Accidents. IEEE Computer 26(7), 18–41 (1993)
8. Netzer, R.H.B., Miller, B.P.: What Are Race Conditions? Some Issues and Formalizations. ACM Letters on Programming Languages and Systems 1(1), 74–88 (1992)
9. Regehr, J.: Random Testing of Interrupt-Driven Software. In: International Conference on Embedded Software, pp. 290–298. ACM (2005)
10. Tchamgoue, G.M., Kim, K.H., Jun, Y.-K.: Testing and Debugging Concurrency Bugs in Event-Driven Programs. International Journal of Advanced Science and Technology 40, 55–63 (2012)

Dynamic Instrumentation for Nested Fork-join Parallelism in OpenMP Programs*

Ying Meng, Ok-Kyoon Ha, and Yong-Kee Jun**

Department of Informatics, Gyeongsang National University,
Jinju 660-701, The Republic of Korea
mengy_candy@hotmail.com, {jassmin,jun}@gnu.ac.kr

Abstract. It is important to determine the logical concurrency of Open-
MP programs, because it helps detecting data races between two threads
in an execution of the program. RaceStand have been developed to detect on-the-fly data races for OpenMP applications. Unfortunately, the
previous tool does not detect data races or reports false positives for
nested fork-join parallelism which uses function calls for the execution
of parallel regions by its defective source code instrumentation. In this
paper, we present an instrumentor to determine logical concurrency of
parallel threads using a dynamic binary instrumentation technique based
on Pin software framework. We implemented a Pin-tool as data race detection tool including our instrumentor, and empirically compared the
correctness of the Pin-tool with previous tool using a set of synthetic
programs considering nested parallelism and function calls.

Keywords: Logical concurrency, nested fork-join parallelism, OpenMP
programs, binary instrumentation.

1   Introduction

OpenMP [2] is an industry standard supporting a serialized program to be executed in parallel with simple compiler directives and libraries that support
standard C/C++ and Fortran 77/90. OpenMP covers only user-directed paral-
lelization and does not enforce to fix concurrency bugs, such as data races, thus
we should be introduce additional techniques or knowledge for detecting data
races. Usually, dynamic techniques detecting data races employ an instrumentation framework to insert monitoring codes for memory accesses and thread
operations. By monitoring thread operations, the logical concurrency of parallel threads can be determined, and it helps detecting data races among parallel
threads in an execution of the program.

---

* "This research was supported by Basic Science Research Program through the Na-
   tional Research Foundation of Korea(NRF) funded by the Ministry of Education,
   Science and Technology(2012-0007434)".
** Corresponding author: In Gyeongsang National University, he is also involved in the
   Engineering Research Institute (ERI).

T.-h. Kim, Y.-h. Lee, and W.-c. Fang (Eds.): FGIT 2012, LNCS 7709, pp. 154–158, 2012.
© Springer-Verlag Berlin Heidelberg 2012

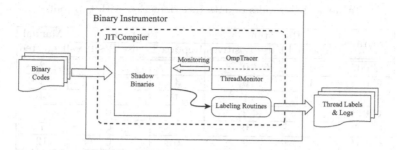

Fig. 1. The overall architecture of dynamic binary instrumentor

RaceStand [3] of GNU (Gyongsang National University) have been developed that is a representative on-the-fly data race detection tool for OpenMP programs. It provides the configuration for efficient verification of the existence of data races with optimal performance. However, the tool reports incorrect results of data race detection including false positives for fork-join parallel programs, such as OpenMP, which use function calls for the execution of parallel regions by its defective source code instrumentation.

This work presents an instrumentor to determine logical concurrency of parallel threads using a binary instrumentation technique based on Pin software framework [1,7,9]. It monitors thread operations considering function calls in an execution of the program and dynamically inserts instrumentation codes into the target programs to determine the logical concurrency of parallel threads using shadow binaries of an OpenMP program. Finally, the instrumentor creates thread identifiers [5] of each parallel thread occurred during an execution of the program. We implemented a Pin-tool [4] as data race detection tool including our instrumentor, and empirically compared the correctness of Pin-tool with previous tool using a set of synthetic programs considering nested parallelism and function calls. The empirical results show that Pin-tool reports at least one data race without any false positive due to the fact that our instrumentor dynamically creates and maintains the correct thread labels for active threads.

2 Determining Logical Concurrency

OpenMP programs determine how many tasks are assigned by consulting the the number of the physical processors and the pre-defined internal control variables, when an execution encounters a parallel region. Thus, we consider to find the instrumentation points which can divide a set of sequential physical threads into logically concurrent threads in binary cods [6]. We developed a binary instrumentor as a Pin-tool [4] on top of Pin instrumentation framework [1,7,9] considering the features of the OpenMP threading model.

Fig 1 shows overall architecture of our dynamic binary instrumentor. Our instrumentor copies shadow binaries from the original input binaries, and Just In Time (JIT) compiler recompiles the shadow binaries to execute the target program. For the instrumentor, we employ two important component, OmpTracer

Table 1. The results of data race detection with two tools

Programs	RaceStand		Pin-tool		Manual
	Reported	False Positives	Reported	False Positives	Detected
C-002	2	0	2	0	2
C-003	3	0	3	0	4
C-012	4	1	4	0	4
C-013	10	2	6	0	8
C-103	0	0	4	0	7
C-104	2	2	6	0	12
C-113	0	0	4	0	14
C-114	2	2	8	0	24

and ThreadMonitor. OmpTracer traces OpenMP directives, such as `parallel for` and `parallel section` directives, and finds instrumentation points by dividing a set of sequential threads on a task region of OpenMP into logical concurrent threads. ThreadMonitor monitor thread operations considering the OpenMP threading model during the execution of input program. It identifies thread creation and thread termination on fork operations and join operations, respectively. Finally, ThreadMonitor generates and manages thread labels to determine logical concurrency for each active thread. Because our instrumentor uses the shadow binaries which generated by JIT compiler and maintains logical concurrency of threads including nested fork-join parallelism by OmpTracer, it can correctly create thread identifiers for the target program only by considering active threads, even if the program employs any function call for parallel regions.

3   Experimental Results

We implemented a Pin-tool as data race detection tool including our instrumentor on top of Pin instrumentation framework which widely used to analyze binary execution, and empirically compared the correctness of Pin-tool with prior tool, RaceStand. For the comparison, we employ a same thread labeling scheme [5] and a detection protocol [8] in each tools, and developed a set of synthetic programs which uses function calls for the execution of parallel regions. The synthetics were considered multilevel nested parallelism and series parallelism, and have at least one access to a shared variable in each thread. Our implementation and experimentation were carried on a system with Intel Xeon 2 CPUs and 2GB main memory under the Kernel 2.6 of Linux operating system. The synthetic programs were compiled with gcc-4.4.3 for the Pin-tool and RaceStand.

Table 1 shows that the results of data race detection with the Pin-tool and RaceStand. In the table, 'Reported' columns contain the number of reported data races by two detection tools, and the false positives of the reported data races are resulted in 'False Positives' columns. The last column contains manually identified data races that consider the execution of parallel threads and accesses to a shared variable. From the results, the Pin-tool reports at least one data race without any false positive due to the fact that our instrumentor dynamically creates and maintains the correct thread labels for active threads. However, RaceStand does not detect data races for C-103 and C-113 that they employ two function calls to contain multilevel nested parallelism. For the four cases, C-012, C-013, C-104, and C-114, RaceStand reports data races including false positives due to the incorrect thread labels by its defective source code instrumentation.

The results from Table 1 show that our dynamic binary instrumentation technique practically determines logical concurrency among the execution of parallel threads for on-the-fly data race detection in nested fork-join parallel programs, such as OpenMP.

4   Conclusion

It is important to determine the logical concurrency of OpenMP programs, because it helps detecting data races among parallel threads in an execution of the program. To detect data races in the programs, previous tool, RaceStand, does not detect data races or reports false positives for nested fork-join parallelism which uses function calls for the execution of parallel regions. We presented a dynamic binary instrumentation technique for on-the-fly data race detection, and implemented a Pin-tool as data race detection tool including our instrumentor on top of Pin instrumentation framework. The experimental results using OpenMP synthetic programs shown that our dynamic binary instrumentation technique practically determines logical concurrency among the execution of parallel threads for on-the-fly data race detection in nested fork-join parallel programs.

References

1. Bach, M., Charney, M., Cohn, R., Demikhovsky, E., Devor, T., Hazelwood, K., Jaleel, A., Luk, C.K., Lyons, G., Patil, H., Tal, A.: Analyzing parallel programs with pin. Computer 43(3), 34–41 (2010)
2. Dagum, L., Menon, R.: Openmp: an industry standard api for shared-memory programming. Computational Science Engineering 5(1), 46–55 (1998)
3. Ha, O.-K., Kim, Y.-J., Kang, M.-H., Jun, Y.-K.: Empirical Comparison of Race Detection Tools for OpenMP Programs. In: Ślęzak, D., Kim, T.-h., Yau, S.S., Gervasi, O., Kang, B.-H. (eds.) GDC 2009. CCIS, vol. 63, pp. 108–116. Springer, Heidelberg (2009)
4. Ha, O.K., Kuh, I.B., Tchamgoue, G.M., Jun, Y.K.: On-the-fly detection of data races in openmp programs. In: Proceedings of the 2012 Workshop on Parallel and Distributed Systems: Testing, Analysis, and Debugging, PADTAD 2012, pp. 1–10. ACM, New York (2012)
5. Ha, O., Jun, Y.: Efficient Thread Labeling for On-the-fly Race Detection of Programs with Nested Parallelism. In: Kim, T.-h., Adeli, H., Kim, H.-k., Kang, H.-j., Kim, K.J., Kiumi, A., Kang, B.-H. (eds.) ASEA 2011. CCIS, vol. 257, pp. 424–436. Springer, Heidelberg (2011)

6. Kuh, I.B., Ha, O.K., Jun, Y.K.: Tracing logical concurrency for dynamic race detection in openmp programs. In: Proceedings of the 1st International Conference on Software Technology, SoftTech 2012. SERSC, pp. 222–224 (2012)
7. Luk, C.K., Cohn, R., Muth, R., Patil, H., Klauser, A., Lowney, G., Wallace, S., Reddi, V.J., Hazelwood, K.: Pin: building customized program analysis tools with dynamic instrumentation. In: Proceedings of the 2005 ACM SIGPLAN Conference on Programming Language Design and Implementation, PLDI 2005, pp. 190–200. ACM, New York (2005)
8. Mellor-Crummey, J.: On-the-fly detection of data races for programs with nested fork-join parallelism. In: Proceedings of the 1991 ACM/IEEE Conference on Supercomputing, Supercomputing 1991, pp. 24–33. ACM, New York (1991)
9. Patil, H., Pereira, C., Stallcup, M., Lueck, G., Cownie, J.: Pinplay: a framework for deterministic replay and reproducible analysis of parallel programs. In: Proceedings of the 8th Annual IEEE/ACM International Symposium on Code Generation and Optimization, CGO 2010, pp. 2–11. ACM, New York (2010)

An Audio Watermarking Algorithm Using Group Quantization of DCT Coefficients

De Li[1], Wenji Quan[1], and JongWeon Kim[2,*]

[1] Dept. of Computer at Yanbian University, China
`leader1223@ybu.edu.cn`, `moongill2008@163.com`
[2] Dept. of Copyright Protection at Sangmyung University, Korea
`jwkim@smu.ac.kr`

Abstract. In this paper, we propose a watermark algorithm based on DCT and audio feature quantization. The proposed algorithm can be easily implemented and has a variety of variable factors to protect user information, such as quantization groups, filtering, and an audio feature extraction formula. If these factors are unknown, it is more difficult for them to be attacked. Our algorithm can extract a watermark without help from the original audio signal, giving it a higher degree of usability. The experimental results show that the proposed scheme is inaudible and robust against common signal processing techniques, including low pass filtering, noise addition, and compression. The proposed algorithm is particularly robust with respect to compression.

Keywords: Audio watermarking, Audio feature, DCT, Quantization, Robustness.

1 Introduction

In the modern world, there is a vast quantity of digital information that can be accessed in various forms: text, images, audio, and video. For digital audio, in particular, it is difficult to secure and protect an author's work from being stolen or copied. This has given rise to an urgent need for protecting the owner's copyright and information. Digital watermarking, which is being developed to meet this need, is the process of embedding information into a digital signal such that it may be used to verify its authenticity or the identity of its owner. Thus, it is an application that embeds a small amount of data but requires the greatest robustness.

Digital watermarking can be used for a wide range of applications, such as copyright protection, source tracking, broadcast monitoring, and covert communication [1-3]. In order to protect copyright information, several watermark methods have been proposed, but most of these are focused on images [4-12]. The few audio watermark algorithms that have been proposed can be grouped into three categories: patchwork in the frequency domain [13], echo hiding in the time domain [14], and spread-spectrum [15].

---

* Corresponding author.

T.-h. Kim, Y.-h. Lee, and W.-c. Fang (Eds.): FGIT 2012, LNCS 7709, pp. 159–166, 2012.

The previously proposed papers on audio watermarking algorithm mostly concentrated in improve the robustness according changed quantization step or using energy-proportion etc. But the robustness of compression is still high and easy to attacking.

In this paper, we propose an audio watermarking algorithm based on the DCT domain using feature group quantization. In our algorithm, we choose the value of low- and mid-frequency components in the DCT domain, because low and mid frequency domain has higher robustness than high frequency domain, and use these components to calculate features. In addition, we quantize the features for these two groups and use the quantized values to calculate the embedding strength. Finally, we embed the digital watermark into the low and mid-domain with the calculated strength. Experimental results show that the proposed scheme is robust against common signal processing techniques, such as audio compression, low pass filtering, and noise addition. Moreover, the watermark is also highly inaudible after being embedded.

This paper is organized as follows. In Section 2, we describe the fundamental theory of the scheme and its construction, and Section 3 describes the algorithm for embedding and extracting the watermark. Section 4 is dedicated to a description of a variety of simulation experiments, which will explain the effectiveness of the proposed scheme. Finally, we present our brief conclusions in Section 5.

2   Fundamental Theory

In our audio watermarking scheme, the watermark can be embedded into the host audio in three steps. Firstly, the host audio is segmented according to the length of the watermark information. Secondly, selecting a small part of each segment, the DCT is performed on the selected parts and the low–mid frequencies are extracted. Finally, we use the low–mid frequencies to calculate the embedding strength, and embed the watermark bits into the low–mid frequency components.

2.1   Embedding Strength Calculation

In order to calculate the embedding strength for the watermark, we firstly segment the audio signal according to the length of the watermark. After segmentation, we calculate each segment's embedding strength and embed one of the watermark bits in each segment. The embedding strength calculation is as follows.

1. Select 640 contents (we want use the two dimensional DCT for each 8×8 blocks so choose 640 contents from each arbitrary segment Fi). Divide the contents into 10 groups of 64, and name each group of 64 contents a block. Reshape the blocks to 8×8.
2. Extract 10 contents from each block and compose them into a sequence of 100 contents. Divide this equally into groups "A" and "B" and use equations (1) and (2) to calculate "SA" and "SB", which representative for characteristic value of the groups "A" and "B".

$$SA = \sqrt{\frac{1}{N} \sum_{t=i-1}^{t=i-1/2} S(t)^2} \tag{1}$$

$$SB = \sqrt{\frac{1}{N} \sum_{t=i-1/2}^{t=i} S(t)^2} \tag{2}$$

3. Use SA and SB to calculate the audio feature F as follows:

$$F = \frac{SA - SB}{SA + SB} \tag{3}$$

In our algorithm, we change the value of the audio feature to embed the watermark according to the following sets:

$$Q_0 = \{-0.7, -0.3, 0.1, 0.1, 0.9\}$$
$$Q_1 = \{-0.9, -0.5, -0.1, 0.3, 0.7\}$$

If the watermark bit is "0," then we use the closest value in group Q0 to quantize F (which is the audio feature in this segment), or if the watermark bit is "1" we use the closest value in Q1 to quantize F.

4. In order to quantize the feature, we use the following formula to calculate the embedding strength "g" for fields A and B.

$$\begin{cases} A : s(t)' = s(t) + gs(t) \\ B : s(t)' = s(t) - gs(t) \end{cases} \tag{4}$$

5. In step five, "g" is calculated by equation (5), in which F is the feature and Q is the quantized value of the feature.

$$g = \frac{1}{2} \frac{Q - F}{1 - QF} \tag{5}$$

3   Embedding and Detection of a Watermark

3.1   Watermark Embedding Scheme

In order to guarantee the robustness and transparency of the watermark, we propose to embed it in the low–mid frequencies of the audio signal. The main steps of the embedding procedure, which is based on feature quantization, can be described as follows.

1. First, the audio signal must be segmented according to the length of the watermark, and each segment reshaped into 8 × 8 blocks.
2. A DCT is performed on each block, and 10 contents are selected from the DCT domain. We choose the low–mid part of the DCT domain and insert 100 contents in every segment.
3. The proposed algorithm is used to calculate the embedding strength of each segment, and one bit of watermark information is embedded in every segment.
4. After embedding the watermark in each segment, an inverse DCT is performed, and each segment is reconstructed. We now have a watermarked digital audio signal. The watermark embedding procedure is shown in Figure 1.

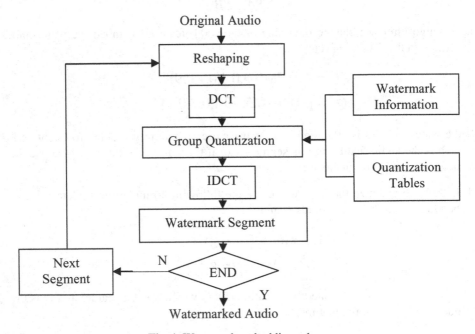

Fig. 1. Watermark embedding scheme

3.2   Watermark Detection Scheme

In our algorithm, the watermark detection procedure does not require the original audio signal. Quantization tables are used to detect the watermark information, and it is easy to change these tables to improve the security of the proposed algorithm.

The watermark detection procedure is summarized as follows.

1. The watermarked audio is segmented according to the length of the watermark.
2. Each segment is reshaped to an 8 × 8 block, and each block has a DCT applied. We then select low- and mid-frequencies from each DCT domain.
3. Using equation (3), we calculate the audio feature of each segment.

4. We compare these features with groups Q_0 and Q_1. For all features closer to a member of group Q_0, we extract a "0"; for all features closer to a member of Q_1, we extract a "1".

In this study, we measure reliability as the bit error rate (BER) of the extracted watermark. This is defined as:

$$BER = \frac{B}{M \times N} \times 100\% \qquad (6)$$

Where B is the number of erroneously detected bits and M × N is the size of the watermark. The watermark detection procedure is shown in Figure 2.

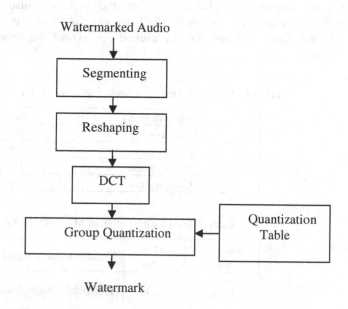

Fig. 2. Watermark extraction scheme

4   Experimental Results

In order to illustrate its inaudible and robust nature, we tested the proposed watermarking scheme on digital mono audio signals of 10 s in length. We used the randomly generated 8 × 8 bit binary image shown in Figure 3 as our watermark.

To evaluate the performance of the proposed watermarking algorithm, we used the StirmarkForAudiov2.0 software, which is widely used to test the robustness of audio watermarking.

Fig. 3. Watermark image

For this study, we chose several common attacks such as a RC low pass, noise addition, and compression to test the robustness of our algorithm. In addition, we experimented with different kinds of audio signals under the above attack types. Table 1 summarizes the proposed watermark detection results against various attacks, and Table 2 shows the signal-to-noise ratio (SNR) of the different audio styles. From Table 2, we can find that the average SNR is 38.85 dB, and Table 3 shows that our method can extract the watermark exactly with a low BER.

Table 1. Watermark Detection Results for Common Signal Processing

Signal Processing	BER
No processing	0%
RC low pass	4%
Noise addition	1%
Compression	3%

Table 2. Data for the Different Music Styles Tested

Audio content	SNR (dB)	Sample audio signal
Classical	34.31	
Dance	40.53	
Hip hop	44.29	
Jazz	34.75	
R & B	38.50	
Rock	40.69	

Table 3. Watermark Detection Results for Different Music Styles

Audio style	BER			
	No processing	Low pass	Noise addition	Com- pression
Classical	0%	4%	1%	1%
Dance	0%	3%	1%	3%
Hip hop	0%	4%	0%	6%
Jazz	0%	3%	1%	3%
R & B	0%	1%	0%	4%
Rock	0%	1%	1%	7%

As can be seen from the Table 1, the algorithm we proposed in this paper has high robustness especially for the compression (other papers for compression robustness in about 9%). In addition, the robustness and SNR for different types of audio is also very high.

5   Conclusion

In this paper, we proposed a robust watermark algorithm based on feature quantization. The robustness of the method is a result of three key steps in our approach: the original digital audio is segmented by the watermark and reshaped into blocks, a DCT is performed on each block, and the proposed algorithm is used to calculate features from each segment. Audio features are quantized using quantization tables, and the watermark is embedded. From our analytical and experimental findings, it was shown that the proposed watermarking method achieved robustness against common audio signal processing techniques, particularly for a compression attack. The SNR of the watermarked audio was above 33 dB. In addition, the watermark was extracted without using the original audio signal, and thus, it can be easily implemented.

Future research will focus on improving the performance of the algorithm to enhance its robustness and reduce the impact of the original audio.

Acknowledgements. This research project was supported by the Ministry of Culture, Sports and Tourism (MCST) and the Korea Copyright Commission in 2011.

References

1. Cox, I.J., Miller, M.L.: The first 50 years of electronic watermarking. J. Appl. Signal Process. 56(2), 225–230 (2002)
2. The Wiki website (2012), http://en.wikipedia.org/wiki/Digital_watermarking
3. Kim, J., et al.: Watermarking two dimensional data object identifier for authenticated distribution of digital multimedia contents. Signal Processing: Image Communication 25, 559–576 (2002)

4. Seok, J., Hong, J., Kim, J.: A Novel Audio Watermarking Algorithm for Copyright Protection of Digital Audio. ETRI Journal 24, 181–189 (2002)
5. Swanson, M., Zhu, B., Tewfik, A., Boney, L.: Robust Audio Watermarking Using Perceptual Masking. Signal Processing 66(3), 337–355 (1998)
6. Bassia, P., Pitas, I., Nikolaidis, N.: Robust Audio Watermarking in the Time Domain. IEEE Trans. on Multimedia 3 (1999)
7. Shin, S.W., Kim, J.W., Choi, J.U.: Development of Audio Watermarking Algorithm using Audio Feature Quantization. Telecommunication Review 5, 653–662 (2002)
8. Seo, J.S., Jin, M., Jang, D., Lee, S., Yoo, C.D.: Audio Fingerprinting Based on Normalized Spectral Subband Moments. IEEE Signal Processing Letters 3, 209–212 (2006)
9. Wang, X.-Y., Niu, P.-P., Yang, H.-Y.: A robust digital audio watermarking based on statistics characteristics. Pattern Recognition 42(11) (2009)
10. Burges, C.J.C., Platt, J.C., Jana, S.: Distortion Discriminant Analysis for Audio Fingerprinting. IEEE Transactions on Speech and Audio Processing (December 2001)
11. Yang, H., Jiang, X., Kot, A.C.: Image watermarking using dual-tree complex wavelet by coefficients swapping and group of coefficients quantization. In: IEEE 2010 Conference on Multimedia and Expo., pp. 1673–1678 (2010)
12. Li, D., Ji, Y., Kim, J.: Audio Watermarking by Coefficient Quantization in the DWT-DCT dual domain. Advanced Science Letters (to be published, 2012)
13. Yeo, I.K., Kim, H.J.: Modified patchwork algorithm: A novel audio watermarking scheme. IEEE Transactions on Speech and Audio Processing 11(4), 381–386 (2003)
14. Gruhl, D., Lu, A., Bender, W.: Echo Hiding. In: Anderson, R. (ed.) IH 1996. LNCS, vol. 1174, pp. 295–315. Springer, Heidelberg (1996)
15. Cui, L., Wang, S., Sun, T.: The application of binary image in digital audio watermarking. Neural Networks and Signal Processing 2, 1497–1500 (2003)

A Study on Optimization Techniques
for the Smart Virtual Machine Platform[*]

YunSik Son[1] and YangSun Lee[2,**]

[1] Dept. of Computer Engineering, Dongguk University
26 3-Ga Phil-Dong, Jung-Gu, Seoul 100-715, Korea
sonbug@dongguk.edu
[2] Dept. of Computer Engineering, Seokyeong University
16-1 Jungneung-Dong, Sungbuk-Ku, Seoul 136-704, Korea
yslee@skuniv.ac.kr

Abstract. SVM(Smart Virtual Machine) is the virtual machine solution that supports various programming languages and platforms, and its aims are to support programming languages like ISO/IEC C++, Java and Objective-C and smart phone platforms such as Android and iOS. Various contents that developed by supported language on SVM can be execute on Android and iOS platforms at no additional cost, because the SVM has the platform independent characteristic by using SIL(Smart Intermediate Language) as an intermediate language. VM(Virtual Machine) is manufactured to software unlike physical system that consists of hardware, it is conceptual computer that have logical system configuration. But, It can assume that optimization of executed code is very important because act thing which VM is slow than that process by real processor. In this paper, we deal with various optimization techniques to optimize stack based virtual machine called SVM which can execute on various smart devices.

Keywords: SVM(Smart Virtual Machine), Smart Platforms, Virtual Machine, SIL(Smart Intermediate Language), VM Optimization, Code Optimizer.

1   Introduction

The previous development environments for smart phone contents are needed to generate specific target code depending on target devices or platforms, and each platform has its own developing language[1,2]. Therefore, even if the same contents are to be used, it must be redeveloped depending on the target machine and a compiler for that specific machine is needed, making the contents development process very inefficient. SVM(Smart Virtual Machine) is a virtual machine solution which aims to

---

[*] This research was supported by Basic Science Research Program through the National Research Foundation of Korea(NRF) funded by the Ministry of Education, Science and Technology(No.20110006884).
[**] Corresponding author.

T.-h. Kim, Y.-h. Lee, and W.-c. Fang (Eds.): FGIT 2012, LNCS 7709, pp. 167–172, 2012.

resolve such problems, and it uses the SIL(Smart Intermediate Language) code which designed by our research team as an input at the execution time.

The SVM solution largely consists of three parts; a compiler, assembler and virtual machine. It is designed in a hierarchical way which minimizes the burden of the retargeting process. In this research, a virtual machine, SVM, has been specifically de-signed and created to be run on various smart devices after receiving a SIL code input. The VM (Virtual Machine) to execute the contents is manufactured to software unlike physical system that consists of hardware, it is conceptual computer that have logical system configuration. But, It can assume that optimization of executed code/VM itself is very important because act thing which VM is slow than that process by real processor.

In this paper, we deal with various optimization techniques to optimize stack based virtual machine called SVM which can execute on various smart devices.

2   Relative Studies

2.1   SVM(Smart Virtual Machine)

The SVM is a platform which is loaded on smart phones. It is a stack based virtual machine solution which can independently download and run application programs. The SVM consists of three main parts; compiler, assembler and virtual machine. It is designed in a hierarchal structure to minimize the burden of the retargeting process.

The SVM is designed to accommodate successive languages, object-oriented languages and etc. through input of SIL as its intermediate language. It has the advantage of accommodating C/C++ and Java, which are the most widely used languages used by developers. SIL was a result of the compilation/translation process and it is changed into the running format SEF(SIL Executable Format) through an assembler. The SVM then runs the program after receiving the SEF.

2.2   SIL(Smart Intermediate Language) & SEF(Smart Executable Format)

SIL, the virtual machine code for SVM, is designed as a standardized virtual machine code model for ordinary smart phones and embedded systems [3]. SIL is a stack based command set which holds independence as a language, hardware and a platform. In order to accommodate a variety of programming languages, SIL is defined based on the analysis of existing virtual machine codes such as bytecode [4], .NET IL [5] and etc. In addition, it also has the set of arithmetic operations codes to accommodate object-oriented languages and successive languages.

SIL is composed of meta-code (shows class declarations and specific operations) and arithmetic codes (responds to actual commands). Arithmetic codes are not subordinate to any specific hardware or source languages and thus have an abstract form. In order to make debugging of the languages such as the assembly language simple, they apply a name rule with consistency and define the language in mnemonics, for higher readability. In addition, they have short form arithmetic operations for optimization. SIL's arithmetic codes are classified into seven and each category has its own detailed categories.

SEF's structure largely consists of a header section which is in charge of expressing SEF files' composition, a program segment section and a debug section expresses debugging related information. The program segment section can be divided again into three sections which express codes and data [6].

2.3 Comparison of the VM and the Native Execution Method

Aspects of executing contents, there are differences between the VM method and the Native.

Firstly, the VM method cans easily executing the same VM application even if H/W changed because it has the H / W independence. Also, it has the stability for the target system when the errors exist in the VM contents and can be easily ported to various H/W. On the other hand, the execution performance of the algorithm code is slower than the native method. In the case of the native method, need the changes of the contents by the characteristics of H/W platforms and OS, and it can affect the system due to the errors in the contents. But, the executing performance of the algorithm code is faster than the VM method[6,7].

3 The Optimization Techniques for the SVM

In the portability of the contents, the SVM has a advantage, but it has the low performance due to the S/W interpretation for the instructions. Optimization techniques for solving these problems can be viewed from two major aspects. Firstly, the optimization of the instruction codes itself in the contents. The optimized code, because it reduces the cost of the interpretation of the virtual machine, is a very important issue in the virtual machine optimization. Next, the optimization of the interpretation method is one of the important issues. The VM requires efficient interpretation method because the stack based interpretation under the general fetch-decode-dispatch method has very poor performance. In this chapter, we will discuss these issues.

3.1 Code Level Optimization

Diverse optimization techniques have been deployed lately in the compilation process of a source program for improving the program's execution speed and reducing the size of the source code. Optimization techniques in the compiler development stage can be categorized into target machine-independent intermediate code optimization and target machine-dependent target code optimization.

Furthermore, since recent attention regarding complier development has been focused on the retargetable optimization compiler that facilitates applications in various target machines, there is an increasing need for target machine-independent intermediate code optimization.

As shown in Fig. 1, if the SIL is optimized by the code optimizer, more efficient code execution is possible and the executing performance is increased. Also, reduce the contents size and improve the performance at the same time by the adding optimization specific SIL code can be abbreviate multiple instructions to smaller command[3,6,7,8].

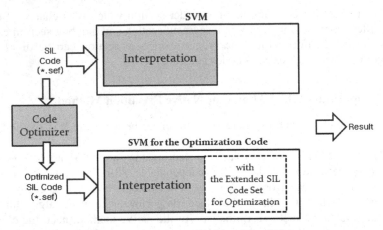

Fig. 1. Code Optimization Model for SVM

3.2   System Level Optimization

Differently from the code level optimization perspective, the VM system optimization may be considered. Especially, There are a variety of methodologies to improve the performance through the interpretation of a stack-based content, because it has a big impact on the degradation of the performance of the VM executing. Firstly, JIT, Back-End, Decompilation and Hotspot Compilation are the native executing method for the contents to avoid the disadvantages of the VM method. Such ways are the method to convert to native code and execute rather than directly executing the intermediate code in the VM[9].

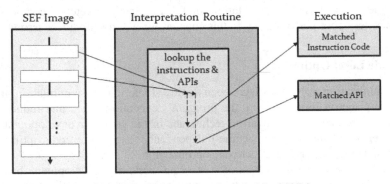

Fig. 2. Typical Interpretation Model of SVM

Next, we will discuss the techniques for enhancing the performance by improving the interpretation model of the VM. Figure 2 shown the execution model of the SVM applied common interpretation technique. In this execution model, a very large degradation of the execution speed occurred because of   frequent searching for to execute the each instruction in the interpretation routine.

To solve the problem, as shown in Fig. 3, the repetitive searching can be removed by the using of the mapping table for instructions/APIs and executing routines instead of lookup routine. In addition, by the executing of the mapped routine on the native level, the executing performance of the VM can be enhanced.

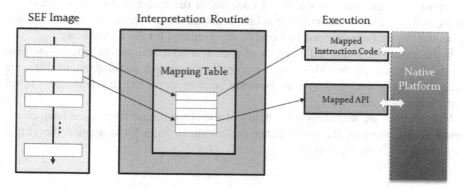

Fig. 3. Enhanced Interpretation Routine Model for SVM

The performance of the SVM applied enhanced interpretation routine are shown in table 1. The test suit was selected as the program with high computational complexity algorithm to verify the performance of the interpretation routine.

Table 1. Performance comparison of the SVM and the Optimized SVM

Test Programs	Performance(millisecond)		Enhanced Performance Rate
	SVM	SVM (using optimized interpretation routine)	
PerfectNumber.sef (parameter: 2000)	3256	2519	23%
PrimeNumber.sef (parameter: 1000)	1780	1130	37%
MagicNumber.sef (parameter: 49)	28	18	36%

VM operation code to interpret the amount of time it takes to measure the performance of IR measurements to be selected arithmetic driven in table 1 because the program is well suited for experiments. The selected test programs in table 1 is suitable the experiment because we need to measure the interpretation time of the VM's arithmetic codes to examine the performance of the interpretation routine. Results of the experiments was confirmed, an average of 32% improvement in performance when applied to the enhanced IR.

4   Conclusions and Further Researches

A virtual machine has the characteristic of enabling application programs to be used without alteration even if processors or operating systems are changed. It is a core technology for executing a variety of contents in the recent mobile, embedded and smart systems. The virtual machine solution has the advantage on the portability, but it has the low performance due to the S/W interpretation for the instructions.

In this paper, we examined a variety of optimization techniques in order to increase the performance of the SVM. Using these optimization techniques, enables the execution of complex and various contents because cover the disadvantage - lower performance - of the VM.

In the future, we will show the validity of the optimization techniques have considered in this paper by the performance evaluation through SVM applied the virtual machine optimization technique.

References

1. Apple, iOS Reference Library, iOS Technology Overview,
   http://developer.apple.com/devcenter/ios
2. Goole, Android-An Open Handset Alliance Project, http://code.google.com/intl/ko/android/
3. Yun, S.L., Nam, D.G., Oh, S.M., Kim, J.S.: Virtual Machine Code for Embedded Systems. In: International Conference on CIMCA, pp. 206–214 (2004)
4. Meyer, J., Downing, T.: JAVA Virtual Machine. O'Reilly (1997)
5. Lindin, S.: Inside Microsoft .NET IL Assembler. Microsoft Press (2002)
6. Lee, Y.S.: The Virtual Machine Technology for Embedded Systems. The Korea Multimedia Society 6, 36–44 (2002)
7. Son, Y., Lee, Y.S.: Design and Implementation of the Virtual Machine for Smart Devices. In: Proc. of the 2011 Fall Conference, Korea Multimedia Society, vol. 14, pp. 93–96 (2011)
8. Son, Y., Lee, Y.S.: Design and Implementation of an Objective-C Compiler for the Virtual Machine on Smart Phone. In: Kim, T.-h., Gelogo, Y. (eds.) MulGraB 2011, Part I. CCIS, vol. 262, pp. 52–59. Springer, Heidelberg (2011)
9. Lee, Y.S., Kim, Y.K., Kwon, H.J.: Design and Implementation of the Decompiler for Virtual Machine Code of the C++ Compiler in the Ubiquitous Game Platform. In: Szczuka, M.S., Howard, D., Ślęzak, D., Kim, H.-K., Kim, T.-H., Ko, I.-S., Lee, G., Sloot, P.M.A. (eds.) ICHIT 2006. LNCS (LNAI), vol. 4413, pp. 511–521. Springer, Heidelberg (2007)
10. Gough, J.: Compiling for the NET Common Language Runtime (CLR). Prentice-Hall (2002)
11. Engel, J.: Programming for the Java Virtual Machine. Addison-Wesley (1999)
12. Lindholm, T., Yellin, F.: The Java Virtual Machine Specification, 2nd edn. Addison-Wesley (1999)

A Real-Time Localization Platform Design in WUSB over WBAN Protocol for Wearable Computer Systems

Kyeong Hur [1], Won-Sung Sohn [1,*], Jae-Kyung Kim [1], and YangSun Lee [2]

[1] Dept. of Computer Education, Gyeongin National University of Education, Gyesan-Dong San 59-12, 45 Gyodae-Gil, Gyeyang-Gu, Incheon, 407-753, Korea
sohnws@ginue.ac.kr
[2] Dept. of Computer Engineering, Seokyeong University Seoul, Korea

Abstract. In this Paper, we propose a Real-Time Localization Platform Built on WUSB (Wireless USB) over WBAN (Wireless Body Area Networks) protocol required for Wearable Computer systems. Proposed Real-Time Localization Platform Technique is executed on the basis of WUSB over WBAN protocol at each sensor node comprising peripherals of a wearable computer system. In the Platform, a WUSB host calculates the location of a receiving sensor node by using the difference between the times at which the sensor node received different WBAN beacon frames sent from the WUSB host. And the WUSB host interprets motion of the virtual object.

Keywords: Localization, Wearable Computer, Wireless USB, Wireless Body Area Networks (WBAN).

1   Introduction

A recent major development in computer technology is the advent of the wearable computer system that is based on human-centric interface technology trends and ubiquitous computing environments [1]. Wearable computer systems use the wireless universal serial bus (WUSB) that refers to USB technology that is merged with WiMedia PHY/MAC technical specifications. WUSB can be applied to wireless personal area networks (WPAN) applications as well as wired USB applications such as PAN. Because WUSB specifications have defined high-speed connections between a WUSB host and WUSB devices for compatibility with USB 2.0 specifications, the wired USB applications are serviced directly. Unlike a wired USB that physically separates the USB host and USB device, WUSB allows a device to separately function as both a WUSB host and WUSB device on a single transceiver; such devices are referred to as the dual role devices (DRD)[2-6].

A wireless body area network (WBAN), which describes the application of wearable computing devices, allows the integration of intelligent, miniaturized, low-power, invasive/non-invasive sensor nodes that monitor body functions and the surrounding environment. Each intelligent node has sufficient capability to process and forward information to a base station for diagnosis and prescription. A WBAN

---

[*] Corresponding author.

T.-h. Kim, Y.-h. Lee, and W.-c. Fang (Eds.): FGIT 2012, LNCS 7709, pp. 173–180, 2012.
© Springer-Verlag Berlin Heidelberg 2012

provides long-term health monitoring of patients under their natural physiological states without constraining their normal activities. The WBAN can be used to develop a smart and affordable health care system, and it can handle functions including basic diagnostic procedures, supervision of a chronic condition, supervising recovery from a surgical procedure, and emergency events [7].

The context awareness and mobility support are major performance measures in the ubiquitous computing environment. To guarantee seamless mobility, research area of localization techniques had gotten large concerns. From that reason, Localization techniques such as Active Badge [8], Cricket [9], RADAR [10] were proposed. The GPS (Global Position System) is not adequate for the indoor environment. But, the above techniques provide indoor location information.

In this Paper, we propose a Real-Time Localization Platform Built on WUSB (Wireless USB) over IEEE 802.15.6 WBAN (Wireless Body Area Networks) protocol required for Wearable Computer systems. Proposed Real-Time Localization Platform Technique is executed on the basis of WUSB over WBAN protocol at each sensor node comprising peripherals of a wearable computer system. In the Platform, a WUSB host calculates the location of a receiving sensor node by using the difference between the times at which the sensor node received different WBAN beacon frames sent from the WUSB host. And the WUSB host interprets motion of the virtual object.

2   WUSB over WBAN Protocol for Wearable Computer Systems

The WUSB channel is a continuous sequence of linked application-specific control packets, called micro-scheduled management commands (MMCs). WUSB maps the USB 2.0 transaction protocol onto the TDMA micro-scheduling feature. Within the WUSB protocol, the micro-scheduled sequence consists of an MMC and the subsequent time slots that are described in the MMC; this sequence is called a transaction group [4].

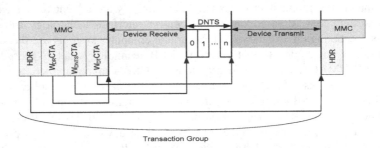

Fig. 1. General structure of WUSB transaction group

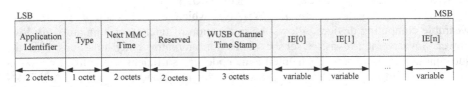

Application Identifier	Type	Next MMC Time	Reserved	WUSB Channel Time Stamp	IE[0]	IE[1]	...	IE[n]
2 octets	1 octet	2 octets	2 octets	3 octets	variable	variable	...	variable

Fig. 2. Format of MMC packet

Figure 1 shows the general model of a transaction group. The WUSB host dynamically manages the size of transaction groups over time according to the demands of the endpoint data streams. Therefore, the number of transactions per transaction group can be variable. MMCs are used by a host to control WUSB channel. The general structure of an MMC control packet is shown in Fig. 2. The type field is used to indicate the MMC command type. The NextMMCTime field indicates the number of microseconds from the beginning of the current MMC packet to the beginning of the next MMC packet. The WUSB channel time stamp field is set to the clock value of the host when MMC transmission starts. The information element (IE) fields in an MMC are called WUSB channel IEs and they include protocol time-slot allocations, device notification time slots (DNTS), and host information [4].

MMCs are used to broadcast command and I/O control information to all devices belonging to the WUSB cluster. In addition, MMCs are used to advertise channel time allocations for point-to-point data communications between the host and the endpoints of the devices in the WUSB cluster. An MMC specifies the linked stream of wireless USB channel time allocation (WCTA) blocks up to the next MMC. The channel time between two MMCs may also be idle time, where no WCTAs are scheduled. The direction of transmission and the use of each WCTA are fully declared in each MMC packet [4]. A WUSB network consists of a WUSB host and several WUSB devices, and this is referred to as a WUSB cluster [4]. In a similar manner, IEEE 802.15.6 WBAN hubs and sensor nodes form a star topology [7].

Figure 3 shows the WUSB over WBAN architecture. Here, the IEEE 802.15.6 WBAN superframe begins with a beacon period (BP) in which the WBAN hub performing the WUSB host's role sends the beacon. This beacon mode of the WBAN is operated in both non-medical and medical traffic environments. The data transmission period in each superframe is divided into the exclusive access phase 1 (EAP1), random access phase 1 (RAP1), Type-I/II access phase, EAP2, RAP2, Type-I/II access phase, and contention access phase (CAP) periods. The EAP1 and EAP2 periods are assigned through contention to data traffic with higher priorities. Further, the RAP1, RAP2, and CAP periods are assigned through contention to data traffic with lower priorities. In the Type-I/II access phase periods, the WBAN hub reserves time slots without contention to exchange data with its input-sensor nodes.

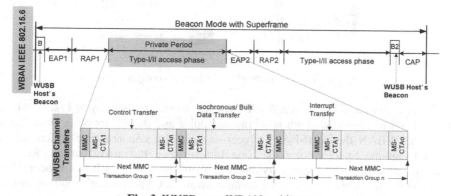

Fig. 3. WUSB over WBAN architecture

In the WUSB over WBAN Architecture, in order to set up a wireless communication link to wearable computer systems, the WUSB channel is encapsulated within a WBAN superframe via Type-I/II access phase periods that enables the WUSB host and the input-sensor nodes to reserve time slots without contention through MMC scheduling. In a user scenario of a wearable computer system using the WUSB over WBAN architecture, the user carries a portable or wearable computing host device. This host device performs roles of the WUSB host and the WBAN hub simultaneously. Therefore, a "wearable" WUSB cluster and a WBAN cluster are formed. The attached input-sensor nodes perform the functions of localization-based input interfaces for wearable computer systems and healthcare monitoring. Furthermore, the attached wireless nodes comprise the peripherals of a wearable computer system, and the central WUSB host exchanges data with the outer peripherals of the WUSB slave devices.

3   Real-Time Localization Platform Design

Active Badge and Active Bat [8] proposed passive ceiling-mounted receivers that obtain information from active transmitters carried by users. Active Badge uses infrared while Active Bat uses both radio frequency (RF) and ultrasound. In contrast, RADAR [10] uses 802.11 RF, and is not as accurate as the systems based on RF and ultrasound. However, RADAR does not require any infrastructure other than 802.11 access points. The Cricket [9] architecture can be taken as an inverse of the Active Badge and Active Bat systems in that ceiling- or wall-mounted active beacons send RF and ultrasound to passive receivers.

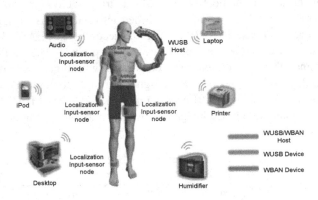

Fig. 4. Wearable computer Workspace configuration

We have built a WUSB over WBAN for the workspace shown in Fig. 4, where each WBAN beacon sends both an ultrasonic pulse and the RF message at the same time. The WBAN device (SLAVE) receiver uses the standard time difference of arrival technique by observing the time lag between the arrival of the RF and ultrasonic signals, and estimates its distance from each WBAN host's beacon. The estimated distances are passed to the context-aware WUSB application server, which computes the location of the WBAN device receiver using the distances.

Our system is different from Cricket [9] in that the receiver is separated from the WBAN host. The receiver can then send context information to an authenticated server looking for a specific service. In the current proof-of-concept implementation, WUSB application service is requested by providing the WUSB/WBAN host with the user's location information. We have developed an ultrasonic WBAN sensor module with a pair of transmitter and receiver. The ultrasonic sensor module is plugged into the main node. The main node consists of the 8-bit AVR MCU, a mobile transceiver of 2.4GHz ISM bandwidth, 128KB memory, etc.

The wireless WBAN sensor nodes are used for both the WBAN beacon node and for the WBAN receiver node. The light-weight WBAN beacon nodes are easy to deploy. They can be placed with few constraints in an body environment. The light-weight WBAN receiver node can be easily attached to a physical object. In the current experiments, the WBAN receiver node communicates with the WBAN application server through serial communication, but can be seamlessly replaced by RF communication.

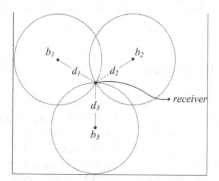

Fig. 5. Trilateration

The context-aware WBAN application server computes the location (x, y, z) of the WBAN receiver using the distances through the trilateration method, as illustrated in Fig. 5. Suppose the location of the i-th WBAN beacon is denoted by b_i, and the estimated distance between the i-th beacon and the WBAN receiver is d_i. Then, we have the following equation for a beacon:

$$(x - b_{ix})^2 + (y - b_{iy})^2 + (z - b_{iz})^2 = d_i^2 \qquad (1)$$

The above equation is solved using Newton-Raphson method. In the current implementation, the initial location (x_0, y_0, z_0) of the WBAN receiver is set to the center of the workspace. Figure 6 describes the modularized frameworks for location-aware application service using WUSB-based WBAN protocol. In addition to the modules for computing and transferring location data (LCM and LTM), the location-aware framework includes Virtual Location Module (VLM), which makes the WUSB application development process independent of the WBAN sensor network. Even with the WBAN sensor network disabled, location-aware application can be tested by running VLM, which takes mouse input in the current implementation. The two frameworks communicate with each other through WBAN.

The location data are passed to Location Receiver Module of the WUSB application Framework, and then to an Input Transformation Module (ITM). ITM is responsible for processing the location data to be suitable for specific applications. Many 3D applications can benefit from such pose-awareness.

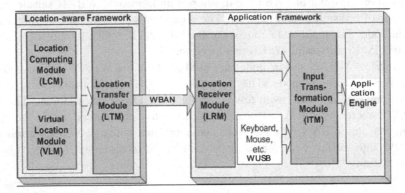

Fig. 6. Location-aware WUSB over WBAN Platform framework

4   Performance Evaluation

The distances between the WBAN beacon nodes and the WBAN receiver node are obtained in an asynchronous mode. The main WBAN node uses a 16-bit timer, and the location of the WBAN receiver is computed at 10Hz. Both of the Location-aware application Frameworks are coded in C++, and run in 1.4GHz core i5 CPU and 2G RAM. The accuracy of the distance estimation has been tested. For a fixed position of the WBAN receiver, the distance from a WBAN beacon is measured by hand. Then, the distance is estimated in the proposed framework. Such estimation is done for 2,000 times. Table 1, Table 2 and Fig. 7 show the statistics for the measured distances of 49.65cm. This distance test proves that the WBAN can be successfully integrated with WUSB applications.

Table 1. Estimated distances at at 49.65 cm

Distance (cm)	Frequency (2000 times in total)
49.569	67
49.604	465
49.638	987
49.709	481

Table 2. Statistical Analysis at 49.65 cm

Statistics	Value
mean	49.644859 cm
variance	0.002045 cm
standard deviation	0.045221 cm

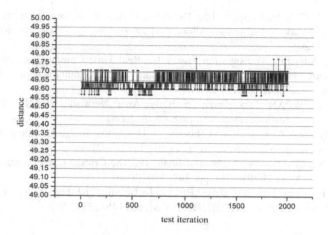

Fig. 7. Test Results at 49.65 cm

5   Conclusion

In this paper, we propose a Real-Time Localization Platform Built on WUSB over IEEE 802.15.6 WBAN protocol required for Wearable Computer systems. The implementation results prove that they can be well integrated, and lead to a new type of natural interface for the Wearable Computer systems. In the current implementation, the location data are computed at 10Hz. For fully supporting real-time applications, more effort should be made to increase the performances. Further, many applications may benefit not only from location-awareness but also from orientation-awareness. To fulfill such needs, the overall performances should be continuously upgraded.

Acknowledgments. This work was supported in part by Basic Science Research Program through the National Research Foundation of Korea (NRF) funded by the Ministry of Education, Science and Technology (MEST) (2010-0002366) and in part by Mid-career Researcher Program through NRF grant funded by the MEST (2011-0016145).

References

1. Rosenberg, R., Slater, M.: The Chording Glove: A Glove-Based Text Input Device. IEEE Transaction on Systems, Man, and Cybernetics-Part C: Applications and Review 29(2), 326–334 (2009)
2. USB 2.0, USB-IF, http://www.usb.org/home/
3. WiMedia Alliance, http://www.wimedia.org/
4. Certified Wireless, U.S.B.1.1, USB-IF (2010),
   http://www.usb.org/developers/wusb/

5. WiMedia MAC Release Spec. 1.5, Distributed Medium Access Control (MAC) for Wireless Networks, WiMedia Alliance (2009), http://www.wimedia.org/en/index/asp
6. Kim, K.-I.: Adjusting Transmission Power for Real-Time Communications in Wireless Sensor Networks. Journal of Information and Communication Convergence Engineering 10(1), 21–26 (2012)
7. IEEE 802.15 WPAN Task Group 6 Body Area Networks (BAN), IEEE (2010), http://www.ieee802.org/15/pub/TG6.html
8. Want, R., Hopper, A., Falcao, V., Gibbons, J.: The Active Badge Location System. ACM Transactions on Information Systems 10(1), 91–102 (1992)
9. Priyantha, N., Chakraborty, A., Balakrishnan, H.: The Cricket Location-Support System. In: Proc. of 6th ACM MOBICOM, pp. 342–350 (2000)
10. Bahl, P., Padmanabhan, V.: RADAR: An In-Building RF-based User Location and Tracking System. In: Proc. of IEEE INFOCOM, pp. 145–153 (2000)

A Study on Improved Similarity Measure Algorithm
for Text-Based Document

Ki-Young Lee[1], Il-Hee Seo[1], Jeong-Joon Kim[2,*], Eun-Young Kang[3],
and Jong-Jin Park[4]

[1] Department of Medical IT and Marketing, Eulji University, Seongnam, Korea
kylee@eulji.ac.kr, ilhee91@gmail.com
[2] Department of Computer Science and Information Engineering,
KonKuk University, Seoul, Korea
jjkim9@db.konkuk.ac.kr
[3] Department of Electronic Communication, Dongyang Mirae University, Seoul, Korea
eykang@dongyang.ac.kr
[4] Department of Internet, Chungwoon University, Hongseong, Chungnam, Korea
jjpark@chungwoon.ac.kr

Abstract. A study on the similarity measurement of document has been active.
We can move the position of word within the sentence. But from these steps,
the probability of the meaning change is extremely rare. Existing research
methods are not enough studies of these parts and the overall accuracy goes
down. Therefore, in this paper, we proposed the algorithm that is improved the
accuracy of the similarity measurement algorithm through moving to the words
in the sentence.

Keywords: Document Similarity, Plagiarism, Forgery.

1 Introduction

Plagiarism has sharply risen through indiscreet information leak from internet.
Plagiarism has emerged as a social issue through plagiarism case of many celebrities.
So, there has been a growing interest in document similarity identity, plagiarism
detection system and a variety of algorithm studies are underway.

Primarily Smith-Waterman[1], Levenshtein[2] algorithm is used in text-based
document similarity method. Sentence is the minimum unit of communication
connected to idea, feeling. First, input sentence vocabulary represents an integer for
implement. For example, "The Woman, the Woman recognized as a beauty to
People" is shown as <1 2 1 2 3 4 5 6 7 8>. Table 1 show that each token mapped to
vocabulary.

As you can see corresponding Table 1, Once the initial lexical analysis phase has
been carried out on all submissions in a corpus, the comparison phase involves only
the result symbol sequences or strings. Hence any of a wide variety of methods that

---

* Corresponding author.

T.-h. Kim, Y.-h. Lee, and W.-c. Fang (Eds.): FGIT 2012, LNCS 7709, pp. 181–187, 2012.
© Springer-Verlag Berlin Heidelberg 2012

can be used to detect similarities in two strings might potentially be used as an aid to collusion detection. Currently not enough studies about moving word in sentence, if you configure a new sentence to plagiarize some of the works created by other people's invention, accuracy of Smith-Waterman, Levenshtein algorithm will go down. Therefore, in this paper, we are improved the accuracy of document similarity measurement through Proposed algorithm about identifying a similar part and moving words in sentence.

Table 1. A mapping of lexemes to tokens

Lexeme	Token
The	1
Woman	2
Recognized	3
As	4
A	5
Beauty	6
To	7
People	8

2   Related Research

2.1   Smith-Waterman Algorithm

In 1981, It was designed for determine between similar protein sequences in the field of molecular biology for the first time. Currently, it was usually used as similarity measurement algorithm in text-based document. The similarity of two sequences is calculated from scoring matrix. The start of the first matrix scoring was filled with 0, matching part to match, not matching part to miss-match, gap part to gap penalty. After the matrix was filled with score, the largest value in the matrix find a similar part from back-track. The following Figure 1 shows an example of the Smith-Waterman algorithm[1].

-	-	G	A	T	T	A	C	G	A
-	0	0	0	0	0	0	0	0	0
G	0	2	1	0	0	0	0	2	1
A	0	1	4	3	2	2	1	1	4
C	0	0	3	2	1	1	4	3	3
G	0	2	2	1	0	0	3	6	5
A	0	1	4	3	2	2	2	5	8
T	0	0	3	6	5	4	3	4	7
T	0	0	2	5	8	7	6	5	6
A	0	0	2	4	7	10	9	8	7
T	0	0	1	4	6	9	8	7	6
T	0	0	0	3	6	8	7	6	5

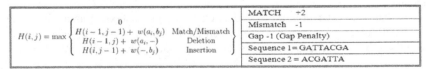

Fig. 1. The example of Smith-Waterman Algorithm

The value of the first string G,A is the value -1 of position S_{i-1j-1}, but max value is 0, so S_{ij} value is filled with 0 and then scoring matrix is filled with value based on above formula.

If you use the S-W algorithm, you can find evolution of the sequence, mutation and find the most On the other side, if the length of sequence is M,N, time complexity is O(MN). That is to say the length of the sentence is the longer, time is the more slowly down. And also, if the sentence is changed portion, you can't find the similar, overlap portion.

2.2   Levenshtein Algorithm

In 1965, it was designed for edit distance about one string and it was the same as the other strings through several operations. Operation includes the insertion, deletion, substitution. Similarity measurement method used scoring matrix which was the same method with Smith-Waterman.

The following Figure 2 shows an example of the Levenshtein algorithm[2]. The sample consists of the same example used in the example of the Smith-Waterman.

	-	G	A	T	T	A	C	G	A
-	0	1	2	3	4	5	6	7	8
G	1	0	1	2	3	4	5	6	7
A	2	1	0	1	2	3	4	5	6
C	3	2	1	1	2	3	3	4	5
G	4	3	2	2	2	3	4	3	4
A	5	4	3	3	3	2	3	4	3
T	6	5	4	3	3	3	3	4	4
T	7	6	5	4	3	4	4	4	5
A	8	7	6	5	4	3	4	5	4
T	9	8	7	6	5	4	4	5	5
T	10	9	8	7	6	5	5	5	6

Fig. 2. The example of Levenshtein Algorithm

In case of Insertion, deletion, substitution, the matrix is filled with value that is the smallest value +1 in S_{i-1j-1}, S_{i-1j}, S_{ij-1}. In the above example, an edit-distance between two sentences is confirmed to 6 through the last value in matrix. The last value is larger, the edit-distance become more distance.

As you can see the above example, if the location does not same, it does not recognize the similar portion even though there is a somewhat similar portion. Also, the length of the sentence is the longer, time complexity is the more slowly down equally as s-w algorithm.

2.3   Smith-Waterman Overlap Candidates

It was designed for complement to S-W algorithm's disadvantage which did not find several similar portions in sentence. It had candidates that can have a set of similar portions as well as the most similar portion[3]. It was possible to find several similar parts in the sentence using the candidate set. An example is shown in Figure 3.

	-	G	A	T	T	A	C	G	A
-									
G	1							1	
A			2	1		1			2
C			1	1			2	1	
G	1						1	3	2
A			2	1				2	4
T			1	3	2	1			3
T				2	4	3	2	1	2
A			1	1	3	5	4	3	1
T				2	2	4	3	3	2
T				1	3	3	3	2	2

Fig. 3. Smith-Waterman Overlap Candidates Explanation

If the value of X(i) is equal to Y(j), value is increased to value +1 of S_{i-1j-1}. And if the value does not match, the matrix filled with the maximum value -1 in S_{i-1j}, S_{i-1j-1}, S_{ij-1} position. Smith-Waterman algorithm found the most similar portion, but it can find all portions more than the threshold. Assuming that threshold value is 4, the most value 5 of ACGA has been the best similar part and value 4 of ACGA is classified as candidate set.

It can find many similar portions in sentence, but it had the disadvantage that surrounding portion can be judged. It seemed to like a similar portion even though it did not similar portion.

In addition, if the threshold is greater, it may not find the similar portion. Therefore, in this paper, we try to improved accuracy of identifying document similarity which includes changing the word location within the sentence.

3   Proposed Algorithm

3.1   An Outline of the Algorithm

S-W algorithm[1] can find many similar parts through overlap candidate, but it may include unnecessary part because it is calculated front part of the S_{ij}. In addition, it is possible to remove the similar portion if the value of the below threshold is judged dissimilar portion. And in case of Levenshtein algorithm[2], it is judged the similar portion which is the only same location between two sequences.

Therefore, we try to increase the accuracy of similarity recognition by using the substitution between the words in sentence after we can find candidate set through S-W algorithm. In Levenshtein, substitution means change the other character. But we used the substitution which is change the word location in sentence.

3.2 Simplified Levenshtein Algorithm

If there is a similar portion at the same location between two sequences, Levenshtein algorithm constants certain value. We used to this advantage through transformation to identify similar parts. We only use the match operator to find a similar part, recognized as wrong part should be initialized to 0. The following formula1 expressed simplified Levenshtein algorithm.

$$S_{ij} = \begin{cases} S_{i-1,j-1}+1 & if\, X(i) = Y(j) \\ O & else \end{cases} \tag{1}$$

If match the position between X(i) and Y(j), we should continue the similar part by the value +1 of S_{i-1j-1}'s location or else the rest of part is initialized to 0. As a result, it is easy to find all similar part within sentence. Also, because it does not apply to threshold we can find all parts that are recognized as similar part.

3.3 Move the Similar Portion

It is based on the long sentence of the two sequences, the words of short sequence is moved. The location of the words in sentence is moved from high score to low score. At this time, if the sentence has a duplicate part, we should identify the value of similarity recognition by moving the parts that are not duplicated. Change of the location is in process until value of the scoring matrix does not change. These steps are represented to Pseudo code. Pseudo code to move the similar portion is as follows.

```
INPUT DATA -> string_x, string_y

function calcScore(string_x, string_y) {
        if string_x == string_y then
                score_table[x][y] += current_score + 1
        else
                score_table[x][y] = 0
        end if

        scoreA[x][y] = max(score_table, 1)
        scoreB[x][y] = max(score_table, 2)

        while(!eof)
                if !isSameChar(scoreA[x][y], scoreB[x][y]) then
                        buf[i] += scoreB[x][y]
                        pasteTo(buf[i], string_x, score[x][y])
                end if
        end while

        calcScore(string_x, string_y)
}
```

An example of applying the above algorithm is shown in Figure 4

Left matrix:

	-	G	A	T	T	A	C	G	A
-									
G	1							1	
A		2			1				2
C					2				
G		1						3	
A		2							4
T			3						
T				4					
A		1				5			
T			2						
T				3					

Right matrix:

	-	C	G	A	T	T	A	G	A
-									
G			1					1	
A				2					2
C		1							
G			2					1	
A				3					2
T					4				
T						5			
A				1			6		
T					2				
T						3			

Fig. 4. The Example of Proposed Algorithm

As you see on the left side of Figure 5, the most value of GATTA is designated as the most similar portion. The location of the words in sentence is moved from high score to low score. Value 5 of GATTA is the largest similar value. GATTA is confirmed to ACGA of the second-largest value 4. C does not overlap between GATTA and ACGA. It is added at the front of GATTA after severance from ACGA. After that, Repeat the process until value of the scoring matrix does not change. So, it connects to the words based on the matching portion. As the result, it recognized all similar portions and it can be able to improve the accuracy of the similar portion through moving the word.

4   Performance Evaluation

Simulation data set is implemented for measurement of document similarity. Data set consists of 1,000,000 Document. About 20 percent of the entire data set, it consists to the similar document which is changed the contents through action such as copy, paste, cut. After that, we are compared speed and accuracy of the S-W using overlap candidates, Levenshtein and proposed algorithm. The result of compared speed and accuracy of the document similarity is shown in Figure 5.

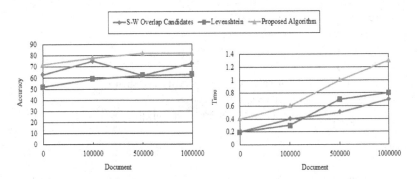

Fig. 5. The results of the comparison algorithms

On average, the amount of token in document consists of 700 to 1000. As you can see the experimental results in Figure 6, the amount of document even more increased, the accuracy of proposed algorithm is greatly improved. The accuracy of the proposed algorithm is about 70%, performance is better than 120 percent of other algorithms.

But the amount document increased, the speed of proposed algorithm is slow down due to increased portion that is related to transformation of document. Proposed algorithm is moved words after recognition about similar portion while the S-W and Levenshtein algorithm search the entire matrix for similar portion. So, Speed of Proposed algorithm not highly lags behind.

5   Conclusions

The similar portion is exactly recognized through a combination of advantages that is identified the similar portion in S-W and is the substitution in Levenshtein. After that, we are able to increase the accuracy of the document similarity through moving the similar portion. However, it is limited method only for moving words. In the future, it is needed on document similarity through inference techniques. In addition, it is expect to need on the fast algorithm in a mass of documents due to disadvantage that is sharply diminished in speed when the amount of documents is increased.

References

1. Smith, T.F., Waterman, M.S.: Identification of Common Molecular Subsequences. J. Mol. Biol. 147, 195–197 (1981)
2. Levenshtein, V.I.: Binary codes capable of correcting deletions, insertions, and reversals. Soviet Physics Doklady 10, 707–710 (1966)
3. Irving, R.W.: Plagiarism and Collusion Detection using the Smith-Waterman Algorithm. University of Glasgow (2004)
4. Su, Z., Ahn, B.-R., Eom, K.-Y., Kang, M.-K., Kim, J.-P., Kim, M.-K.: Plagiarism Detection Using the Levenshtein Distance and Smith-Waterman Algorithm. Innovative Computing Information and Control (2008)

Design of Order System Using NFC Based Smart Phone

Myung-Jae Lim[1], Hyun-Jun Seo[1], Eun-Ser Lee[2], and Ki-Young Lee[1,*]

[1] Department of Medical IT and Marketing, Eulji University,
553, Sanseong-daero, Sujeong-gu, Seongnam-si, Gyeonggi-do, 461-713, Korea
[2] Department of Computer Engineering, Andong National University
Seongcheon-dongn 1375 Gyeongdong-ro, Andong-si Gyeongsangbuk-do, 760-749, Korea
{lk04,kylee}@eulji.ac.kr, final0807@naver.com,
eslee@andong.ac.kr

Abstract. Recently, mobile communication service is rapidly spreading, the number of smart phone users is sky-rocketing. As mobile market is growing, people are getting more interested in order and payment system of products using smart phones. Therefore, this paper suggests an order system which is combined with smart phone using NFC among local wireless communication. This paper applied a reader reacting to create RF field from generator among NFC communication modes for security purpose during payment process and also applied manual communication mode which enables communication between reader and tags reacting to commands generated from generator. Through this system, smart phone based order system that provides rapid and correct ordering and convenience for users is expected to be available.

Keywords: NFC, RFID, Order system, Smart Phone.

1   Introduction

Nowadays, as the number of smart phone users is rapidly increasing due to an era of smart phone, market of smart phone is rapidly growing. Smart phone market, which had approximately 7 million people in 2010, reached at as many as 15 million people for 2011 and 25 million people for 2012. In 2013, as many as 30 million people are expected to use smart phones which is approximately 80% of total mobile phone users. Its growing pace is expected to persistent for few years and mobile market is also expected to grow continuously.

As mobile market is rapidly growing, people are getting more interested in ordering and payment system using NFC. Not only overseas manufacturers for smart phone but also domestic manufactures mostly apply NFC technology for their smart phones. NFC smart phone is expected to be produced by 30 million sets in 2012, 35 million sets in 2013, 35 million sets in 2014 and 45 million sets in 4500.

Therefore, this paper is intended to design order system to improve service in a specific facilities using continuous growing smart phone and a local wireless communication technology, NFC.

---

* Corresponding author.

T.-h. Kim, Y.-h. Lee, and W.-c. Fang (Eds.): FGIT 2012, LNCS 7709, pp. 188–193, 2012.

This paper consists of related researches in Chapter 2, NFC-based order system in Chapter 3, implementation cases in Chapter 4 and conclusion in Chapter 5.

2   Related Works

NFC, as one of RFIDs is a local wireless communication technology using a bandwidth of 13.56Mhz. This, unlike RFID, makes it possible to not only read but also write data. NFC, which transfers data within 10 cm or so, is able to provide data connected with smart phone and also provides compatibilities with conventional RFID. NFC is widely used for securities purposes such as payment, travel information, traffic and controlling access.

2.1   NFC TAG

NFC TAG consists of IC chip for data input and antenna and attachable to objects. Data stored in TAG uses wireless frequency and it is transferred to terminal with built-in NFC function. TAG consists of a total 4 types and they are classified by speed and use. Table 1 shows characteristics for each NFC TAG and the 2nd type, NFC TAG is most widely used.

Table 1. Type of NFC tag

Division	1	2	3	4
RF Interface	14443A	14443A	18092	14443
Speed(Kbps)	106	106	212	424
Memory	1KB	2KB	1MB	64KB
Protocol	Self-instruction	Self-instruction	FeliCa	ISO 1443-4, 7816-4
Applications	single low-dose	single low-dose	Multi-high-capacity	Multi-high-capacity

2.2   NFC Function

NFC supports 3 functions including card emulation, Reader/Writer and P2P. Card emulation mode is always recognized regardless of power of terminal while it has power saving effects. Reader/Writer works by recognizing TAG in NFC-supported mode while it needs power to recognize TAG and makes it possible to acquire information directly and connect to linked site. P2P mode processes data communication for all devices supporting NFC by one contact and this mode can be simply connected and used as it needs to be contacted by users unlike other wireless communication.

2.3   Wireless Communication

NFC is a wireless communication technology which makes it possible to exchange data in local area within 10 cm and it is a supplemented technology from a reading function which was supported by conventional RFID.

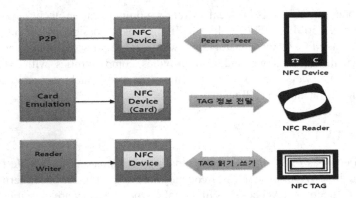

Fig. 1. NFC operational mode

This technology is very distinctive in a way that not only reading but also writing is available. Moreover, NFC provides higher security than RFID. Although NFC is low in data transferring speed compared to other communication technologies such as Zigbee, IrDa and Bluetooth, its malfunctioning is rare with short set time. Table 2 shows a comparison between NFC and other local area wireless communication.

Table 2. Wireless communication

Division	NFC	Zigbee	IrDa	Bluetooth
Range	10cm	20cm	5m	30m
Price	Low	Usually	Usually	Usually
Speed(bps)	848K	250K	4M	24M
RFID	O	X	X	X
Setup time	0.1S	-	0.5S	6S

3   NFC Based Order System Design

3.1   System Configuration

Figure. 2 shows a system configuration for NFC. Internal structure for NFC based smart phone consists of antenna for RF transmission and NFC chip to process transferred data and SE (Secure Element). NFC chip, antenna to transfer or receive RF of 13.56Mhz and security component to manage payment and user information are core technologies for NFC technology. This system uses reader which enables a generator to create RF field and react to command of generator and also uses passive communication mode making it possible to communicate with tags. Fig . 3 shows a passive communication mode and it reacts by same transferring speed as target once initiator starts to communicate by a designated transferring speed. Initiator provides carrier field and target is operated by modulating provided one. Operating power for target works as a transceiver acquired by electromagnetic filed Self power is not supported.

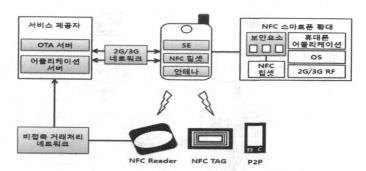

Fig. 2. NFC system configuration

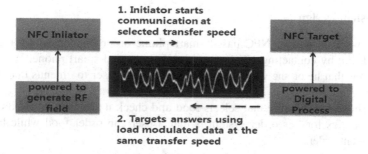

Fig. 3. Passive communication mode

As a case study for NFC based order system, this paper attempted to simulate Professional base ball stadium that many people look for. Recently, users are benefited by more convenient services due to market growth for smart phone and advancement of NFC local area wireless communication. Baseball, which is called a national sport, exceeded 6 million audience in 2012 as the number of audience has been increasing every year. To cope with this sky-rocketing number of audience, this paper applied a order system using NFC in mobile phone which most of people own. This paper designed feasibility for this order system targeting audience seats and convenience facilities. This paper designated audience's seats which can be primarily recognized such as designated seats and family seats. Procedures for order consist of selecting providers that users want, receiving order, inquiring order and confirmation of order to varify finished order. Based on this, this paper is intended to provide order system. Figure 4 shows a system configuration for NFC based order system for public sport facilities. User accesses the order system by contacting NFC TAG attached to a seat where a user sits on via smart phone. When user connects a corresponding linked web page by contacting NFC TAG through smart phone, the system is connected to ordering page for corresponding shop located in facilities with seat information. User orders his or her food. When a user completed his or her order, the corresponding order is received by a corresponding shop.

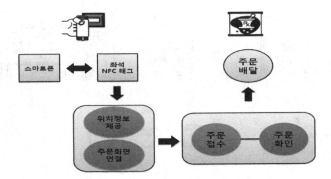

Fig. 4. NFC system configuration

3.2   System Design

Fig. 5 shows a design for NFC based smart phone order system, which indicates a connected link by contacting NFC tag with NFC-enabled smart phone. When a user clicks menus that he or she wants, this system connects user to   menus that he or she can select.

Fig. 6 shows a procedure that selects food and check it and then adjust its amount. A characteristics for this order system is that a user can order food while he or she checks current orders.

Fig. 5. Design for order system

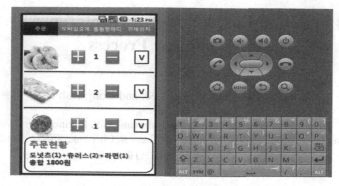

Fig. 6. Screen for order

4 Conclusion

This paper suggested an order system using NFC based smart phone for public sport facilities. NFC-based smart phone order system, which improved complicated interface for conventional order system, is expected to be positioned as a service to increase sales for shops in facilities based on service for audience and help to maintaining and managing facilities.

In following up research, an order system which is available anywhere NFC TAG exists regardless of location using NFC based smart phone will be suggested.

References

1. Yi, O.: Study on NFC Security Analysis and UICC Alternative Effect. Korean Institute of Communication Sciences 36(1), 29–36 (2011)
2. Chavira, G., Nava, S.W., Hervas, R., Villarreal, V., Bravo, J., Barrientos, J.C., Azuara, M.: Touching Services: The Tag-NFC Structure. AISC, vol. 51, pp. 117–124. Springer, Berlin (2009)
3. Lahtela, A., Hassinen, M., Jylha, V.: RFID and NFC in healthcare: Safety of hospitals medication care (2008)
4. Pasquet, M., Reynaud, J., Rosenberger, C.: Secure Payment with NFC Mobile Phone in the SmartTouch Project. In: IEEE, The 2008 International Symposium on Collaborative Technologies and System (2008)
5. GSMA, mobile NFC ServiceV1.0 (2007)
6. NFC Forum. NFC Specification 1.1, http://www.nfc-forum.org
7. e-Business AJ –NFC, http://e-businessaj.wikispaces.com/NFC
8. ISO/IEC, http://iso.org
9. RFID Introduction, http://www.rfemfo.co.kr/RF_Introduce
10. GoogleWallet, http://www.google.com/wallet/

Hard Partition-Based Non-Fuzzy Inference System for Nonlinear Process

Keon-Jun Park, Jun-Myung Lee, and Yong-Kab Kim

Department of Information and Communication Engineering,
Wonkwang University, 344-2, Shinyong-dong, Iksan-si, Chonbuk, 570-749 South Korea
{bird75,junmyung87,ykim}@wonkwang.ac.kr

Abstract. We introduec a non-fuzzy inference system based on hard partition to contruct model for nonlinear process. In fuzzy modeling, the generation of fuzzy rules has the problem that the number of fuzzy rules exponentially increases. To solve this problem, the rules of non-fuzzy inference systems are generated by partitioning the input space in the scatter form using HCM clustering algorithm. The premise parameters of the rules are determined by membership matrix by means of HCM clustering algorithm. The consequence part of the rules is represented in the form of polynomial functions. The proposed model is evaluated with the performance using the data widely used in nonlinear process.

Keywords: Hard Partition of Input Space, Non-Fuzzy Inference Systems, Hard C-Means Clustering Algorithm, Rule Generation, Nonlinear Characteristics.

1 Introduction

Fuzzy modeling has been studied to deal with complex, ill-defined, and uncertain systems in many other avenues and there has been a diversity of approaches to fuzzy modeling [1]. Linguistic modeling [2] and fuzzy relation equation-based approach [3] were proposed as primordial identification methods for fuzzy models. The general class of Sugeno-Takagi models [4] gave rise to more sophisticated rule-based systems. The generation of the fuzzy rules and the adjustment of their membership functions were conducted by trial and error and/or on the basis of the operator's experience. The designers find it difficult to develop adequate fuzzy rules and membership functions to reflect the essence of the data. Some enhancements to the model have been proposed by many researchers, yet the problem of finding "good" parameters of the fuzzy sets and of partitioning spaces in the rules remains open.

In this paper, we introduce a non-fuzzy inference system (NFIS) based on hard partition of input space. Hard partition realized with HCM clustering [5] help determine the rules of non-fuzzy model. The premise part of the rules is realized with the aid of the scatter partition of input space generated by HCM clustering algorithms. The number of the partition of input space equals the number of clusters and the individual partitioned spaces describe the rules. The consequence part of the rules is

T.-h. Kim, Y.-h. Lee, and W.-c. Fang (Eds.): FGIT 2012, LNCS 7709, pp. 194–201, 2012.
© Springer-Verlag Berlin Heidelberg 2012

represented by polynomial functions. The proposed model is evaluated with numerical experimentation for nonlinear process.

The paper is organized as follows. Section 2 is concerned with the design of Non-Fuzzy Inference System. Section 3 presents results of numeric experimentation. Finally Section 4 concludes the paper.

2   Non-Fuzzy Inference System

The identification procedure for this model is split into the identification activities dealing with the premise and consequence parts of the rules.

2.1   Premise Identification

The premise part of the NFIS is developed by means of the Hard C-Means clustering algorithm [5]. This algorithm divides the input space by the clusters and each partitioned local space represents the rules. Therefore, the number of clusters is the number of rules. This algorithm is aimed at the formation of 'c' clusters (relations) in $\mathbf{R}^n$. We obtain the matrix representation for hard c-partition, defined as follows.

$$M_C = \left\{ \mathbf{U} \mid u_{ik} \in \{0,1\}, \ \sum_{i=1}^{c} u_{ik} = 1, \ 0 < \sum_{k=1}^{n} u_{ik} < n \right\}. \tag{1}$$

[Step 1] Fix the number of clusters $c(2 \leq c < n)$ and initialize the partition matrix $\mathbf{U}^{(0)} \in M_C$

[Step 2] Calculate the center vectors $\mathbf{v}_i$ of each cluster:

$$\mathbf{v}_i^{(r)} = \{v_{i1}, v_{i2}, \cdots, v_{ij}, \cdots, v_{im}\}. \tag{2}$$

$$v_{ij}^{(r)} = \sum_{k=1}^{n} u_{ik}^{(r)} \cdot x_{kj} \bigg/ \sum_{k=1}^{n} u_{ik}^{(r)}. \tag{3}$$

Where, $[u_{ik}] = \mathbf{U}^{(r)}$, $i = 1, 2, \ldots, c, j = 1, 2, \ldots, m$.

[Step 3] Update the partition matrix $\mathbf{U}^{(r)}$; these modifications are based on the standard Euclidean distance function between the data points and the prototypes,

$$d_{ik} = d(\mathbf{x}_k - \mathbf{v}_i) = \|\mathbf{x}_k - \mathbf{v}_i\| = \left[\sum_{j=1}^{m} (x_{kj} - v_{ij})^2 \right]^{1/2}. \tag{4}$$

$$u_{ik}^{(r+1)} = \begin{cases} 1 & d_{ik}^{(r)} = \min\{d_{jk}^{(r)}\} \ for \ all \ j \in c \\ 0 & otherwise \end{cases}. \tag{5}$$

[Step 4] Check a termination criterion. If

$$\left\| U^{(r+1)} - U^{(r)} \right\| \le \varepsilon \text{ (tolerance level)} \tag{6}$$

Stop ; otherwise set $r = r+1$ and return to **[Step 2]**

Figure 1 visualizes the example of the hard partitioned spaces of input space with four clusters by means of HCM clustering algorithm. The resulting partitioned local spaces represent the rules of system.

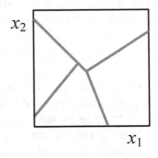

Fig. 1. Hard partition of input space based on HCM clustering algorithm

2.2   Consequence Identification

The identification of the conclusion parts of the rules deals with a selection of their structure that is followed by the determination of the respective parameters of the local functions occurring there.

The conclusion is expressed as follows.

$$R^j : If \ x_1 \ and \ \cdots \ and \ x_d \ is \ H_j \quad Then \ y_j = f(x_1,...,x_d) \cdot \tag{7}$$

Type 1 (Simplified Inference):

$$f = a_{j0} \tag{8}$$

Type 2 (Linear Inference):

$$f = a_{j0} + \sum_{k=1}^{d} a_{jk} x_k \tag{9}$$

Type 3 (Quadratic Inference):

$$f = a_{j0} + \sum_{k=1}^{d} a_{jk} x_k + \sum_{k=1}^{d} a_{j,(d+k)} x_k + \sum_{k=1}^{d} \sum_{l=k+1}^{d} a_{jz} x_k x_l \tag{10}$$

Type 4 (Modified Quadratic Inference):

$$f = a_{j0} + \sum_{k=1}^{d} a_{jk} x_k + \sum_{k=1}^{d} \sum_{l=k+1}^{d} a_{jz} x_k x_l \tag{11}$$

Where R^j is the j-th rule, x_k represents the input variables, H_j is a membership grade obtained using HCM clustering algorithm, a's are coefficient of polynomial function, z is the number of combinations of input variables.

The calculations of the numeric output of the model, based on the activation (matching) levels of the rules there, are carried out in the well-known format

$$y^* = \frac{\sum_{j=1}^{n} w_{jp} y_j}{\sum_{j=1}^{n} w_{jp}} = \sum_{j=1}^{n} \hat{w}_{jp} y_j . \tag{12}$$

Here, as the normalized value of w_{jp}, we use an abbreviated notation to describe an activation level $\hat{w}_{jp}$, which values is determined by the partition matrix $\mathbf{U}$;

$$w_{jp} = u_{ip} . \tag{13}$$

Therefore, the inferred output value y^* can be expressed as

$$y^* = \sum_{j=1}^{n} w_{jp} y_j \tag{14}$$

If the input variables of the premise and parameters are given in consequence parameter identification, the optimal consequence parameters that minimize the assumed performance index can be determined. In what follows, we define the performance index as the mean squared error.

$$PI = \frac{1}{m} \sum_{p=1}^{m} \left(y_p - y_p^* \right)^2 \tag{14}$$

The minimal value produced by the least-squares method is governed by the following expression:

$$\hat{\mathbf{a}} = \left(\mathbf{X}^T \mathbf{X} \right)^{-1} \mathbf{X}^T \mathbf{Y} \tag{15}$$

3   Experimental Studies

We discuss numerical example in order to evaluate the advantages and the effectiveness of the proposed approach. This time series data (296 input-output pairs) coming from the gas furnace nonlinear process has been intensively studied in the previous literature [6]. The delayed terms of methane gas flow rate $u(t)$ and carbon dioxide density $y(t)$ are used as input variables organized in a vector format as $[u(t-3), u(t-2), u(t-1), y(t-3), y(t-2), y(t-1)]$. $y(t)$ is the output variable. The first part of the data set (consisting of 148 pairs) was used for training purposes. The remaining part of the series serves as a testing data set. We consider the MSE as a performance index.

We construct the model for a two-dimensional system by configuring 2-input 1-output system using $u(t-3)$ and $y(t-1)$ as inputs. Figure 2 shows the distribution of $u(t-3)$ and $y(t-1)$ data.

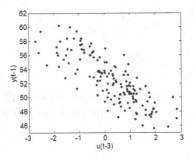

Fig. 2. The distribution of $u(t-3)$ and $y(t-1)$ data

Figure 3 shows hard-partitioned input spaces generated by increasing the number of clusters from 2 to 10 using HCM clustering algorithm in two-dimensional input space. The boundaries of each local space indicate the binary boundary by the membership matrix with a value of 0 or 1. An increase of the number of clusters can be seen that the input space is finely divided in the dense part of the data.

Table 1 summarizes the performance index for training and testing data by setting the number of clusters and inference type. Here, PI and E_PI stand for the performance index for the training data set and the testing data set, respectively. From the table 1, linear inference, quadratic inference and modified quadratic inference shows better performance than Simplified inference. In general, NFIS shows a better performance, if it has more rules. We selected the best model with 8 rules (clusters) with quadratic inference that exhibits PI = 0.013 and E_PI = 0.300.

Figure 4 shows the space plane of the input and output for selected models according to both the partitioning of the input space and the reasoning methods. In case of the simplified inference, each partitioned local space shows the characteristic plane of the constant term due to the simplified inference. In case of the other inferences, each partitioned local space represents the characteristic plane of linear, quadratic and modified quadratic polynomial. In addition, local spaces show independent input and output characteristics not to overlap with each other.

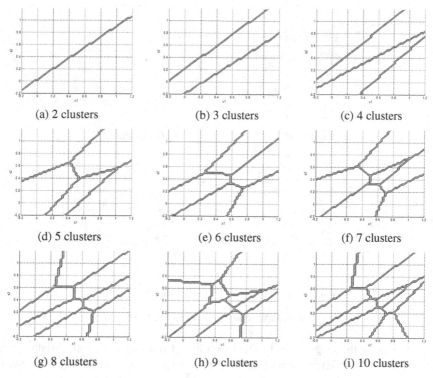

(a) 2 clusters   (b) 3 clusters   (c) 4 clusters

(d) 5 clusters   (e) 6 clusters   (f) 7 clusters

(g) 8 clusters   (h) 9 clusters   (i) 10 clusters

Fig. 3. Input spaces partitioned by means of HCM clustering algorithm

Table 1. Performance evaluation for two input system

No. of Clusters	Type	PI	E_PI	No. of Clusters	Type	PI	E_PI
2	Type 1	3.459	4.104	6	Type 3	0.015	0.352
	Type 2	0.022	0.335		Type 4	0.016	0.344
	Type 3	0.022	0.337	7	Type 1	0.825	1.957
	Type 4	0.022	0.347		Type 2	0.016	0.327
3	Type 1	1.671	2.161		Type 3	0.014	0.309
	Type 2	0.021	0.346		Type 4	0.015	0.325
	Type 3	0.020	0.339	8	Type 1	0.713	1.460
	Type 4	0.021	0.354		Type 2	0.018	0.302
4	Type 1	1.054	1.706		Type 3	0.013	0.300
	Type 2	0.020	0.347		Type 4	0.015	0.302
	Type 3	0.018	0.337	9	Type 1	0.803	1.673
	Type 4	0.019	0.350		Type 2	0.017	0.330
5	Type 1	1.026	1.747		Type 3	0.013	0.374
	Type 2	0.018	0.347		Type 4	0.016	0.329
	Type 3	0.016	0.324	10	Type 1	0.623	1.379
	Type 4	0.017	0.346		Type 2	0.016	0.300
6	Type 1	0.898	1.857		Type 3	0.010	0.338
	Type 2	0.019	0.341		Type 4	0.014	0.311

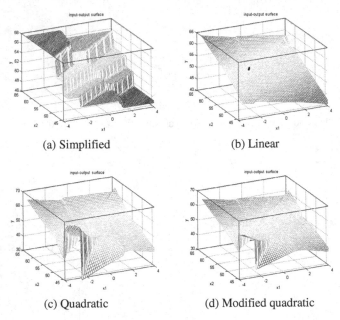

(a) Simplified   (b) Linear

(c) Quadratic   (d) Modified quadratic

Fig. 4. Input-output spaces (8 clusters)

Fig. 5 depicts the original and model outputs of training and testing data for the selected model. This figure shows that the model output is approximately the same for original output.

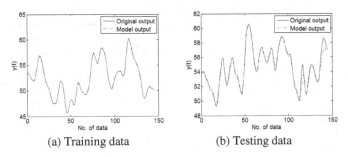

(a) Training data   (b) Testing data

Fig. 5. Model output (8 clusters, Quadratic)

4   Conclusions

In this paper, we have developed a non-fuzzy inference system based on hard-partition of input space. The input spaces of the proposed model were divided as the scatter form using HCM clustering algorithm to generate the rules of the system for nonlinear process. By this method, we could alleviate the problem of the curse of dimensionality and design the NFIS that are compact and simple.

From the results in the previous section, we were able to design preferred model. Through the use of a performance index, we were able to achieve a balance between the approximation and generalization abilities of the resulting model. Finally, this approach would find potential application in many fields.

References

1. Jang, J.S.R., Mizutani, E., Sun, C.T.: Neuro-Fuzzy and Soft Computing. In: A Computational Approach to Learning and Machine Intelligence. Prentice Hall, NJ (1997)
2. Pedrycz, W.: Numerical and application aspects of fuzzy relational equations. Fuzzy Sets Syst. 11, 1–18 (1983)
3. Tong, R.M.: Synthesis of fuzzy models for industrial processes. Int. J. Gen. Syst. 4, 143–162 (1978)
4. Takagi, T., Sugeno, M.: Fuzzy identification of systems and its applications to modeling and control. IEEE Trans. Syst., Cybern. SMC 15(1), 116–132 (1985)
5. Krishnaiah, P.R., Kanal, L.N. (eds.): Classification, pattern recognition, and reduction of dimensionality. Handbook of Statistics, vol. 2. North-Holland, Amsterdam (1982)
6. Box, G.E.P., Jenkins, G.M.: Time Series Analysis: Forecasting and Control, 2nd edn. Holden-Day, San Francisco (1976)

A Study on Location DB Matching of IPS in Specific Area Using LED Lights and Image Sensor

Jaesang Cha and Seungho Lee[*]

Dept. of Electronic & IT Media Eng., Seoul National Univ. of Science and Tech., Seoul, Korea
checkmemo@gmail.com

Abstract. In this paper, we researched DB(Data Base) matching algorithm for distinction of specific area of indoor based on image sensor using the LED. Existing positioning technology are positioning based on communication and visible light communication. Among them, visible light communication due to sending carrier wave in positioning inforrmation, occurs to computational increase by complexity of location-aware process. In addition, visible light communication occurs constraints of light source interference. Therefore, in this paper, Studied the location-aware algorithm to matched specific area through compare coordination value to specific area collected in advance server DB after location value obtained through image sensor using LED. It was simulated using four LED. And then, it was proved usefulness to perception in position local through experiments.

Keywords: LED, Image sensor, DB matching, positioning.

1   Introduction

Current the visible light wireless communication technology is spotlighted as the next generation of wireless technology. This technology is transmitted digital signal using LED, the receiver receiving digital data to determine the presence or absence of light through PD(Photo Diode)[1-3]. Among them, visible light communication using location-aware services are issues technology that be studied in a variety of applications in the service sector[4-5]. However, existing wireless communication using visible light of existing location-aware services positioning errors can occur due to the NLOS (Non-Line of Sight) in indoor environments. Also, It occurs problem that computational complexity of light to increase the overload due to the signal information each of. In this paper, we proposed the DB matching algorithm for distinguish a specific area based on image sensor using LED. The experimental environment construct LED of four that recognize to realize to   image sensor.

In chapter 2, DB matching algorithm using image sensor and LED will be explain and in chapter 3, DB matching algorithm is applied was simulation design in chapter 4, finally conclusion will be written.

---

[*] Corresponding author.

T.-h. Kim, Y.-h. Lee, and W.-c. Fang (Eds.): FGIT 2012, LNCS 7709, pp. 202–205, 2012.

2   DB Matching Algorithm Using the LED and Image Sensor

There are connected four LED, the image sensor, Server PC for save the DB value. And then, it is to detect the location of a particular color LED that is captured by the video camera. Figure 1. is proposed algorithm flowchart to DB Matching algorithm for specific area discernment using the LED and image sensor.

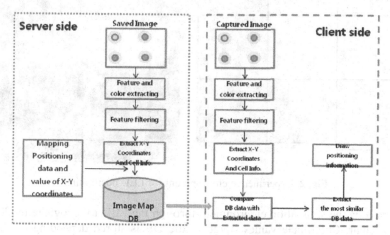

Fig. 1. Algorithm flowchart of DB matching algorithm using the LED and image sensor

After It compare Captured LED coordinate values and ImageMapDB value. It selects the minimum error value of a specific place of the coordinate value. And indicate the area corresponding to the user's location information.

3   DB Matching Algorithm Applied Simulation

In this paper, we were simulated the DB matching algorithm by applying for indoor location-aware using the proposed image sensor with LED in an indoor.

Table 1 is a environment for the simulation.

Table 1. Channel simulation parameters of LED communication in indoor

Items	Values
Simulation Tool	MATLAB 2011
Image Sensor	Cam Camera(Wire)
LED	RGB Lamp
Measure the distance	50cm
Capture Total Frame	1000
Capture Resolution	240X320

Figure 2.shows the configuration of the experimental environment. Resolution of image sensor is 240x320.

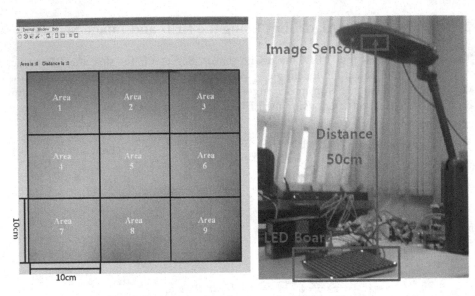

Fig. 2. Experimental environment for LED positioning

Figure 3. is the simulation environment through the LED to recognize the location of a particular. Coordinate values stored in the DB is stored depending on the unit. Between the LED and the image sensor, length measured 50cm distance from LED 10cm by moving coordinate value unit basis is stored. Between the LED and the image sensor, the 50cm distance. And then, when it moves 10cm ever time, LED is stored coordinate value unit. It compared capture location and the value of the DB, we can display the user's location.

Fig. 3. Result screen of LED positioning using DB matching algorithm

When LED light source is moved to another Area, it is recognized that area the less error in the two Area. It does not recognize if the LED light source is their escape from Area. In addition, LED light source has the separation distance. Therefore, there may be errors because of escape from Area. We are able to confirm the accuracy of Sensor position and image position values via standard DB.

4   Conclusion

In this paper, DB matching algorithm using LED (received national attention) and image sensor was proposed, which is possible to distinguish the position and area. Also we demonstrated the possibility of positioning through the experiment using LED and image sensor. And this study decreased the complexity and operation time in comparison to the existing positioning method based on visible light communication. Therefore this result is possible to apply to the application of positioning infra oriented to low price.

Acknowledgement. This work was partially supported by the IT R&D program of MKE/KEIT [10035362, Development of Home Network Technology based on LED-ID].

References

1. Kim, J.Y. (ed.): LED Visible Light Communication Systems. Hongreung Science Publishers, Seoul (2009)
2. Tanaka, Y., et al.: Indoor Visible Light Data Transmission System Utilizing White LED Lights. IEICE Transactions on Communications E86-B, 2440–2454 (2003)
3. Tanaka, Y., et al.: Wireless optical transmissions with the white colored LED for the wireless home links. In: Proc. of the 11th Int. Symp. Personal, Indoor and Mobile Radio Commun. (PIMRC 2000), pp. 1325–1329 (September 2000)
4. Roberts, R., et al.: Visible Light Positioning: Automotive Use Case. In: proc. of IEEE Vehicular Networking Conference, pp. 309–314 (December 2010)
5. Yoshino, M., et al.: High-accuracy Positioning System using Visible LED Lights and Image Sensor. In: proc. of IEEE Radio and Wireless Symposium, pp. 439–442 (January 2008)

Implementation Microprocessor Controller
for LED Lights Emotional Match Digital Sounds

Jaesang Cha[1], Jaekwon Shin[2], and Junghoon Lee[1,*]

[1] Dept. of Electronic & IT Media Eng., Seoul National Univ. of Science and Tech., Seoul,
Korea
[2] Dept. R&D Center, Fivetek Co., Sungnam, Korea
dwarfxx@gmail.com

Abstract. Recently, an interest of application based on the emotion has been
increased. And the LED control based system according to sound has been
proposed. However existing system is adopted the temporary and simple
method for the LED control according to sound change and it is impossible to
explain a variety of human emotion sufficiently. Therefore, we proposed the
efficient emotional matching structure based on microprocessor, DMX and
LED driver. Also we proved the usefulness of proposed system structure and
micro process by conducting the experiment based on hardware device.

Keywords: Microprocessor, LED, Emotional Light, LED Control Driver,
DMX Protocol.

1   Introduction

Emotional light links human emotion with lighting technology, associated study is
focused on illumination, temperature, humidity[1][2]. And associated technologies
which consider sound level and color have been developed. Previous LED light
control system is adopted the temporary and simple method for the LED control
according to sound change and it is impossible to explain a variety of human emotion
sufficiently[3][4]. Therefore, matching algorithm is acquired, which is possible to
control the consecutive emotional flow and reflect variety visual effects.

Emotional factor of LED lighting is variously extended and it is acquired to
express the various emotions through the emotional matching algorithm of digital
sound and LED emotional lighting. And we propose this emotional matching system.
Also we conduct the experiment based on microprocessor and proposed system.

2   Structure of LED Emotional Matching System

A sound signal or digital sound is transmitted to microprocessor included with the
codec. Then result data transfers to the microprocessor output port after received

---

* corresponding author.

T.-h. Kim, Y.-h. Lee, and W.-c. Fang (Eds.): FGIT 2012, LNCS 7709, pp. 206–208, 2012.
© Springer-Verlag Berlin Heidelberg 2012

signal is analyzed as the spectrum. And LED control server received serial signal adopted by emotional algorithm.

In order to control the signal according to emotional matching algorithm, we design the system structure as shown Figure 1.

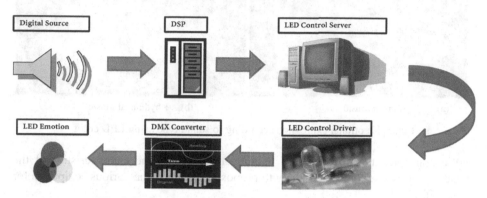

Fig. 1. The structure of system for LED emotional direction

First, a digital sound classifies the characteristic according to the sound type through the PC based audio interface. Then the spectrum is analyzed by microprocessor. And lighting source is controlled according to the emotion of digital sound based on emotional mapping table after processing result is transmitted to LED control driver.

3   Experiment of LED Based Emotional System

We conduct the experiment based on the direction of emotional lights. Micro processor acquires the digital sound signal and conducts the emotional direction. The fabricated system based on proposed system is as show Figure 2.

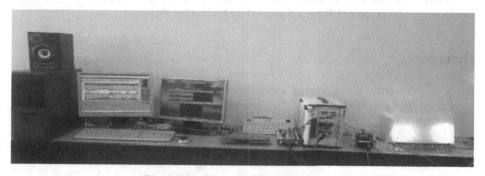

Fig. 2. LED emotion Implement system

Micro processor controller includes the digital sound, frequency to features according to the sound. LED based emotional system expresses the rhythm and features of sound. And emotional LED differently expressed the emotional information according to the sound type.

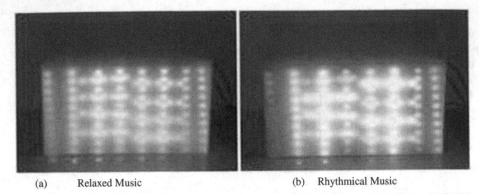

(a)   Relaxed Music   (b)   Rhythmical Music

Fig. 3. Emotional expression according to sound type using LED color

We confirmed the difference of lighting according to the characteristics of the sound. It is possible to use and apply to proposed system at the various sculptures for visual effects.

4   Conclusion

In this paper, we proposed the emotional matching system using LED and sound. Also we demonstrated the usefulness of proposed system by conducting the experiment based on micro processor according to the sound characteristic.

The natural and emotional direction using LED is possible through the proposed system. Also it is possible to provide the high scalability and flexibility by using emotional matching algorithm and LED variable matching table. Also the proposed system can be applied to the various application of the LED converged technology.

Acknowledgment. This research was supported by a grant(C-12-5) from Gyeonggi Technology Development Program funded by Gyeonggi Province.

References

[1] Kim, J.Y. (ed.): LED Visible Light Communication Systems. Hongreung Science Publishers, Seoul (2009)
[2] Tanaka, Y., et al.: Indoor Visible Light Data Transmission System Utilizing White LED Lights. IEICE Transactions on Communications E86-B, 2440–2454 (2003)
[3] Tanaka, Y., et al.: Wireless optical transmissions with the white colored LED for the wireless home links. In: Proc. of the 11th Int. Symp. Personal, Indoor and Mobile Radio Commun. (PIMRC 2000), pp. 1325–1329 (September 2000)
[4] Roberts, R., et al.: Visible Light Positioning: Automotive Use Case. In: proc. of IEEE Vehicular Networking Conference, pp. 309–314 (December 2010)
[5] Yoshino, M., et al.: High-accuracy Positioning System using Visible LED Lights and Image Sensor. In: proc. of IEEE Radio and Wireless Symposium, pp. 439–442 (January 2008)

Determination of a Pair of Single Stationary Zeros in Cross-Coupled Systems

Keehong Um[1,*], Yong-Soon Im[2], Gye-Kuk Kim[3], and Jeong-Jin Kang[4]

[1] Department of Information Technology, Hansei University
Gunpo-city, Kyunggi-do, Korea
[2] Department of Broadcasting, Kookje University
Pyeongtaek-city, Kyunggi-do, Korea
[3] Department of Information & Telecommunication, Gangneung-Wonju National University
Wonju-city, Gangwon-do, Korea
[4] Department of Information and Communication, Dong Seoul University
Sungnam-city, Kyunggi-do, Korea
um@hansei.ac.kr, ysim@kookje.ac.kr,
woodo123@gwnu.ac.kr, jjkang@du.ac.kr

Abstract. We present a theoretical method in order to trace the complex transmission zero (TZ) locations of dielectric-loaded lumped systems, by using chain matrices for subsystems, obtained from the whole system by partitioning into several parts. By deriving the closed-form expressions of transmission zero characteristic equation (TZCE), in terms of impedances of elements. We prove an important result that integer pairs of complex zeros are shown to result solely from the cross-coupled portion of the system. We can locate TZs using only the TZCE obtained from canonical transfer functions, without evaluating the entire transfer function of the whole system.

Keywords: Chain matrix; Ladder networks; Voltage transfer function, Dynamic zeros.

1 Introduction

A new technique is presented to theoretically determine transmission zeros (TZs) from the cross-coupled (CC) systems obtained from the initially-synthesized ladder systems. By adding a feed forward CC bridge on the ladder systems an *integer* pair of TZs can be produced in a complex *s*-plane. The transfer function of isolated passive networks composed of R's and C's with a cross-coupled section was derived to discuss complex and real zeros[1]. Chen discussed the design of cross-coupled filter by coupling matrix[2]. We demonstrate in this paper the finite-frequency complex pairs of TZs are produced solely from the CC portion of the circuit.

1.1 Chain Matrices

The complex zeros – a result of perturbing the element values – are determined from the numerator polynomial of the transfer function. The *chain matrix* is especially

---

* Corresponding author.

T.-h. Kim, Y.-h. Lee, and W.-c. Fang (Eds.): FGIT 2012, LNCS 7709, pp. 209–215, 2012.

useful in analyzing a cascade of two-port networks since the matrix for the overall network is simply the product of the individual chain matrices. The chain matrix T of n cascaded networks is given by [3].

$$T = \begin{bmatrix} A & B \\ C & D \end{bmatrix} = \prod_{i=1}^{n} \begin{bmatrix} A_i & B_i \\ C_i & D_i \end{bmatrix} = \prod_{i=1}^{n} T_i , \tag{1}$$

where T_i is the chain matrix of the i-th system. The entry A of (1) is given by the element (1,1) of chain matrix T, obtained by open-circuiting the output port, i.e., A is found by applying a voltage V_i at port 1, and measuring the open-circuit voltage V_o at port 2. The voltage transfer function $H(s)$ can thus be expressed as [4]

$$H(s) = \left.\frac{V_o}{V_i}\right|_{I_o=0} = \frac{1}{A} = \frac{1}{T(1,1)} = \frac{N(s)}{D(s)} , \tag{2}$$

Where $N(s)$ and $D(s)$ are the numerator and the denominator polynomials of $H(s)$. Therefore, if the entry (1, 1) of the chain matrix is known the transfer function can be obtained. After the cancellation process, the remaining canonical form of zeros and poles of the transfer function will be considered. The canonical form of the numerator polynomial is defined as the characteristic polynomial of the TZs. Equating the polynomial to zero, the *transmission zero characteristic equation* (TZCE) is obtained, which is to be solved to find out TZs. The TZs are classified into two different types. One is called a *stationary zero*, which does not change its location with any variations in network element values, and is located at the origin of the s-plane; the other is a *dynamic zero*, which, when element values change, is located anywhere but at the origin. We define positively cross-coupled (PCC) network: a network where the sign of the cross-coupling is the same as the sign of the main line coupling (i.e., inductive cross-coupling in an inductively coupled circuit *or* capacitive cross-coupling in an capacitively coupled circuit)[5].

We also define negatively cross- coupled (NCC) network: a network where the sign of the cross- coupling is the opposite of the sign of the main line coupling (i.e., inductive cross-coupling in a capacitively coupled circuit *or* capacitive cross-coupling in a inductively coupled circuit). Depending on the existence of a positive or negative CC subsystem and the particular connection of cross-coupled elements, the dynamic zero can be integer pairs of complex conjugates. In this paper, we will consider the NCC and PCC filter networks required to produce complex zeros to obtain TZ locations and/or locus.

1.2   Ladder Networks

An initially-synthesized ladder network, with shunt- connected LC resonators without any cross-coupling element, is a building block in the design of a cross-coupled system. Each LC resonator has impedances of L and C in parallel [6]. The series- connected elements could be inductors or capacitors. There are several possibilities for adding cross-coupling elements to the circuit: (1)Without skipping any resonators (adjacent resonators), (2) Skipping one resonator, and (3) Skipping two resonators. More complicated cross-coupling configurations are used to optimize the filter response and satisfy specific requirements. In this paper, we consider the first case. by calculating the Laplace impedance to obtain a transfer function. and a canonical form of the numerator polynomial, i.e., TZCE, and plot locus of TZs from the TZCE.

2   CC Circuits without Skipping Any Resonators

We consider a cross-coupled system, obtained from the ladder network, by connecting a cross-coupling element (inductor or capacitor) without skipping any resonators.

2.1   Negatively Cross-Coupled (NCC) Systems

The system in Fig. 1 is an example of an NCC filter.Another case is when the inductive cross coupling is in a capacitively coupled main (ladder) line. We proved that both of these NCC filters have the same characteristic equations [5]. By (1), chain matrix of each subsystem is expressed as follows:

$$T_1 = \begin{bmatrix} 1 & 50 \\ 0 & 1 \end{bmatrix}, T_5 = \begin{bmatrix} 1 & 0 \\ 1/50 & 1 \end{bmatrix}, T_i = \begin{bmatrix} A_i & B_i \\ C_i & D_i \end{bmatrix}, i = 2,3,4 \tag{3}$$

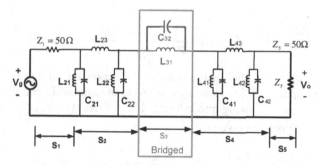

Fig. 1. Negatively cross-coupled (NCC) filter network without skipping any resonators

These are the chain matrices of the series source with impedance R of 50Ω (S_1 in Fig.1), a π -network (S_2) , series- connected LC-parallel subsystem (S_3) , another π -network (S_4) , and the load impedance R of 50Ω (S_5), respectively [7, 8]. The 1st subnetwork is composed of impedance $Z_1 = 50\Omega$ and the ground line. Equation (3) defines the chain matrices of each subsystem, and all entries should be expressed in terms of Laplace impedances. The impedances of the five subsystems are given by

$$Z_1 = Z_5 = 50 \; ; \quad Z_{21} = \frac{sL_{21}}{L_{21}C_{21}s^2 + 1} , \quad Z_{22} = \frac{sL_{22}}{L_{22}C_{22}s^2 + 1} ,$$

$$Z_{23} = sL_{23} \; ; \quad Z_3 = \frac{sL_{31}}{L_{31}C_{32}s^2 + 1} ;$$

$$Z_{41} = \frac{sL_{41}}{L_{41}C_{41}s^2 + 1} , \quad Z_{42} = \frac{sL_{42}}{L_{42}C_{42}s^2 + 1} , \quad Z_{43} = sL_{43} , \qquad (4)$$

where all the element values of the filter are assumed to be non-zeros. All entries of matrix T_1 are constants, so T_1 is not a function of s. Therefore, the 1st system does not have zeros nor poles in the s-plane. The value 50 of entry $(2, 1)$ affects the magnitude of the transfer function for the whole system. The 5th subsystem is composed of load impedance $Z_L = 50\Omega$ shunt-connected to the ground line. All entries of matrix T_5 are also constants. Therefore, the 5th system also does not have zeros nor poles in any s-plane. The 2nd subsystems in a π-network is composed of Z_{21}, Z_{22}, and Z_{23}. The shunt-connected Z_{21} is a network of parallel connection of L_{21} and C_{21}. The shunt-connected Z_{22} is a network of parallel connection of L_{22} and C_{22}. The series-connected Z_{23} is just an impedance of the single inductor L_{23}. The four entries of the chain matrix T_2 in (1) are expressed as [4]

$$T_2 = \begin{bmatrix} A_2 & B_2 \\ C_2 & D_2 \end{bmatrix} , \qquad (5)$$

with

$$A_2 = 1 + \frac{Z_{23}}{Z_{22}} , \quad B_2 = Z_{23} , \quad C_2 = \frac{1}{Z_{21}} + \frac{1}{Z_{22}} + \frac{Z_{23}}{Z_{21}\,Z_{22}} , \quad D_2 = 1 + \frac{Z_{23}}{Z_{21}} , \qquad (6)$$

where each impedance of the matrix entries is expressed in terms of Laplace impedances. The impedances in (4) are used in (6) to obtain matrix entries. Each entry is calculated with the following procedures. The entries A_2, B_2, C_2, and D_2 are rational polynomial functions given by

$$A_2 = \frac{(L_{22}C_{22}L_{22})s^2 + (L_{22} + L_{23})}{L_{22}} , \qquad B_2 = L_{23} \cdot s ,$$

$$C_2 = \frac{\begin{bmatrix} (L_{21}L_{22}C_{21}L_{23}C_{22})s^4 \\ + (L_{21}L_{22}C_{21} + L_{21}L_{22}C_{22} + L_{21}L_{23}C_{21} + L_{22}L_{23}C_{22})s^2 \\ + (L_{21} + L_{22} + L_{23}) \end{bmatrix}}{sL_{21}L_{22}} ,$$

$$D_2 = \frac{(L_{21}C_{21}L_{23})s^2 + (L_{21} + L_{23})}{L_{21}} . \qquad (7)$$

2.2   Locus of Transmission Zeros

The 3rd subsystem has impedance Z_3. The chain matrix T_3 is given by

$$T_3 = \begin{bmatrix} 1 & Z_3 \\ 0 & 1 \end{bmatrix}. \tag{8}$$

The 4th subsystem is another π-network composed of Z_{41}, Z_{42} and, Z_{43}. The procedure to get the chain matrix T_4 is the same as the 2nd subsystem case by replacing (L_{21}, L_{22}, L_{23}, C_{21}, and C_{22}) with (L_{41}, L_{42}, L_{43}, C_{41}, and C_{42}), respectively. After cancellations of the common terms in numerator and denominator polynomials, the canonical form of the numerator polynomial, i.e., TZCE in the transfer function in (2) is obtained as a 3rd degree polynomial, namely

$$N(s) = 50\, L_{21} L_{22} L_{41} L_{42}\, s \cdot [L_{31} C_{32} s^2 + 1]. \tag{9}$$

Equating (9) to zero, i.e., $N(s) = 0$, the TZCE of the network shown in Fig. 1 is expressed as a product of two functions

$$f(s) = s \cdot (a_{32} s^2 + 1) \equiv f_1(s) \cdot f_2(s) = 0, \tag{10}$$

With

$$f_1(s) = s, \qquad f_2(s) = a_{32} s^2 + 1 \tag{11}$$

where the non-zero coefficient a_{32} due to cross-coupling is given as

$$a_{32} = L_{31} C_{32}. \tag{12}$$

When there is no cross-coupling (i.e., $C_{32} = 0$), there is only a sole stationary zero at origin, but there are no dynamic zeros. So, there will be no complex zeros (in this case, complex doublet zeros). Therefore, to have a cross-coupled circuit, the condition is that C_{32} should not be zero. Otherwise, if the value of the cross-coupling element C_{32} is zero, the complex doublet zeros are not located in the *finite* s-plane. Another case is for the inductive cross coupling in a capacitively coupled main line. We can prove similarly that both of these CC filters have the same characteristic equations [10]. Equation (10) gives three finite TZs: a single stationary zero at the origin from (11.a) and two dynamic zeros from (11.b), which are given by

$$s = \pm j \sqrt{\frac{1}{a_{32}}}. \tag{13}$$

Note that dynamic zeros can exist only when $C_{32} (\neq 0)$ has the range of values

$$0 < C_{32} < \infty. \tag{14}$$

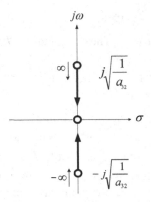

Fig. 2. Zero locus of the NCC filter network

For the sake of convenience, the very small positive value almost equivalent to zero and the very big positive value almost equivalent to (very close to) infinity are noted as 0^+ and ∞_-, respectively. Accordingly, as the value of C_{32} increases from 0^+, the zeros move from $\pm\infty$ to locations very close to the origin (but not the origin) along the $j\omega$-axis. Perturbed element values of the filter network generate a different coefficient. From (13) and (14), the TZ locus can be calculated and shown in Fig. 2. Thus, without skipping any resonators, a single TZ results solely from the tank circuit (S_3) resonator. This is the expected result and simply helps validate the generality of the theory.

3   Positively Cross-Coupled (PCC) Filter Systems

In Fig. 1, if L_{32} is used in place of C_{32}, the PCC network is obtained. With $Z_3 = L_{31} /\!/ L_{32}$, the series impedance of subsystem S_3 is given by

$$Z_3 = \frac{sL_{31}L_{32}}{L_{31}+L_{32}}. \tag{15}$$

Using (15) and (2), and after cancellations of the common terms, the canonical form of the numerator polynomial is calculated as the 1st degree monomial

$$N(s) = 50L_{21}L_{22} \cdot (L_{31}+L_{32}) \cdot L_{41}L_{42} \cdot s. \tag{16}$$

From (16), the TZ characteristic equation is given by

$$f(s) = s = 0. \tag{17}$$

Equations (16) and (17) show that there is a single stationary zero at the origin. There are no dynamic zeros. Again, there is no cross-coupling in S_3 and the result is expected from conventional network theory, merely helping to validate the generality of this theory.

4   Conclusion

We have presented a theoretical investigation of a practical method to determine quantitatively the locations and locus of complex transmission zeros (TZs) of positively and negatively cross-coupled band pass systems, without skipping any resonators .We have shown that a pair of complex doublets and two pairs of complex doublet of TZs are shown to result solely from the cross-coupled portion of the filter network. A cross-coupled (CC) filter network is formed by adding a cross-coupling bridge on the initially-synthesized ladder network. Based on the varying coefficients, the TZCE gives different solutions. The continuous change of solutions due to the changing of cross-coupling elements of capacitors and inductors produces the TZ locus on the complex s-plane. The case of the two resonators skipped will be considered more fully in future work.

Remark   1. This work is the modified and revised versions of the presentations in the conference; ENGE 2102 (Sep. 16-19, 2012, Jeju, Korea) and the 2012 MulGrab Int'l (Dec. 16-19, 2012, Gangneung, Korea).

Remark   2. This work was supported by Hansei University.

References

1. Bernd, G., Rudolf, R., Alexander, S.: Signals and systems, 2nd edn., p. 50. Wiley (2001) ISBN 0-471-98800-6
2. Cheng-Chung, C., Yi-Ru, C., Chi-Yang, C.: Miniaturized Microstrip Cross-Coupled Filters Using Quarter-Wave or Quasi-Quarter-Wave Resonators. IEEE Trans. Microwave Theory and Technique MTT-51(1), 120–131 (2003)
3. Peter, R.A.: Microwave Engineering: Passive Circuits. Prentice-Hall, Englewood Cliffs (1988)
4. Hong, G., Lancaster, J.M.: Microstrip Filters for FR/Microwave Applications. John Wiley & Sons, Inc. (2001)
5. Keehong, U.: Method for Theoretically Determining the Locus and Locations of the Transmission Zeros in Microwave Filter Networks. Ph.D. Dissertation. New Jersey Institute of Technology (2003)
6. Gorski-Popiel, J., Drew, A.J.: RC active ladder networks. Proc. of the IEEE on Electrical Engineers 112, 2213–2219 (1965)
7. Pozar, D.M.: Microwave Engineering. John Wiley & Sons, Inc. (2001)
8. Van Valkenberg, M.E.: Network Analysis, 3rd edn. Prentice-Hall (1974)

Secure Contents Design and Implement of Smart Home Management System in OISCS

Minkyu Choi[1], Goreti Marreiros[1], Myunggwon Hwang[2], Zita Vale[1], and Hoon Ko[1]

[1] Knowledge Engineering & Decision Support Research Group (GECAD),
Institute of Engineering-Polytechnic of Porto (ISEP/IPP),
Rua. Dr. Antonio Bernardino de Almeida, 431, 4200-072, Porto, Portugal
freeant7@naver.com, {mgt,zav,hko}@isep.ipp.pt
[2] Korea Institute of Science and Technology Information (KISTI)
245 Daehak-ro, Yuseong-gu, Daejeon, 305-806, Republic of Korea
mg.hwang@gmail.com

Abstract. Optimal Intelligent Supervisory Control System (OISCS) is the program which has an evaluation / a monitor and a control functions for home / office devices from outdoor [1][2]. For their controlling, we usually use Mobile Devices (MD). Also, we can avoid energy wasting by using MDs. However, because they use a network system, all security problems will belong to MD's such as a man in the middle attack. If attackers take transferring contents between MDs and a home/a office, they can see inside. It will be potential troubles. To avoid it, we designed and implemented to all contents which are transferring in network.

1 Introduction

Various smart devices are able to connect between energy areas to IT areas easily. Jeremy said the 3rd industrial revolution will come through a union of between energy and IT in near future. It means that all buildings have each generator in all buildings, and they will be connected to share. It is a strategy which they take and/or give all energy by connecting together. They need a special program to use it. The existing system that still we are studying is an Optimal Intelligent Supervisory System (OISCS) that have an evaluation/ a monitor and a control function to manage all devices in a home and in an office [1][2]. Because this system uses the existing network, they can be uneasiness elements in OISCS (in Smart Grid) in future. In case they send them without an encryption, if attackers take them and look inside, they can catch all of information including home address, ID/Password etc. To solve these problems, various modules have been developing so far, one of them is the contents encryption (data and signals from all equipment and MD). So, in this paper, we designed and implemented the encryption algorithm of contents. This paper consists of next; it describes the secret encryption algorithm (the related works) in section 2, Section 3 explains Optimal Intelligent Supervisory Control System (OISCS). In section 4, we write about design and implementation, at last, we put our conclusion in section 5.

T.-h. Kim, Y.-h. Lee, and W.-c. Fang (Eds.): FGIT 2012, LNCS 7709, pp. 216–223, 2012.

2   Secret Encryption Algorithm

Symmetric-key algorithms are a class of algorithms for cryptography that use trivially related, often identical, cryptographic keys for both decryption and encryption. The encryption key is trivially related to the decryption key, in that they may be identical or there is a simple transform to go between the two keys. The keys, in practice, represent a shared secret between two or more parties that can be used to maintain a private information link [3][4]. Symmetric-key algorithms can be divided into stream ciphers and block ciphers. Stream ciphers encrypt the bytes of the message one at a time, and block ciphers take a number of bytes and encrypt them as a single unit [4]. Since encrypting a message does not guarantee that a message is not changed while encryption process is performed, symmetric ciphers are also used to achieve other cryptographic primitives than just encryption. A message authentication code is added to a ciphertext to ensure that changes to the ciphertext will be noted by the receiver. Message authentication codes can be constructed from symmetric ciphers. The symmetric ciphers can also can be used for non-repudiation purposes by ISO 13888-2 standard. Another application is to build hash functions from block ciphers [5][6].

3   Optimal Intelligent Supervisory Control Systems

Figure 1 shows Optimal Intelligent Supervisory Control System (OISCS) module [1][2]. To SCADA safety, before sending to user device, first it should process 'One-way Authentication', and then they encrypt all data with hash value, which generate from 'One-way Authentication'. That is, it sends control / evaluation information and control signal after encrypting which are in control, evaluation and monitor area. In this paper, we implemented encryption module.

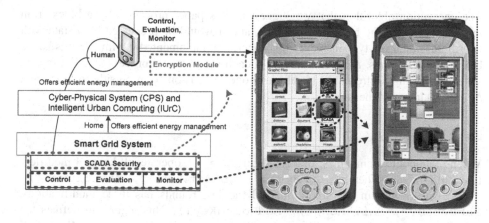

Fig. 1. Menu of OISCS

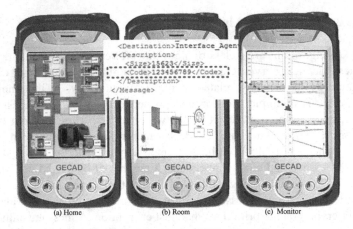

Fig. 2. Estimated values (Three areas)

In the Figure 2, '(a) Home' shows the whole area of home. If a user clicks (or touches) each area, the user can see the next steps (b). In '(b) Room', the user selected '(b) Room'. That room has some electronic devices. The user monitors all devices status of the room. According to each area, all users have to click or touches the area, then the device show the next steps to the user. '(c) Monitor' shows the energy flows. The users can know the amount used energy in real time through '(c) Monitor'. As we see in figure 2, there are no security modules such as encryptions in OCISC. So, if attackers take transferring contents and try to look them inside, all information can be opened. It will be serious troubles soon. Therefore, we designed and implemented the encryption modules for them.

4   Design and Implementation

The encryption algorithm that we suggest in this paper processes by a block from input and output. The basic unit is a byte, and it would be processed by a state with two-dimension array type inside. In this paper, we implemented it with 128 bits key, a block and ten rounds. All modifications in each round take a process the all arrays in state after changing from 128 bit block in one-dimension from outside to four line× N_b (N_b =4) in two-dimension.

4.1   Encryption

When plain contexts incomes, first AddRoundKey() operates. It keeps 4 modifications till r-1 round. There are SubBytes(), ShiftRows(), MixColumns(), AddroundKey() in the algorithm, and the last rounds has three modifications, SubBytes(), ShiftRows(), AddRoundKey(). This algorithm defines tag security encryption because all contents which are transferring between MD and all users is consist of XML types. We explain (a) Communication between interface and house, (b) onConnection (Client Code) and (c) getPriceEnergy below;

```
//Encryption Processing
Rijndael (byte State, byte CipherKey) {
    KeyExapansion(CipherKey, ExpandedKey);
        AddRoundKey(State, ExpandedKey);
        for(i=1;i<Nr;i++)
                Round(State, ExpandedKey+Nb*i);
        FinalRound(State, ExpandedKey+Nb*Nr);
}


//(a) <MaxPower> encryption in communicationBetweenInterfa-
ceAndHouseEncryptor.java
if (nChildNode.getNodeType() == Node.ELEMENT_NODE) {
    if (nChildNode.getNodeName().equals("MaxPower")) {
        encryptElement((Element) nChildNode, true);
}


//(b) <ValueKwH> encryption in onConnectionEncryptor.java
if (nChildNode.getNodeType() == Node.ELEMENT_NODE) {
    if (nChildNode.getNodeName().equals("ValueKwH")) {
        encryptElement((Element) nChildNode, true);
}


//(c) <Code> encryption in priceOfEnergyEncrypto.java
if (nChildNode.getNodeType() == Node.ELEMENT_NODE) {
    if (nChildNode.getNodeName().equals("Code")) {
        encryptElement((Element) nChildNode, true);
}
```

4.2   Decryption

Once the cyber text comes into the system, it also takes AddRoundKey() first like an encryption, it keeps four modifications till $r-1$ round, InvShiftRows(), InvSubBytes(), AddroundKey(), and InvMixColumns(), And there are three modifications, InvShiftRows(), InvSubBytes(), AddRoundKey() in last round.

```
//Decryption Processing
InvRijddael(byte State, byte CipherKey)
{
        InvKeyExpansion(CipherKey, InvExpandedKey);
        AddRoundKey(State, InvExpandedKey+Nb*Nr);
        for(i=Nr-1;i>0;i--)
                InvRound(State, InvExpanedKey+Nb*i);
        InvFinalRound(State, InvExpandedKey);
}
```

1) SubBytes()/InvSubBytes()

A SubBytes() modification independently changes in non-linear byte by each state byte which used a S-Box. S-Box came from two modifications. In this algorithm, it make inverse value of $GF(2^8)$ or it takes a process next notation for $GF(2^8)$. Once it processes, it will be implemented by S-Box in $2^8 \times 8$ lookup table type. InvSub-Bytes() modification is an inverse modification of byte replacement. Each inverse S-Box is going to be applied in each state.

//SubBytes() / InvSubBytes()

```
alog[0]=1;
    for(i=1;i<256;i++){
                j=(alog[i-1]<<1)^alog[i-1];
                if((j&0x100)!=0)j^=ROOT;
                alog[i] = j;
    }
    byte[][] A = new byte[][] {
    :
    };
    byte[] B = new byte[] { 0, 1, 1, 0, 0, 0, 1, 1};
```
---

2) ShiftRows() / InvShiftRows()

A ShifeRow() let bytes which is the last three line in state shifts as much as the number of different byte. A InvShiftRows() is the inverse modification of a ShifeRow().

// ShiftRows() / InvShiftRows()

```
for(i=0;i<256;i++){
        S[i]=(byte)(cox[i][0]<<7);
        for(t=1;t<8;t++)
        S[i]^=cox[i][t]<<(7-t);
        Si[S[i]&0xFF]=(byte)i;
}
```
---

3) MixColumns() / InvMixColumns()

Each line is expressed a polynomial expression in $GF(2^8)$., that is, fixed notation $a(x)$does multiplication into x^4+1. A InvMixColumns() is the inverse modification of MixColumn(), it will be processed by column-by-column. Each line is expressed a polynomial expression in $GF(2^8)$.

// MixColumns() / InvMixColumns()

```
static final int multiplication (int a, int b) {
              return (a != 0 && b != 0) ?
              alog[(log[a & 0xFF] + log[b & 0xFF]) % 255] :
              0;
      }
      //InvMixColumns()
      for(int r=1;r<ROUNDS;r++)
              for(j=0;j<BC;j++){
              tt=Kd[r][j];
                      Kd[r][j]=U1[(tt>>>24)&0xFF]^
                      U2[(tt>>>16)&0xFF]^
                      U3[(tt>>>8)&0xFF]^
                      U4[tt&0xFF];
      }
```

---

4) AddRoundKey()

AddroundKey() modification will be processed by XOR operation between state value and round key.

//AddRoundKey(State, RoundKey);

5) Key Expansion

This algorithm has an encryption key, K, and the key extension routine will come from Key schedules. The extension key is expressed in *(w[N_b(N_r+1)])* which is 4 bytes and liner array. In this step, N_b is necessary to be initial process, each round N_r has to the key data as much as N_b word.

//KeyExpansion(byte CipherKey, word ExpandedKey);

4.3   Implementation Result

The figure 3 shows the result of implementation. There are three items to be encrypted, (a) Communication between interface and house, (b) onConnection (Client Code) and (c) getPriceEnergy. In this research, we didn't study all contents encryption; just we implemented it to special tag because all contents in OCISC use a XML Tags. At the result, <MaxPower> in (a), <ValueKwH> in (b), and <Code> in (c) had encrypted. We can compare <Code> from Figure 2 and from 3, whether it is in encryption or not. With figure 3, we confirmed that <Code> was encrypted by security algorithm.

```
▼<Load>                                    ▼<Message>
  <IDType>3</IDType>                         <Type>setPriceEnergy</Type>
  <On>true</On>                              <Source>Agent_Source</Source>
  <Power>50</Power>                          <Destination>Agent_Destination</Destination>
  <Range>15</Range>                        ▼<Description>
  <Type>Variable</Type>                      ▼<ValueKwH>
  <Description_load>Motor 2</Description_load>    ▼<EncryptedData xmlns="http://www.w3c.org/xmlenc">
  ▼<MaxPower>                                      <CipherText>cgksGz8j2Bw=</CipherText>
    ▼<EncryptedData xmlns="http://www.w3c.org/xmlenc">    </EncryptedData>
        <CipherText>2L3978G9p/0=</CipherText>      </ValueKwH>
      </EncryptedData>                          </Description>
    </MaxPower>                              </Message>
</Load>
```
(a) Communication between Interface and House   (b) onConnection (Client Code)

```
                    ▼<Message>
                      <Type>clientCode</Type>
                      <Source>Agent_Server</Source>
                      <Destination>Agent_Client</Destination>
                    ▼<Description>
                      ▼<Code>
                        ▼<EncryptedData xmlns="http://www.w3c.org/xmlenc">
                            <CipherText>F+YmVEVyPLjEGbzSshEbQ==</CipherText>
                          </EncryptedData>
                        </Code>
                      </Description>
                    </Message>
```
(c) getPriceEnergy

Fig. 3. Encryption Results

5   Conclusion

We studied a contents encryption for OISCS, and we designed and implemented it in this paper. There are appearing various / many contents from a home and/or an office in smart ages. And we can catch and check them over our MD; also we can control all devices by MD. However, because all information which send between a home/an office and MD (Users) don't have security modules, they only have ID/Password/PIN code in their MD, if attackers take them and look inside, then many information may be opened. So, to apply an encryption algorithm can be the one of solutions. But, if we encrypt all contents inside, it will be another troubles to be delayed from decryption them. That's why; we designed and implemented special tags. As the result, we suggested an encryption way to special tags which keep important content, and designed / implemented. We expect this encryption algorithm held the OISCS to be safety.

Acknowledgement. This work is supported by FEDER Funds through the "Programa Operacional Factores de Competitividade - COMPETE" program and by National Funds through FCT "Fundação para a Ciência e a Tecnologia" under the project: FCOMP-01-0124-FEDER-PEst-OE/EEI/UI0760/2011.

References

1. Ko, H., Marreiros, G., Morais, H., Vale, Z., Ramos, C.: Intelli-gent Supervisory Control System for Home Devices using a Cyber Physical Ap-proach. Integrated Computer-Aided Engineering 19(1), 67–79 (2012)
2. Ko, H., Vale, Z.: Optimal intelligent Supervisory Control System in Cyber-Physical Intelli-gence. In: Jeju, S.K. (ed.) The 2010 International Conference on Security Technology, December 11-13, pp. 171–178 (2010)
3. Ko, H., Freitas, C., Marreiros, G., Ramos, C.: A study on Users Authentication Methods for Safety Group Decision System in Dybanic Small Group. Journal of Convergence Information Technology 4(4), 68–76 (2009)
4. Robles, R.J., Choi, M.-K.: Symmetric-Key Encryption for Wireless Internet SCADA. In: Ślęzak, D., Kim, T.-h., Fang, W.-C., Arnett, K.P. (eds.) SecTech 2009. CCIS, vol. 58, pp. 289–297. Springer, Heidelberg (2009)
5. RSA Laboratories, What is RC4? (2009), http://www.rsa.com/rsalabs/node.asp?id=2250
6. Diffie, W., Hellman, M.E.: Privacy and Authentication: An Intro-duction to Cryptography. Proc. IEEE 67(3), 397–427 (1979)

Development of 3D Visibility Analysis Models Implementing NURBS[1] Data

Choong Sik Kim

Dept. of Environmental Landscape Architecture, Gangneung-Wonju National University,
South Korea

Abstract. Landscape Visibility Map has advantages of assessing landscape character and expects any planning scenarios. The research aimed to develop a visibility analysis programme based on NURBS in order to improve accuracy of the process and result. Seoul Forest Apartment and Kum-Ho 14 Redevelopment District have been chosen as case study and site in order to review terrain, high rise building blocks and any built up structures at the same time. After case study, VE3D which was developed for visibility analysis from vectorised datasets was able to illustrate high level of detail in visibility identification better than using Arcview 3.3 programme. Moreover, VE3D can produce a visibility analysis in reflecting complicated structures such as flyovers and high rise tower blocks.

Keywords: Visibility Analysis, 3D Simulation, NURBS, VE3D, Arcview, Visibility Map, Visual Exposure.

1 Introduction

Recently, it has been efficient to produce Visibility Models using grid based DTM[2] in order to implement in planning process. Moreover, Landscape Visibility Map has advantages of assessing landscape character and expects any planning scenarios. In particular, Visibility Analysis using GIS[3] can be processed at high speed, efficient and doesn't require special expertise to carry out (HE Jie et al, 2002).

Furthermore, Visibility Analysis using GIS and its accumulative exposure map is able to produce a synthetic analysis which cannot be carried out through intuitive method (Kim et al, 2011). However, it could be biased depending on height cell size; moreover, each cell (unit) only contains single height information (value) which cannot deal with irregular built up structures and floating bridges.

On the other hand, commercial software such as Ecotect or Geoweb3D can be used for a vectorised Visibility Analysis models in order to overcome rasterised lattice structure model. These vectorised models can simulate bridges, flyover, built ups, terrain information as close to the real world. Moreover it uses ray tracing to increase realism and efficiency; whereas, there is not tools for Visibility Analysis yet.

---

[1] Non Uniform Rational B Spline.
[2] Digital Terrain Model.
[3] Geographic Information System.

T.-h. Kim, Y.-h. Lee, and W.-c. Fang (Eds.): FGIT 2012, LNCS 7709, pp. 224–232, 2012.

Therefore, this research aims to develop vectorised 3D Visibility Analysis programme in order to increase accuracy using NURBS which deals with terrain data efficiently.

2   Literature Review

2.1   Methodology Comparison Based on Dataset Structure

Rasterised Visibility Analyses employ ground models based on the datasets such as TIN[4], sRSG[5], tRSG[6]. In particular, sRSG datasets are widely used because its faster data processing speeds as well as enabling simulations with smaller sizes of datasets.

Visibility Analysis based on sRSG data models draws visible sprays from viewpoints to targets, then analyses and calculates any obstruction within the sprays. Grid methods, however, calculate from ground models to built up structures; therefore, it is difficult to analyse high rise tower blocks or flyovers.

While vector data driven Visibility Analyses principally calculates between viewpoint and target points and renders results based on the sprays, the Visibility Analyses used mesh and surface have benefits of accurate form making and efficiency on realistic modelling. However, in order to increase the level of detail in terrain, significant numbers of meshes are needed then, consequently increase computing time. Moreover, computing can be bottlenecked when it calculates the visual sprays (Pottmann et al., 2007).

Conversely, NURBS models use splines and they can express complicated terrains quickly with relatively small number of nodes. Moreover, NURBS can provide tools such as rendering, shades, visibility, and transformation for terrain analysis. Models produced by NURBS curves can be used for Visibility Analysis with ray tracing and division methods; therefore, computing process is very fast and deal with terrains in relatively small file sizes (Kaihuai et al., 1996).

2.2   Calculation of Cumulated Visibility Analysis with Human Visual Perception

Producing Visibility Analysis is divided into two depending on number of viewpoints; view shed and cumulative view shed. Cumulative view shed is adding results of more than one singular viewpoint and normally used for multiple viewpoint analysis in highly sensitive areas. However, it has been limited for reflecting visual perceptions and visibility distances since it simply accumulates visibility values of single viewpoints using bit data (0 and 2 datasets). Therefore, Cumulative Visibility Analysis which takes human perception into accounts has been required (Caldwell et al., 2003). Vector methods can compute visible distance from targets; whereas, raster based methods only produce Visibility Analysis with simple accumulation bits by bits.

---

[4] Triangular Irregular Network.
[5] Stepped Regular Square Grid.
[6] Triangulated RSG.

3   Methodology

3.1   Site Selection and Viewpoint

Seoul Forest Apartment and Kum-Ho 14 Redevelopment District have been chosen as case study and site in order to review terrain, high rise building blocks and any built up structures at the same time. Because the site is located in the area where green open space is adjacent and within a high dense high rise apartment blocks as well as there is Du Mo Bridge, which is a concrete built flyover within walking distance. This enables us to review various structures and terrain.

Total 15 viewpoints were selected on the basis of visibility mainly from (1) footpath towards Ung-Bong Mountain, Du Mo Bridge and (3) Han River Ferry routes.

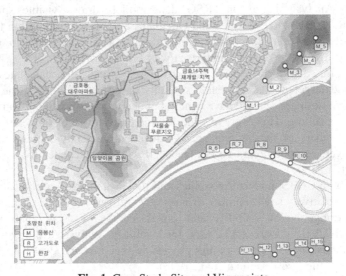

Fig. 1. Case Study Site and Viewpoints

3.2   Research Methodology and Process

Database was constructed by both rasterised and vectorised software. Then, Visibility and Cumulative Visibility Analysis have been carried out. In case of Rasterised datasets, Arcview 3.3 was employed to assemble grids from DTM 1:1000 and the analysis was carried out from the grids.

Whereas, for vectorised datasets, Rhinoceros 5.0 was implemented for authorising NURBS surfaces for the terrain of the area, then other built up structures such as apartment blocks and concrete flyover were also converted as surface in order to combine with the terrain. VE3D module were utilised for analysing the datasets.

For the both datasets, 1x1, 5x5, and 10x10m grids terrains were compared allowing differences in level of detail. However, in the grid 1x1, VE3D could not handle the amount of time for analysis and consequently excluded in the research.

The both analyses were carried out using same hardware; Intel Core i5 760 2.80GHz CPU, 4GB DDR3 RAM, NVIDIA GeForce GTS 250, 7200 RPM SATA HDD and Windows 7 operating system.

Fig. 2. 3D Terrain and Buildings Used in Visibility Analysis 1 (from Arcview – Elevation)

Fig. 3. 3D Terrain and Buildings Used in Visibility Analysis 2 (from Rhinoceros – NURBS)

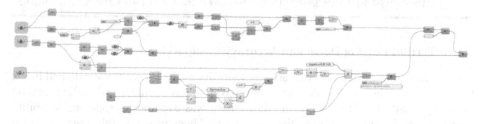

Fig. 4. Visibility Analysis Process by VE3D

4   Result and Findings

4.1   Visibility Analysis Processing Time - VE3D

Before the actual construction start, Visibility Analysis processing time by VE3D for 5x5 grids is minimum 10 minutes 26 seconds (viewpoint 3, 4) and maximum 13 minutes 24 seconds (viewpoint 7), which the average time become 11 minutes 8 seconds. For 10x10 grids, processing time is minimum 2 minutes 49 seconds (viewpoint 3) and maximum 3 minutes 3 seconds (viewpoint 15), which the average time become 2 minutes 54 seconds.

There is an increase for analysis after completion. For instance, for 5x5 grids Visibility Analysis processing time was minimum 13 minutes 27 seconds (viewpoint 10) and maximum 25 minutes 33 seconds (viewpoint 7), which the average time become 18 minutes 1 second. For 10x10 grids, processing time is minimum 3 minutes 5 seconds (viewpoint 13) and maximum 5 minutes 37 seconds (viewpoint 14), which the average time become 3 minutes 52 seconds.

This incensement could be explained by the fact that there were increase number of built up structures such as 30 tower blocks in after completion, the process time for this blocks' concealment and openness increased the processing time by approximately 1.5 – 2 times. We can therefore, conclude that multiple viewpoint Visibility Analysis for 5x5m grids models is less efficient since it processes longer than 30 minutes. However, for 10x10m grids models process within around 3 minutes and therefore, they have potential to use for multiple Visibility Analysis.

Table 1. VE3D's Visibility Analysis Processing Time (unit - min:sec)

View change	Grids	Viewpoint															Ave.
		1	2	3	4	5	6	7	8	9	10	11	12	13	14	15	
Before	5x5m	10:41	11:24	10:26	10:26	10:29	11:29	13:24	10:51	10:51	10:51	11:15	11:04	11:00	11:14	11:42	11:08
	10x10m	02:50	02:50	02:49	02:50	02:50	02:54	02:59	02:53	02:53	02:52	02:57	02:57	02:53	02:54	03:03	02:54
After	5x5m	17:36	16:46	20:03	20:03	13:33	19:30	25:33	20:07	20:07	13:27	16:41	16:41	14:17	14:17	21:29	18:01
	10x10m	03:50	04:40	03:32	03:33	03:34	03:32	03:50	03:26	03:26	03:25	04:13	03:10	03:05	05:37	05:01	03:52

4.2   Terrain Level of Detail and Accuracy Comparison

The research also carried out comparisons visibility analysis' accuracy ratio and limits by grids sizes. In case of Arcview, there were large numbers of differences on visibility based on grid sizes. For instance, there was even error producing Visibility Analysis on viewpoint 7 during the case study. There was a visible point in 1x1m grids; whereas, Arcview calculated the point was not visible within 10x10m grids.

However, Arcview and VE3D produced similar results for 1x1m grids models. Therefore, it is reasonable to conclude that VE3D can be employed with 5x5m grids models for visibility analysis and evaluation with benefits of processing time and accuracy levels. Moreover, since there were negligible error on 1x1m and 5x5m grids models from Arcview, it is reasonable to compare Arcview with VE3D in 5x5m grids models.

Table 2. Visibility from Each Viewpoint (unit – per cent)

View Change	Software	Grids	Viewpoint														
			1	2	3	4	5	6	7	8	9	10	11	12	13	14	15
Before	Arcview	1×1m	59.6	64.4	64.4	66.4	67.6	42.2	43.0	40.2	33.8	29.5	15.1	16.2	17.2	17.9	18.6
		5×5m	64.0	67.6	68.8	69.3	70.3	56.9	52.8	48.9	36.3	30.6	17.1	18.3	19.5	20.0	20.6
		10×10m	67.5	70.5	72.4	71.8	72.7	50.0	11.5	45.5	40.9	36.4	19.5	21.1	21.8	22.2	23.2
	VE3D	5×5m	56.6	60.6	63.1	63.3	63.9	52.5	48.4	41.1	35.3	34.1	24.2	26.1	27.5	28.6	28.7
		10×10m	54.7	58.9	61.3	61.5	62.4	50.4	45.9	38.4	33.4	31.9	23.3	24.4	26.1	27.5	27.2
After	Arcview	1×1m	8.9	8.8	7.3	9.8	11.9	9.9	9.4	9.7	9.1	8.7	11.7	12.1	12.4	12.8	12.9
		5×5m	7.7	7.6	7.7	8.9	10.4	12.3	10.2	10.5	7.8	6.1	13.1	13.4	13.8	14.0	14.2
		10×10m	9.8	9.9	11.1	11.4	13.0	11.7	3.0	10.5	10.6	10.9	14.3	15.0	15.6	15.4	15.2
	VE3D	5×5m	10.2	10.0	13.9	13.5	15.8	17.4	12.4	10.7	10.9	11.2	13.4	14.0	14.2	14.7	15.1
		10×10m	10.8	10.7	14.2	13.7	16.2	17.2	12.1	10.4	10.5	10.7	13.0	13.6	13.9	14.6	14.7

Nevertheless, it appears to be negligible differences on grid sizes for VE3D resulting visibility. Comparing differences of VE3D and Arcview on visible areas based on grids sizes, ArcView results have average 10-17%; whereas, VE3D results revealed less than 5% error rates. VE3D was found to be taken less impact from grid sizes; therefore, using 10x10m grids models, VE3D would be able to process Visibility Analysis efficiently without compromising accuracy.

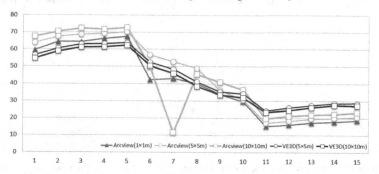

Fig. 5. Relative Error Rates of Visible Areas (After the construction)

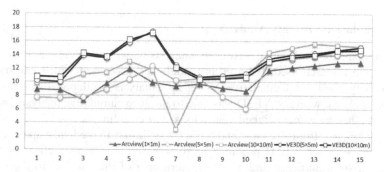

Fig. 6. Relative Error Rates of Visible Areas (Before the construction)

4.3   Visibility Analysis Comparison

The research compared ArcView 3.3 and VE3D processes in 5x5 and 10x10m grids models. Then, visibility results in individual grids models were simulated with three dimensional models in order to compare human eye views to simulated results.

There were a few areas where only ArcView analysis could identify within the before the construction analysis; however, there were large amount of areas where only VE3D analysis could identify in particular, around the concrete flyover and between tower blocks.

This results explained that VE3D, NURBS/vector dataset based, is able to handle visibility analysis process in higher accuracy than ArcView which is based on raster type methods.

Fig. 7. Visibility Analysis before the Construction of Tower Blocks (in grids 5x5, 10x10, and simulation)

Fig. 8. Visibility Analysis after the Construction of Tower Blocks (in grids 5x5, 10x10, and simulation)

4.4   Cumulative Visibility Analysis

In order to compare Cumulative Visibility Analysis between ArcView 3.3 and VE3D generated, the research used 5x5m grids models and processed with same datasets. ArcView only used for Cumulative Visibility Analysis produced from rasterised individual analysis; whereas, VE3D was able to produce cumulative analysis based on distance-weighed and area-weighed values by x, y, z coordinates.

Visual frequency from ArcView and VE3D was similar in the landscape before the construction; however, VE3D provided more intensive results as well as generated different results in northeast and north southern area of the site due to the existing flyover structures. Within the landscape after the construction, visual frequencies were very similar each other results from both ArcView and VE3D because of high rise tower blocks were placed in the site.

The both distance and area weighed measures were produced by divisions from distance or double distance. Distance weighed method indicated that southern part of the site had excellent visibility and area weighed method results shows clear visibility in the southeast part of the site. This could be interpreted as different result to visual frequency. In short, if analysis weights more in viewpoints near the site rather than far off, visibility would be increased in the central or southern parts of the site. Therefore, it is reasonable to conclude that visibility is highly sensitive in central and eastern part of the site.

5   Conclusion

The research aimed to develop a Visibility Analysis programme based on NURBS in order to improve accuracy of the process and result. After case study, VE3D which was developed for Visibility Analysis from vectorised datasets, was able to illustrate high level of detail in visibility identification better than using ArcView 3.3 programme. Moreover, VE3D can produce a Visibility Analysis in reflecting complicated structures such as flyovers and high rise tower blocks.

Carrying out a Visibility Analysis within 10x10m grids models, VE3D can perform the process efficiently as well as contain high level of detail. The research also suggests that VE3D is able to contribute to in-depth and credible Visibility Analysis and this can be achieved by further research on application within various terrains and built up structures.

References

1. Park, B.-J., Furuya, K., Kasetani, T., Takayama, N., Kagawa, T., Miyazaki, Y.: Relationship between psychological responses and physical environments in forest settings. Landscape and Urban Planning 102(1), 24–32 (2011)
2. Kirkpatrick, J.B., Daniels, G.D., Davison, A.: Temporal and spatial variation in garden and street trees in six eastern Australian cities. Landscape and Urban Planning 1021(3), 244–252 (2011)
3. Domingo-Santos, J.M., de Villarán, R.F., Rapp-Arrarás, Í., de Provens, E.C.-P.: The visual exposure in forest and rural landscapes: An algorithm and a GIS tool. Landscape and Urban Planning 101(1), 52–58 (2011)
4. Domon, G.: Landscape as resource: Consequences, challenges and opportunities for rural development. Landscape and Urban Planning 100(1), 338–340 (2011)
5. Jorgensen, A.: Beyond the view: Future directions in landscape aesthetics research. Landscape and Urban Planning 100(1), 353–355 (2011)
6. Anastasopoulos, P.C., Islam, M.B., Perperidou, D., Karlaftis, M.G.: Hazard-Based Analysis of Travel Distance in Urban Environments: Longitudinal Data Approach. Journal of Urban Planning and Development-ASCE 138(1), 53–61 (2012)

7. Zheng, Z., Bohong, Z.: Study on Spatial Structure of Yangtze River Delta Urban Agglomeration and Its Effects on Urban and Rural Regions. Journal of Urban Planning and Development-ASCE 138(1), 78–89 (2012)
8. Lee, D., Choe, H.: Estimating the Impacts of Urban Expansion on Landscape Ecology: Forestland Perspective in the Greater Seoul Metropolitan Area. Journal of Urban Planning and Development-ASCE 137(4), 425–437 (2011)
9. Oakil, A.T.M., Ettema, D., Arentze, T., Timmermans, H.: Longitudinal Model of Longer-Term Mobility Decisions: Framework and First Empirical Tests. Journal of Urban Planning and Development-ASCE 137(3), 220–229 (2011)
10. Hui, E.C.-M., Ng, I.M.-H., Lo, K.-K.: Analysis of the Viability of an Urban Renewal Project under a Risk-Based Option Pricing Framework. Journal of Urban Planning and Development-ASCE 137(2), 101–111 (2011)

A Multi-set Relational Algebra in View of Universal Query Language

Piotr Wiśniewski

Faculty of Mathematics and Computer Science
Nicolaus Copernicus University
Chopina 12/18, 87-100 Toruń
pikonrad@mat.umk.pl

Abstract. The Unified State Model (USM) is a single model that allowed conveying objects of popular programming languages and databases. The USM model exploits and emphase common properties of all objects. The mapping between popular data models and USM has been already shown. In consequence the Universal Query Language (UQL) has been proposed as a set of base operators. UQL pretends to cover most popular query languages and construction of USM and base operators of the UQL has been performed. Examples of simple SQL queries expressed via UQL has been already demonstrated. In this paper we present how operators of a multi-set extended relational algebra can be expressed by UQL operators.

1 Introduction

Our research concentrates on the data models and data languages. There is a lot of data models defined in totally different ways, based on irrelevant theories. As the consequence it is difficult to map precisely map data from one model to another and to compare results of different query languages working on different types of databases. The problem of such mismatch has been already discussed [1]. The universal state model has been proposed which covers most of the models used in databases and programing languages.

The next challenge was construct a language, which can cover the most popular query languages. The relational model proposed in [2] eventually became dominant in data storage there is no sign of a change despite known limitations. Thus we have decided to construct the language, which can cover the SQL language. The proposed language is called *Universal Query Language* and has been presented in [3]. Some SQL examples expressed by the UQL has been presented there.

2 Contribution

Once the UQL has been sucessfule used to express selected SQL querys one would like to extend it to cover all laguage capabilities. The SQL language is based on the relational algebra. So to cover the base of SQL language is enough

T.-h. Kim, Y.-h. Lee, and W.-c. Fang (Eds.): FGIT 2012, LNCS 7709, pp. 233–240, 2012.
© Springer-Verlag Berlin Heidelberg 2012

to cover the relational algebra operators. In the [1] we present the relational model by meaning of Grefen [4] so consequently by the operators of relational algebra we mean operators of multiset relational algebra defined by Grefen. The main contribution of this paper is expression of operators of multiset relational algebra using UQL operators.

3 Universal State Model

In this Section we remind some definition of the Unified State Model (USM) introduced in [1] and we remind the definitions of the multiset relational model proposed by Grefen in [4]

We use the following symbols. V is a set of atomic values. We assume that it contains all simple values. $N \subset V$ is a set of *external* names of objects with a chosen value $\eta \in N$ to tag nameless objects. External names are used by designers and programmers to access objects. Nameless objects can only be accessed through object references. $I \subset V$ is a set of *identities* with a chosen value $\mathbf{nil} \in I$ to represent empty identifier/address. We assume that $N \cap I = \emptyset$.

For any set S we denote by $S^* = \bigoplus_{t \in \mathcal{N}} S$, i.e. the set of all finite sequence of elements of S.

3.1 Simple Object

Definition. *A state of an object of the level* 0 *is a triple* $(i, n, v) \in I \times N \times V$. By O_0 we mean the set of all states of the level 0. This set is also denoted by S_0.

The simple objects can represent cels in relational model or properties of objects in programing language as is presented on following exaple:

$$o_1 = (i_1, name, "Jan")$$
$$o_2 = (i_2, sname, "Kowalski")$$
$$o_3 = (i_3, address\_id, 2)$$

3.2 Complex Objects

Definition. Let $t \in \mathcal{N}$ be a positive natural number and assume that we have defined states of objects of the level k for all $k < t$ and S_{t-1} denotes the set of all states of objects of the levels lesser than t. A state of an object of the level t is a triple $(i, n, L) \notin S_{t-1}$ where $i \in I, n \in N$ and $L \in S_{t-1}^*$ is a finite sequence of elements of S_{t-1} and $L \notin S_{t-2}^*$ (with assumption $S_{-1} = \emptyset$).

The set of all states of objects of the level t will be denoted by O_t. By $S_t = O_t \cup S_{t-1}$ we denote the set of all states of objects of the levels not greater than t. Members of the list L will be called states of subobjects of the object state o.

In [1] we have formally defined the notion of *proper* states. In a proper state no object identity is repeated and all object references are valid, i.e. there are no dangling pointer objects.

We also provide some notions:

- S_∞ is the set of all states of objects of all natural levels.
- **S** is the set of all proper states.

3.3   Relational Model

The aim of the paper is to express the multiset relational algebra operators in UQL, thus we need also to remind some information on the mapping between USM and the relational model presented in [1]. Our analysis of the relational data model is based on the multi-set extended relational algebra [4].

Let $\mathcal{R}$ be a relational schema, also called the type of a relation denoted by $dom(R)$ such that $dom(R) = dom(A_1) \times ... \times dom(A_n)$, where $dom(A) \subset V$ is some domain.

We define a tuple of a relation of type $dom(R)$ as a state of an object $o = (i, R, o_1, ..., o_n)$ such that for $k = 1, ..., n$; $o_k = (i_k, A_k, v_k)$ is an atomic object such that $v_k \in dom(A_k)$. In particular, a tuple $o \in O_1$ is a state of the first level. Let us recall a definition from [1]:

Definition. The tuples $o = (i, R, o_1, ..., o_n), o' = (i', R, o'_1, ..., o'_n)$ shall be called *relationally equal* if for all $k = 1, ..., n$ it holds that $v_k = v'_k$.

Let us consider the table **person** with five columns **id, name, sname,** and **address**. The two object states o and o':

$$o = (i, (person, \qquad\qquad o' = (i', (person,$$
$$(i_0, id, 1) \qquad\qquad\qquad (i'_0, id, 1)$$
$$(i_1, name, "Jan") \qquad\qquad (i'_1, name, "Jan")$$
$$(i_2, sname, "Kowalski") \qquad (i'_2, sname, "Kowalski")$$
$$(i_3, address\_id, 2) \qquad\qquad (i'_3, address\_id, 2)$$
$$)) \in O_1 \qquad\qquad\qquad)) \in O_1$$

represent the followind tuple:

```
id | name |   sname   | address
---+------+-----------+---------
 1 | Jan  | Kowalski  |    2
```

Although they are different, they are relationally equal.

Next we deal with relations that are defined by Grefen [4] as multisets of tuples.

The state of a relation R is any object (i, R, T), where T is a sequence of tuples of the type R.

Definition. Let the states $o = (i, R, T) \in O_2$ and $o' = (i', R, T') \in O_2$ be of the second level, where T and T' are sequences of states of the first level. Assume also that $o \approx_R o'$. States o and o' are called relationally equal iff $|T| = |T'|$ and there is a permutation p of the sequence T, such that for each $t = 1, ..., |T|$ the states of the tuples $p(T)_t$ and T'_t are relationally equal.

Note that the *relational equality* of states defined above is an equivalence relation and:

- The simple objects represent cels.
- The first level object represent tuples.
- The second level objects represent relations (tables).
- The third level objects represent relational databases.

Let $\mathcal{R} = (i, R, T)$ be a state of a relation R of a type $dom(R)$. For any tuple $v = (v_1, ..., v_n) \in dom(R)$ we define

$$\Psi_{\mathcal{R}}(v) = |\{o \in T; Rel(o) = v\}|,$$

as a number of tuple objects corresponding to the tuple v.

Such function establishes the multiset of tuples of a relation of type $dom(R)$. Such multiset is called the instance of a relation of a type $dom(R)$ in [4]. By using this function we may characterize than states $\mathcal{R} = (i, R, T), \mathcal{R}' = (i', R, T')$ of a relation R are relationally equal iff $\Psi_{\mathcal{R}}(v) = \Psi_{\mathcal{R}'}(v)$ for any $v \in dom(R)$ Such characteristics leads us to the following conclusion:

There exists a mutual correspondence between instances of relations defined in [4], and the equivalence classes of relational equality of states defined above.

This considerations show that the relational model in terms of the multiset theory is expressible as equivalence classes of the relational equality of states in USM. The corresponding states of the matching relation instances are included in the S_2, while the states corresponding to the tuples are included in the S_1.

4   UQL Operators

In this Section we remind operators of the Universal Query Language (UQL). The most of them have been presented in [3]. In this text we will assume, that the set of identifiers is well ordered, and in the result of operators are constructed with the minimal identifiers bigger than identifiers used in arguments. Thus all result are proper states.

4.1   Build

Assume that we have some objects $o_1, o_2, ..., o_t$. Operator build construct the enveloping object of them.

$$build(o_1, o_2, ..., o_t) = (i, \eta, (o_1, o_2, ..., o_t))$$

4.2   Flattening

For a complex object the operator $flatten$ replaces its subjects with the contents of these subobjects. If the argument complex object is simple or has any simple subjects, $flat$ returns an empty object. Assume $o = (i, n, (o_1, o_2, \ldots, o_k))$. If for all $t = 1 \ldots k$ $o_t \notin O_0$ and $o_t = (i_t, n_t, (o_{t,1}, \ldots, o_{t,j_t}))$, then

$$flatten(o) = (i, n, (o_{1,1}, o_{1,2}, \ldots, o_{1,j_1}, o_{2,1}, \ldots, o_{k,j_k}))$$

Otherwise:

$$flatten(o) = (i, n, nil)$$

4.3 Mapping

The purpose of the operator map is the application of a function to all subobjects of the given object. The functor $map : \mathbf{S}^{\mathbf{S}} \to \mathbf{S}^{\mathbf{S}}$ is defined as follows. Let $f : \mathbf{S} \to \mathbf{S}$ be the function to be applied. Then:

$$map(f)(o) = \begin{cases} (i, n, (f(o_1), \ldots, f(o_n))) & \text{if } o = (i, n, (o_1, o_2, \ldots, o_k)) \notin O_0 \\ (i, n, nil) & \text{if } o \in O_0. \end{cases}$$

4.4 Getting k-th Subobject

Let $o = (i, n, (o_1, o_2, \ldots, o_t))$ be a state of an object. We define:

$$get_k(i, n, (o_1, \ldots, o_t)) = \begin{cases} o_k & \text{if } k < t \text{ and} \\ (i', \eta, \mathbf{nil}) & \text{otherwise.} \end{cases}$$

4.5 Filtering

Filtering is also performed by a functor. Assume a function $p : \mathbf{S} \to V$ that returns Boolean values. Then:

$$filter(p)(o = (i, n, (o_1, o_2, \ldots, o_k))) = (i, n, (o_{i_1}, o_{i_2}, \ldots, o_{i'_k}))$$

where the sequence $(o_{i_1}, o_{i_2}, \ldots, o_{i'_k})$ is the subsequence of $(o_1, o_2, \ldots, o_k)$ composed of all objects o_j such that $eval_1(p(o_j)) = true$.

4.6 Nesting

The operator $nest$ creates a new nameless object and puts the argument object into it:

$$nest(o) = (i', \eta, o)$$

4.7 Product

Let $o = (i, n, (o_1, ..., o_t))$, $o' = (i', n', (o'_1, ..., o'_{t'}))$ be complex objects. The *cross* product operator is defined as follows:

$$cross(o, o') = (i, \eta, ((o_{11}, ..., o_{1t'}, ..., o_{tt'}), \text{ where } o_{jk} = (i_{jk}, \eta, (o_j, o'_k))$$

4.8 Grouping

Let $\approx$ be an equivalence relation on a subset of states $S \subset S_\infty$. Let $o = (i, n, (o_1, ..., o_t))$ be a complex object such that $\{o_1, ..., o_t\} \subset S$. The operator *abstract* is defined as follows:

$$abstract_\approx(o) = (i', n, (u_1, ..., u_k))$$

where $u_j = (i_j, n, (o_{j1}, ..., o_{jt_j}))$ and the following conditions are satisfied:

a. The sequence $(o_{j1}, ..., o_{jt_j})$ is a subsequence of $(o_1, ..., o_t)$ for all $j = 1, ..., k$ and the sequence $o_{11}, ..., o_{k1}$ is a subsequence of $(o_1, ..., o_t)$.

b. The items in $(o_{j1}, ..., o_{jt_j})$ are pairwise related with respect to $\approx$.

c. For any $j \neq j'$ and m, m' it is true that $o_{jm} \not\approx o_{j'm'}$.

4.9   Subtraction

When we think about subtraction, we cannot expect direct set subtraction. Assume that we have to objects $o' = (i', n', (o'_1, ..., o'_t))$, $o'' = (i'', n'', (o''_1, ..., o''_k))$ or $o'' = (i'', n'', nil)$ and the object who envelops them $o = (i, n, (o', o''))$. We define a difference operator as follows:

$$differ(o) = \begin{cases} (i, n, (o'_1, ..., o'_{t-k})) & \text{, if } t > k \\ (i, n, nil) & \text{, if } t \leq k \\ (i, n, (o'_1, ..., o'_t)) & \text{, if } o'' = (i'', n'', nil) \end{cases}$$

5   Multiset Relational Algebra

This section presents the standard relational algebra operators expressed by UQL operators.

5.1   Base Tuple Operators

Grefen presents a tuple concatenation operator $r_1 \oplus r_2$. It is an easy observation, that if o_1, o_2 represents tuples r_1, r_2 then $flatten(build(o_1, o_2))$ represents the tuple $r_1 \oplus r_2$.

Selection π_σ where σ is a subset of attributes of type of relation is also easy :

$$\pi_\sigma(o) = filter_{name \in \sigma}(o)$$

where o is an object representing a tuple.

5.2   Union

For two o, o' relational states of type $dom(R)$ we want to obtain the state being their (multi)set-theoretic union. We simply use $flatten$ on the enveloping object:

$$o \uplus o' := flatten(build(o, o'))$$

5.3   Distinct

For a relational state $o = (i, R, T)$ we want to obtain the new state without duplicates in terms of some equivalence $\approx$ on tuples. Thus:

$$distinct(o) = flatten(map(get_1, (abstract_{\approx_R}(o))))$$

5.4   Difference

Let $o, o' \in O_2$ are object represents relations R_1, R_2 of the same relation type$\mathcal{R}$ and let $db = (i, n, o_1, o_2)$. We want tu calculate $R_2 -_{Rel} R_2$

In the first step we group equivalence tuples of the left side and nest R_2 on the right side.

$$abne = (map(abstract \approx \otimes nest, db)$$

Next we make Cartesian product of such sequences.

$$cr = cross(abne)$$

The pairs in the product contain on the left sequences of equivalent tuples, on the right all R_2. Now we can filter right sides of the pairs.

$$fltr = map(id \otimes filter_{get_1(get_1)} \approx ..., cr)$$

Each subobject of the fltr contain two sequences of equivalent tuples or sequence on left and the nil object on the right. First sequence come from R_1 second from R_2. If there is a nil object on the right means there was no corresponding tuple in R_2. Then the last step is to subtract and "smooth" result.

$$diff_{Rel}(db) = map(flatten, filter_{isnotnil}(map(differ, fltr)))$$

Thus the relational difference of two relation $db = (i, n, o_1, o_2)$ in UQL is:

$$
\begin{aligned}
diff_{Rel}(db) = map(&flatten, filter_{isnotnil}(map(differ, \\
&map(id \otimes filter_{get_1(get_1)} \approx (...), cross(\\
&map(abstract \approx \otimes nest, db) \\
&)) \\
&)))
\end{aligned}
$$

5.5   Product

The product of two relations $R_1 \times R_2$ represented by the objects $o, o' \in O_2$ enveloped by $db = (i, n, o_1, o_2)$ is represented by the following object:

$$map(flatten, cross(db))$$

5.6   Selection

Selection $\sigma_\phi R$ is easy realized by the $filter$ operator:

$$filter_\phi(o)$$

where o represents a relation R.

5.7   Projection

The projection is nothing else then selection mapped into tuples, thus for a relation R represented by an object o the projection π_σ on the attributes σ is as follows:

$$\pi_\sigma(o) = map(filter_{name \in \sigma}, o)$$

5.8   Intersetction and Joins

Following the theorem 3.1 from the [4] The join and intersection operators are redundant, they can be constructed as follows:

$$R_1 \cap R_2 = R_1 -_{Rel} (R_2 -_{Rel} R_1)$$
$$R_1 \bowtie_\phi R_2 = \sigma_\phi(R_1 \times R_2)$$

6   Conclusions

In the prequel paper the SQL examples expressed in UQL has been presented. This work describes how the operators of the multiset standard relational algebra proposed by Grefen could be expressed using UQL. The next challenge is to construct operators of a multi-set extended relational algebra.

References

1. Wiśniewski, P., Burzańska, M., Stencel, K.: The impedance mismatch in light of the unified state model. Fundam. Inform. (to appear, 2012)
2. Codd, E.F.: A relational model of data for large shared data banks. Commun. ACM 13, 377–387 (1970)
3. Wiśniewski, P., Stencel, K.: Universal query language. In: Proceedings of the CS&P Conference, Berlin (2012)
4. Grefen, P.W.P.J., de By, R.A.: A multi-set extended relational algebra - a formal approach to a practical issue. In: ICDE, pp. 80–88. IEEE Computer Society (1994)

Using Particle Swarm Optimization
for Image Regions Annotation

Mohamed Sami[1,*], Nashwa El-Bendary[2,*], Tai-hoon Kim[3,*],
and Aboul Ella Hassanien[1,*]

[1] Cairo University, Faculty of Computers and Information, Cairo, Egypt
{mohamed.sami,abo}@egyptscience.net
[2] Arab Academy for Science, Technology, and Maritime Transport, Cairo, Egypt
nashwa.elbendary@ieee.org
[3] School of Information Science, University of Tasmania, Australia
taihoonn@empas.com

Abstract. In this paper, we propose an automatic image annotation approach for region labeling that takes advantage of both context and semantics present in segmented images. The proposed approach is based on multi-class K-nearest neighbor, k-means and particle swarm optimization (PSO) algorithms for feature weighting, in conjunction with normalized cuts-based image segmentation technique. This hybrid approach refines the output of multi-class classification that is based on the usage of K-nearest neighbor classifier for automatically labeling images regions from different classes. Each input image is segmented using the normalized cuts segmentation algorithm then a descriptor created for each segment. The PSO algorithm is employed as a search strategy for identifying an optimal feature subset. Extensive experimental results demonstrate that the proposed approach provides an increase in accuracy of annotation performance by about 40%, via applying PSO models, compared to having no PSO models applied, for the used dataset.

1   Introduction

With advent of digital imaging modalities, such as the increasingly affordable digital cameras and the widespread of personal computers, lead to build up a huge volume of digital images that are available in the digital libraries and on the web. This growth raises the demand to increase the usefulness of these large images archives. There is a growing need to have applications that effectively search and index these images. By using text query, images could be found in a manner that would meet the different needs of many users as most users prefer textual keyword search instead of content based image retrieval systems that ask user to enter image samples or low level features descriptions as query. Therefore, the importance of image annotation techniques for automatically assigning labels to images in order to fill the gap between the visual features search and the semantic means is rapidly increasing.

In this paper, we present an approach based on multi-class K-nearest neighbor (K-NN) classifier, K-means clustering, and particle swarm optimization (PSO) algorithm.

---

* Scientific Research Group in Egypt (SRGE), http://www.egyptscience.net

T.-h. Kim, Y.-h. Lee, and W.-c. Fang (Eds.): FGIT 2012, LNCS 7709, pp. 241–250, 2012.
© Springer-Verlag Berlin Heidelberg 2012

The common PSO [1], Trelea [2], and Clerc [3] models have been applied. We used the same normalized cuts-based algorithm for segmentation, visual features, and data-set as in [4]. Particle swarm optimization algorithm is used in our proposed approach for weighting feature vectors. The PSO fitness function includes the usage of K-NN and K-means algorithms as well as training and testing data. We used K-means to find the centroid of each class training data, and we use K-NN to find the closest class for each new feature vector.

The rest of this paper is organized as follows. Section 2 gives an overview of K-NN and particle swarm optimization algorithms. Section 3 presents the different phases of the proposed hybrid image annotation approach. Section 4 shows the obtained experimental results. Finally, Section 5 addresses conclusions and discusses future work.

2   K-Nearest Neighbor (K-NN) and Particle Swarm Optimization (PSO): Preliminaries

Due to space limitations we provide only a brief explanation of the basic framework of K-NN theory and particle swarm optimization algorithm, along with some of the key definitions. A more comprehensive review can be found in sources such as [1–3, 5–7].

2.1   K-Nearest Neighbor (K-NN)

The K-nearest neighbor (K-NN) method was first introduced by Fix and Hodges in 1951, and was one of the most popular nonparametric methods used for classification of new object based on attributes and training samples. The K-NN consists of a supervised learning algorithm where the result of a new instance query is classified based on the majority of the K-nearest neighbor category [8]. The K-NN method has been successfully applied in many areas: statistical estimation, pattern recognition, artificial intelligence, categorical problems, and feature selection. One advantage of the K-NN method is that it is simple and easy to implement.

K-NN is not negatively affected when training data are large, and indifferent to noisy training data. Disadvantages of the K-NN method are the need to determine parameter K (number of nearest neighbors), calculate the distances between the query instance and all the training samples, sort the distances and determine the nearest neighbors based on the Kth minimum distance, as well as determine the categories of the nearest neighbors.

2.2   Particle Swarm Optimization (PSO)

The concept of particle swarms, although initially introduced for simulating human social behaviors, has become very popular these days as an efficient search and optimization technique. Particle swarm optimization [1–3], does not require any gradient information of the function to be optimized, uses only primitive mathematical operators and is conceptually very simple. PSO has attracted the attention of a lot of researchers resulting into a large number of variants of the basic algorithm as well as many parameter automation strategies. The canonical PSO model consists of a swarm of particles, which are initialized with a population of random candidate solutions. They move iteratively through the d-dimension problem space to search the new solutions, where the fitness, f, can be calculated as the certain qualities measure. Each particle has a position represented by a position-vector x_i (i is the index of the particle), and a velocity represented by a velocity-vector v_i. Each particle remembers its own best position so far in a vector $x_i^{\#}$, and its j-th dimensional value is $x_{ij}^{\#}$. The best position-vector among the swarm so far is then stored in a vector x^*, and its j-th dimensional value is x_j^*. During the iteration time t, the update of the velocity from the previous velocity to the new velocity is determined by equation (1). The new position is then determined by the sum of the previous position and the new velocity by equation (2).

$$v_{ij}(t+1) = wv_{ij}(t) + c_1 r_1 (x_{ij}^{\#}(t) - x_{ij}(t)) + c_2 r_2 (x_j^*(t) - x_{ij}(t)) \tag{1}$$

$$x_{ij}(t+1) = x_{ij}(t) + v_{ij}(t+1) \tag{2}$$

Where w is called as the inertia factor, which governs how much the previous velocity should be retained from the previous time step, r_1 and r_2 are the random numbers, which are used to maintain the diversity of the population, and are uniformly distributed in the interval $[0,1]$ for the j-th dimension of the i-th particle. c_1 is a positive constant, called as coefficient of the self-recognition component, c_2 is a positive constant, called as coefficient of the social component. From equation (1), a particle decides where to move next, considering its own experience, which is the memory of its best past position, and the experience of its most successful particle in the swarm. In the particle swarm model, the particle searches the solutions in the problem space with a range $[-s, s]$ (if the range is not symmetrical, it can be translated to the corresponding symmetrical range). In order to guide the particles effectively in the search space, the maximum moving distance during one iteration must be clamped in between the maximum velocity $[-v_{max}, v_{max}]$ given in equation (3):

$$v_{ij} = sign(v_{ij}) min(|v_{ij}|, v_{max}) \tag{3}$$

The value of v_{max} is $p \times s$, with $0.1 \leq p \leq 1.0$ and is usually chosen to be s, i.e. $p = 1$. The end criteria are usually one of the following:

– maximum number of iterations
– number of iterations without improvement
– minimum objective function error

3 Automatic Image Regions Annotation Approach

The intelligent PSO-based image regions annotation approach proposed in this paper is composed of four phases; namely, *segmentation phase*, where the input image is segmented into regions using normalized cuts algorithm, *feature extraction phase*, where a feature vector per segmented region is extracted, *feature optimization phase*, which applies a particle swarm optimization for features weighting per class, and finally *classification and annotation phase*, where the optimized weights are used with K-NN and K-Means for classification. This section describes each of these phases in details. An overview of the proposed approach is depicted in figure 1.

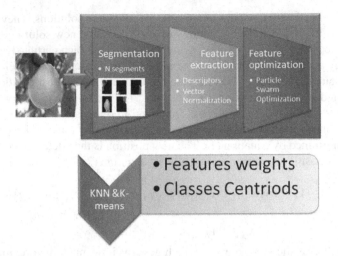

Fig. 1. Intelligent automatic image regions annotation system architecture

3.1   Segmentation Phase

In our proposed approach we aim to automatically annotate images based on regions. Therefore, the need for an image segmentation step is evident. For this, we applied the normalized cuts segmentation algorithm [9, 10], which formulates image segmentation as a graph partitioning problem and uses the normalized cut value between different graph groups.

In the employed graph theoretic formulation of grouping, a set of points in an arbitrary feature space is represented as a weighted undirected graph $G(V,E)$, where the nodes of the graph are the points in feature space, and an edge is formed between every pair of nodes. The weight on each edge $w(i,j)$ is a function of the similarity between nodes i and j. A graph $G(V,E)$ is partitioned into two disjoint sets A and B, where $A \bigcup B = V$ and $A \bigcap B = \phi$, by removing edges and hence performing a cut. The segment cut between A and B is defined as presented in equation (4).

$$cut(A,B) = \sum_{u \in A, v \in B} w(u,v) \tag{4}$$

The optimal partitioning is the one that minimizes the cut value. In order to avoid partitioning out small sets of points, instead of looking at total edge weights between the two parts, a fraction of cut cost for total edge connections to all the nodes in graph is calculated resulting what is called normalized cut given by equation (5).

$$Ncut(A,B) = \frac{Cut(A,B)}{assoc(A,V)} + \frac{Cut(A,B)}{assoc(B,V)} \tag{5}$$

Where, $assoc(A,V) = \sum_{u \in A, t \in V} w(u,t)$ is the total connection from nodes in group A to all nodes in the graph and $assoc(B,V)$ is similarly defined. In our approach, we segment every input image into five regions.

3.2   Feature Extraction Phase

During this phase, each image segment is represented by a visual feature vector characterizing its color, texture, and shape contents. A comprehensive list of the 83 features we have employed is given in Table 1.

Table 1. Region features

Feature Name	Length	Type	Details
Color Mean	3	Color	For RGB
Color StdDev	3	Color	For RGB
Segment size	1	Global	Number of pixels in image
Entropy	1	Global	
Moment	3	Global	For RGB
Dominant Color	4	Color	Color percentage to image with RGB
Eccentricity	1	Shape	Scalar that specifies the eccentricity of the ellipse that has the same second-moments as the region
Orientation	1	Shape	The angle (in degrees ranging from -90 to 90 degrees) between the x-axis and the major axis of the ellipse that has the same second-moments as the region
Convex Area	1	Shape	Scalar that specifies the number of pixels in the binary image that specifies the convex hull
Filled Area	1	Shape	Scalar specifying the number of on pixels in the binary image of the same size as region
Euler Number	1	Shape	Scalar that specifies the number of objects in the region minus the number of holes in those objects
Equiv Diameter	1	Shape	Scalar that specifies the diameter of a circle with the same area as the region
Solidity	1	Shape	Scalar specifying the proportion of the pixels in the convex hull that are also in the region
Perimeter	1	Shape	The distance around the boundary of the region
Gabor Filter	60	Texture	5 scales, 6 orientations
Total	83		

3.3   Feature Optimization Phase

A computational iterative PSO method, which works on a population of candidate solutions that are called particles. These particles follow mathematical formula and moving in search space. There are a local best position that influence each particle in this space. This best position is updated if a better position is found during the iterative search process. By this particle's movement the swarm should move toward the best solution available. The K-means algorithm is used to find the centroid of each class based on its belonged feature vectors. For the classification of any new non-labeled feature vector, the K-NN classifier with euclidian distance is used to find the closet class's centroid.

For the proposed approach, we used PSO coupled with K-means in order to optimize the feature set for image annotation per class. We applied real number particle swarm candidate solutions as weight. We have used four models for PSO algorithm, namely; common PSO, Trelea-1, Trelea-2, and Clerc models [1–3]. The length of each particle swarm is calculated according to equation (6).

$$Length = NumberOfClasses * NumberOfDescriptors \qquad (6)$$

The fitness function of the PSO is based on K-NN evaluation with instance particle. Each class has its own training data and its own part of particle candidate that is used as feature weighting. After calculating all the centroids based on the training data and the weights, test data is used for evaluating the current weights. A fitness function is used to evaluate every particle using the centroids that have calculated and the K-NN for test data classification. Algorithm (1) describes the fitness value calculation. Table 2 defines the meaning of each parameter used in algorithm (1).

Table 2. Parameters used in Algorithm (1)

Parameter	Description
N	Number of classes including the background class
IndexTrain	Current training data item from certain class
T	Total number of test data
Centroid	Array of all classes centroids
Distance	Array distances between a specific data to all centroids
ExpectedClass	Correct current label of testing data

3.4   Classification/Annotation Phase

In this phase, we experiment particle swarm optimization algorithm with four different models, namely; the common PSO, Trelea-1, Trelea-2, and Clerc models [1–3]. K-means algorithm was used for evaluating the centroids of different data classes and K-NN classifier was used as well for the classification of test data. We assumed that there are N classes including a background class. For a new unknown feature vector, it is firstly normalized, then weighted and classified based on the already calculated centroids. The distance for all centroids is calculated and also the minimum distance points to the corresponding class.

4   Experimental Results

The proposed approach has been evaluated using six classes of fruit images: apple, banana, grapes, mango, orange, and watermelon, in addition to a class for background. Each class has in average about 15 training feature vectors and 10 for testing feature vectors, however the background class has the highest number of vectors which is 216 in training and 101 in testing. Each image is segmented, as previously mentioned, into five segments using the normalized cuts algorithm. Each segment was manually annotated to provide a ground truth. Table 3 and table 4 show the number of testing regions in

Algorithm 1. Fitness value calculation algorithm

```
1:  for i=1 to N do
2:      Compute: TrainingDataWeighted(j) = TrainingData(i) * Weights(i)
3:      Train: Centroid(i)=Caculate-Centroid-KMeans(TrainingDataWeighted, TrainingLabels)
4:  end for
5:  Result = Array of centroids for each class
6:  for x=1 to T do
7:      for y=1 to N do
8:          Compute: TestingDataWeighted = TestingData(x) * Weights(y)
9:          Compute: Distance(y) = KNN.classify((TestingDataWeighted),Centroid(y))
10:     end for
11:     Result =Find index of minimum value in Distances array
12:     if Result = ExpectedClass then
13:         Increase the total number of correct labels
14:     end if
15: end for
16: Compute: the fitness value of current iteration as:
```

$$FitnessValue = \frac{TotalNumberOfCorrectLabels}{TotalTestData} \qquad (7)$$

(A:actual) when using Trelea-1 parameter set for PSO and (E:expected) which is the ground truth for each class and the distribution of classes feature vectors, respectively. Figure 2 shows some normalized cuts segmentation results.

Table 3. Number of testing regions in (A:actual) and (E:expected) for each class

Class	A:actual:	E:expected
Grapes	1	9
Apple	6	6
Banana	5	8
Mango	7	12
Orange	5	8
Watermelon	3	6
Background	100	101
Total Number Of regions	127	150
Accuracy	84.67%	

For the PSO algorithm we have used a population size of 200, maximum iteration equal 400, inertia weights equal 0.9 and 0.6. acceleration constant equals 2.1, and the lowest error gradient tolerance value is 1e-99. The starting particle positions are random, and the particle values range is -100 to 100.

Table 5 shows obtained accuracy using the proposed approach without using any PSO model and through applying the four previously mentioned PSO models. As illustrated in table 5, the maximum accuracy achieved was via using the Trelea PSO models $\simeq 84\%$ compared to $\simeq 45\%$ without having any PSO models used.

248   M. Sami et al.

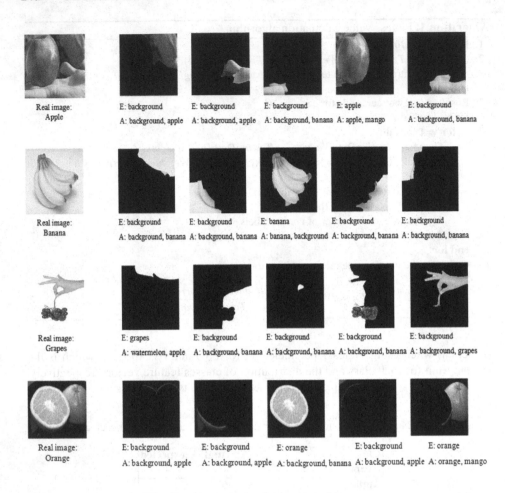

E: Expected label, A: Actual results (First closest, Second closest)

Fig. 2. Examples of normalized cuts segmentation results

Table 4. Distribution of classes feature vectors

Class	Training vectors	Testing vectors
apple	13	6
banana	13	8
grapes	19	9
mango	11	12
orange	14	8
watermelon	14	6
background	216	101

That obtained annotation accuracy percentage is not optimal due to a number of reasons such as the limited dataset used with addition to mistakes happen sometimes in our manual annotation of training and testing regions. Also, the wrong segmentation of images taking in mind the variation in size and quality of images dataset represent another reason for the accuracy achieved. Moreover, some images are poorly segmented and wrongly classified as the number of regions representing fruits classes is very small compared to background classes.

For watermelon and mango classes, poor labeling results have been obtained due to poor segmentation as segmentation doesn't precisely segment objects and errors are generated due to manual labeling. Also, the number of regions representing background classes is very large compared to other fruits classes. Moreover, the number of test segments for watermelon and the number of training segments for the mango were the lowest. Furthermore, grapes class has the maximum number of training segments and also most of the misclassified mango segments were labeled as grapes, we have to mention that the worst segmentation results are in the grapes class images. These reasons for poor labeling results will be considered for further research.

Table 5. Results for different PSO Models

Models	Accuracy
Without-PSO	44.67%
Common PSO	82.00%
Trelea-1	84.67%
Trelea-2	84.00%
Clerc	82.00%

5   Conclusions and Future Work

In this paper, we have presented an automatic image regions annotation approach for region labeling that takes advantage of both context and semantics present in segmented images. The proposed approach is based on KNN classifier, K-means and particle swarm optimization (PSO) algorithms. The PSO was used for weighting the features vectors and this has increased the annotation performance by about 40% with achieving maximum annotation accuracy $\simeq 84\%$. Our focus in the future work is validating the current work proposed in this paper using a larger dataset, and also implementing new techniques for optimizing weighting and features selection. Moreover, we are going to consider using different image segmentation techniques in order to overcome the miss segmentations in our model. Currently, we are working on the imageclef [11] dataset.

References

1. Kennedy, J., Eberhart, R.: Particle Swarm Optimization. In: Proceedings of IEEE International Conference on Neural Networks, vol. 4, pp. 1942–1948 (1995)
2. Trelea, I.C.: The Particle Swarm Optimization Algorithm: convergence analysis and parameter selection. Information Processing Letters 85(6), 317–325 (2003)

3. Clerc, M., Kennedy, J.: The particle swarm - explosion, stability, and convergence in a multidimensional complex space. IEEE Transactions on Evolutionary Computation 6(1), 58–73 (2003)
4. Sami, M., El-Bendary, N., Hassanien, A.E., Schaefer, G.: Hybrid Intelligent Automatic Image Annotation Using Machine Learning. In: The 2011 Online Conference on Soft Computing in Industrial Applications WWW (WSC16) (2011)
5. Viswanath, P., Sarma, T.H.: An improvement to k-nearest neighbor classifier. In: Proceedings of IEEE Int. Conference on Recent Advances in Intelligent Computational Systems (RAICS), pp. 227–231 (2011)
6. Qiang, H., Aibing, J., Qiang, H.: Multiple Real-valued K nearest neighbor classifiers system by feature grouping. In: Proceedings of IEEE International Conference on Systems Man and Cybernetics (SMC), pp. 3922–3925 (2010)
7. Lin, L., Qi, L., Jun-yong, L., Chuan, L.: An improved particle swarm optimization algorithm. In: Proceedings of IEEE International Conference on Granular Computing (GrC 2008), pp. 486–490 (2008)
8. Castillo, O., Xu, L., Ao, S.I.: Trends in Intelligent Systems and Computer Engineering. Springer (2008)
9. Cai, W., Wu, J., Chung, A.C.S.: Shape-based image segmentation using normalized cuts. In: IEEE Int. Conference on Image Processing, pp. 1101–1104 (2006)
10. Shi, J., Malik, J.: Normalized cuts and image segmentation. IEEE Trans. Pattern Analysis and Machine Intelligence 22(8), 888–905 (2000)
11. Imageclef dataset website, http://www.imageclef.org/datasets

On Architecture Warehouses
and Software Intelligence

Robert Dąbrowski*

Institute of Informatics
Warsaw University
Banacha 2, 02-097 Warsaw, Poland
r.dabrowski@mimuw.edu.pl

Abstract. By architecture of a software system we typically denote the knowledge about the organization of the system, the relationships among its components and the principles governing their design. By including artifacts coresponding to software engineering processes, the definition gets naturally extended into the architecture of a software system and process. This paper recalls theoretical model for representing architectural knowledge based on directed multi-graph, defines an *architecture warehouse* implementation of the model capable of representing the complete architecture of a software system and process, and shows how it can be harnessed to create a *software intelligence* layer providing software architects with a toolset for software analysis and visualisation. The reasoning is supported by examples depicting warehouse implementation and results obtained from its application to a sample software project.

Keywords: architecture, graph, intelligence, metric, model, software, warehouse.

1 Introduction

As long as there were no software systems, managing their architecture was no problem at all; when there were only simple systems, managing their architecture became a mild problem; and now we have gigantic software systems, and managing their architecture has become an equally gigantic problem (to paraphrase Edsger Dijkstra).

Nowadays software systems are being developed by teams that are: changing over time; working under time pressure; working over incomplete specification and changing requirements; integrating unfamiliar source-code in multiple development technologies, programming languages, coding standards; productively delivering only partially completed releases in iterative development cycles. When development issues arise (bugs, changes, extensions), they frequently lead to refactoring of the software system, the software process or both. Even if the issues get addressed promptly, they often return in consecutive releases due

---

* Supported by the Polish National Science Centre grant 2011/01/B/ST6/03867.

T.-h. Kim, Y.-h. Lee, and W.-c. Fang (Eds.): FGIT 2012, LNCS 7709, pp. 251–262, 2012.

to volatile team structure, insufficient flow of information, inability to properly manage architectural knowledge about the software system and the software process. Unsurprisingly such challenges have already been identified and software engineering is focused on their resolution. There emerged a number of software development methodologies (e.g. structured, iterative, adaptive), design models (e.g. Entity Relationship Diagram, Data Flow Diagram, State Transition Diagram), development languages (e.g. functional, object-oriented, aspect-oriented) and production management tools (e.g. issue trackers, build and configuration managers, source-code analyzers). Although they address important areas, it still remains a challenge to integrate those methodologies, standards, languages, metrics, tools into a consistent environment suitable for a software architect to browse and analyse the system's architecture. For software practitioners this current lack of integration of architectural knowledge is a historical condition: while software was limited to a small number of files delivered in one programming language and built into a single executable, it was possible to browse the artifacts in a *list* mode (file by file; or procedure by procedure). Next, as software projects evolved to become more complex and sophisticated, the idea of a software project organized according to a *tree* (folders, subfolders and files; or classes, subclasses and methods) emerged to allow browsing artifacts in a hierarchical approach. This is no longer enough. Although software engineering is going in the right direction, the research will lack the proper momentum without a sound model to support integration of current trends, technologies, languages. A new vision for architectural repository of a software system and software process is a must and this paper defines one. It assumes all software system and software process artifacts being created during a software project are modelled as vertices of a graph connected by multiple edges that represent multiple kinds of dependencies among those artifacts. Then the key aspects of software production like quality, predictability, automation and metrics are conveniently expressible in graph-based terms. Such integration of system and process artifacts in a single model opens new possibilities, that include ie. defining new metrics and qualities that take into account all architectural knowledge, not only the source code.

The paper is organized as follows. Section 2 analyzes the background that motivated presented approach. Section 3 recalls the theoretical model for representing *warehouse of architectural knowledge* based on directed multigraphs and presents its proof-of-concept implementation using current technologies. Section 4 defines a *software intelligence* layer providing tools for software analysis and visualisation. Section 5 concludes the paper and enumerates challenges for further research. The reasoning is supported by examples demonstrating a proof-of-concept warehouse implementation and usage of its analysis and visualisation toolset on a real software project.

2   Related Work

The idea described in this paper has been contributed to by several existing approaches and practices.

Osterweil [14] perceived software systems as large, complex and intangible objects developed without a suitably visible, detailed and formal descriptions of how to proceed. He suggested that not only the software, but also software process should be included in software project as programs with explicitly stated descriptions. According to Osterweil, software architect should communicate with developers, customers and other managers through software process programs indicating steps that are to be taken in order to achieve product development or evolution goals. Osterweil postulated that developers would benefit from communicating by software process programs, as reading them should indicate the way in which work is to be coordinated and the way in which each individual's contribution is to fit with others' contributions. In that sense software process program would be yet another artifact in the graph recalled in this paper.

Modern software models often describe systems by a number of (partially) orthogonal views (e.g. state machine, class diagram). Abstract models are often transformed into platform-specific models, and finally into the code. During such transformations it is usually not possible to keep a neat separation into different views (e.g. the specification language of the target models might not support all such views). The target model, however, still needs to preserve the behavior of the abstract model. Therefore, model transformations have to be capable of moving behavioral aspects across views. Kühne, Selic, Gervais and Terrier [12] have noticed that an automated transition from use cases to activity diagrams would provide significant, practical help. Additional traceability could be established through automated transformation, which could then be used to relate requirements to design decisions and test cases. They proposed an approach to automatically generate activity diagrams from use cases while establishing traceability links. Such approach has already been implemented (e.g. RAVEN, *ravenflow.com*). Derrick and Wehrheim [8] studied aspects of model transformations from state-based views (e.g. class specifications with data and methods) into protocol-based views (e.g. process specifications on orderings of methods) and vice versa. They suggested that specification languages for these two views should be equipped with a joint, formal semantics which enables a proof of behavior preservation and consequently derives conditions for the transformations to be behavior-preserving. Also Fleurey, Baudry, France and Ghosh [9] have observed that it is necessary to automatically compose models to build a global view of the system. The graph-based approach allows for a generic framework of model composition that is independent from a modeling language.

Gossens, Belli, Beydeda and Dal Cin [10] considered view graphs for representation of source code. Such graphs are convenient for program analysis and testing at different levels of abstraction (e.g. white-box analysis and testing at the low level of abstraction; black-box analysis and testing at the high level of abstraction). A graph-based approach integrates the different techniques of analysis and testing. Graph relations *vertex-egde-vertex* can be translated to RDF triples *subject-predicate-object*, that are usually stored in textual formats, ie. XML or N3. Several languages have already been proposed to query this formats, like Sesame [3] and SPARQL [15].

As software engineering strives for quantitative assessment of software quality and software process predictability, this is typically achieved by different metrics. Frequently there are many contradicting definitions of a given metric (i.e. they depend on the implementation language). It has been suggested by Mens and Lanza [13] that metrics should be expressed and defined using a language-independent metamodel based on graphs. Such graph-based approach allows for an unambiguous definition of generic object-oriented or higher-order metrics.

3   Architecture Warehouse

3.1   General Idea

Architecture evolves over time. It is a constant process that takes place during entire lifecycle of a software project. Artifacts and their relations get created, updated, removed. Thus the architectural knowledge has to be constantly collected and preserved, monitored over time and assesed, its quality constantly measured and improved. This section defines *architecture warehouse*, describes how it can be implemented based on software architecture graphs (directed multigraphs), formulates analytical and visual transformations that software architects use to obtain *software intelligence*, and demonstrates those by examples. The overall concept of the warehouse is depicted on Figure 1.

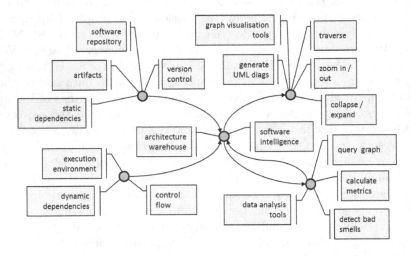

Fig. 1. Graph-based visualisation of architecture warehouse general idea

In further reasoning I assume existence of a typicall software project setting, where *project repository* is the collection of files organized hierarchically (in a tree-like fashion) and maintained under supervision of a version controlling system (etiquetted with revision numbers). The project repository is the source for *static acquisition* of architectural data. I further assume existence of a software *execution environment* (runtime environment) being the source for *dynamic acquisition* of architectural data. Both - static and dynamic acquisition - result in sediment of data in the database founding the *architecture warehouse*. The data collected in the warehouse is subject to further transformations (ie. updates, subgraphs, closures, etc.) that provide software architects with more explicit representation thus with a better understanding of the complexity and quality of the software in question; the latter is called here *software intelligence*.

3.2 Theoretical Foundations

Model I recal the theoretical model [6] for unified representation of architectural knowledge. The key reason for introducing such model is the need for representation of the architectual knowledge that is scallable by nature, abstract from programming paradigms, languages, specification standards, testing approaches, etc., and complete, that is allows for representation of all software system and process artifacts.

Definition of the model is based on directed labeled multigraph. According to the model, the *software architecture graph* is an ordered triple $(\mathcal{V}, \mathcal{L}, \mathcal{E})$ where $\mathcal{V}$ is the set of vertices that reflect all artifacts created during a software project, $\mathcal{E} \subseteq \mathcal{V} \times \mathcal{L} \times \mathcal{V}$ is the set of directed edges that represent dependencies (relations) among those artifacts, and $\mathcal{L}$ is the set of labels which qualify the artifacts and their dependencies. There can be more than one edge from one vertex to another vertex (multigraph), as artifacts can be in more than one relation. The relations are typically not reflexive (the graph is directed).

Vertices of the project graph are created when artifacts are produced during software development process. By default vertices represent parts of the source code, like: modules, classes, methods, tests (ie. unit tests, integration tests, stress tests). Other examples of vertices are: documents (ie. requirements, use cases, change requests), coding guidelines, source codes in higher level languages (ie. yacc grammars), configuration files, make files or build recipes, tickets in issue tracking systems etc. Therefore, vertices may be of different granularities (densities). The containment relation is easily represented in the model using a special containment label to relate vertices representing artifacts for different granularities; on graph print-outs it can be presented as an arrow or more preferably using vertex nesting. During software development vertices are subject to changes (due to changes in requirements, implementation process or bug fixing and code refactoring), therefore the vertices must be versioned. This is easily represented in the model using a special label containing version number (revision) attached to each vertex and/or label. It means that multiple vertexes can exist for the same artifact in different version; however graph print-outs usually show vertices from one revision only, ie. the most recent one. For more details on artifacts visualisation see Section 4.

Example 1. Each artifact can be described by a set of labels that may have additional properties. A method can be described by labels showing that ie.: it is a part of project source code (*code*); it is written in Java programming language (*java*); its revision is 456 (*r:456*). There can be also some language specific labels, ie.: *abstract, public*. Edges are directed and may have multiple labels as well, ie.: a package *contains* a class (while a class *is a part of* a package); a method *calls* another method; a package *depends on* another package. Other typicall labels include ie.: *generates*; *verifies*; *tests*; *defines*; *implements*.

Transformations The graph model is general and scalable, fits both small and huge project. It has been tested in practice [7] which proved however, that in case of a large project it becomes too complex to be human-tractable as a whole. This confirmed, that some rules for graph transformation are a must, since software architects are interested both in an overall picture and in particular details that satisfy certain restrictions. Intuitions for such transformations are ie.: return the subgraph including only methods that call the given method; return the subgraph of all public methods for the given class (either including or excluding inherited ones). Obviously, in the graph model the queries that compute such transformations are computationally inexpensive, as usually they only need to traverse the graph (or even its small fraction).

Example 2. For a given software graph $\mathcal{G} = (\mathcal{V}, \mathcal{L}, \mathcal{E})$ and $t : \mathcal{L} \times \mathcal{L} \mapsto \mathcal{L}'$, its *closure* is a transition $\mathcal{G}^t = \{\mathcal{V}, \mathcal{L}', \mathcal{E}'\}$, where $\mathcal{E}'$ is the set of new edges resulting from a transitive closure of t calculated on pairs of neighboring edges from E. The vertices V remain unchanged.

Example 3. For a given software graph $\mathcal{G} = (\mathcal{V}, \mathcal{L}, \mathcal{E})$ and $f : \mathcal{V} \mapsto bool$, its *subgraph* is a transformation $\mathcal{G}|_f = (\mathcal{V}', \mathcal{L}, \mathcal{E}')$, where $\mathcal{V}' = \{v \in \mathcal{V} | f(v) = true\}$ and $\mathcal{E}' = \mathcal{E} \cap (\mathcal{V}' \times \mathcal{L} \times \mathcal{V}')$.

Metrics For complex projects, quantitive evaluation of software is a must. The graph-based approach is in line with best practices for metrics [1,16], allows for easy translation of existing metrics into graph terms [4], ensures that they can be efficiently calculated using graph algorithms and allows for designing new metrics, in particular ones that integrate both software system and software process artifacts are particularly interesting.

Example 4. For a given software graph $\mathcal{G} = (\mathcal{V}, \mathcal{L}, \mathcal{E})$, its *metric* is a transformation $m : \mathcal{G} \mapsto \mathcal{R}$ where $\mathcal{R}$ denotes real numbers and m can be effectively calculated by a graph algorithm on G.

Example 5. For given software architecture graph G let CF denote a *counting function* defined as $CF(n, \eta_1, \eta_2, \eta_3) = \#\{m \in \mathcal{V} \mid type(n) \ni \eta_1 \wedge type(m) \ni \eta_2 \wedge \exists e \in \mathcal{E}: source(e) = n \wedge target(e) = m \wedge type(e) = \eta_3\}$, where $n \in \mathcal{V}$, $\eta_1, \eta_2, \eta_3 \in \mathcal{L}$. For a node n with a label in set η_1, CF counts the number of nodes m with a label in set η_2 and such that there is an edge e of label η_3 from n to m. Obviously CF can be implemented on G effectively, namely in time $O(|V| + |E|)$ [5].

Example 6. Let NOC (Number Of Children) denote metric counting the number of direct subclasses. Using the counting function NOC is implemented simply as: $NOC(c) = CF(c, class, class, inherits)$.

Example 7. Let *WMC* (Weighted Method per Class) denote metric counting $\sum_{i=1}^{n} c_i$ where c_i is the complexity of the i-th method in the class. If each method has the same complexity, WMC is just the number of methods in the class. Using the *counting function* the number of methods in a class is implemented simply as: $WMC(c) = CF(c, class, method, contains)$.

Please note that graph metrics depend only on the graph's structure, thus they are programming language independent. Moreover, storing and integrating all architectural knowledge in one place facilitates tracing not only dependencies in the source code but also among documentation and meta-models. This opportunity gives raise to new graph-defined metrics concerned with software processes.

Example 8. Consider a software architecture graph G with the relationships *calling, called, using* and *used*. Let *CHC* (Cohesion of Classes) denote metric counting the number of strongly connected components of this graph. Software is cohesive if this metric is 1. The computation of this metric is cheap as it can be done in time $O(|G|)$ with respect to the size of the graph G [5].

The transformations and metrics recalled give the foundation for *software intelligence* layer of tools covered in Section 4. Please note that the list of transformations is not exclusive and there still remains a challenge to provide a canonical classification for all such operations (including basic operations like adding or deleting graph nodes, or graph edges).

3.3 Proof-of-Concept Implementation

The platform for storing architectural knowledge was designed in a warehose-like fashion. The fundamental aspect was the decision on separation of the repository of architectural knowledge in question from the repositoriy of project products (ie. source code) that the software developers use for commiting artifact revisions. This follows the principle that currently is a standard de-facto for business-type systems that separates transactional part of the system from its data warehouse.

The proof-of-concept version of the warehouse has been implemented using open-source graph database *neo4j* [18]. Neo4j offers scalability and high-availability facilities that make it feasible to build repositories for large projects. It fits the needs as its definition of a vertex contains a map of properties and every edge has a type (besides a map of parameters) which can be accessed during graph traversal. Additional reasons for choosing Neo4J databases were good integration with Lucene full text indexer, which can improve significantly typical searches and graph querying language Gremlin. Gremlin is a path language similar to XPath, however a number of additional facilities like backtrack and loops make Gremlin Turing-complete. Thus we can code in Gremlin any transformation that constitutes the theoretical foundations for the warehouse.

To test the implementation, a project *jUnit* from the *Source Forge* repository was selected.

For the purpose of the proof-of-concept static data acquisition, a tool called *Mikroskop* [7] was used. Mikroskop is a Java application that performs static analysis of Java program tree, exports collected facts into an XML format that is later uploaded into the graph database. For the purpose of the proof-of-concept dynamic data acquisition, a tool called *Kieker* [17] was used. Kieker is a Java framework for application performance monitoring and dynamic software analysis. The upload process first took the software project source code as an input, and Mikroskop retrieved information on those architectural artifacts (like packages, classes, methods, variables) and their relationships (like methods owned by classes, classes belonging to packages) that could be determined statically. Another stream of facts about the software project was uploaded dynamically when execution of the software project was eardropped using Kieker. This made it possible to collect data on dynamic relationships between software artifacts (ie. count the numbers of executed call).

4   Software Intelligence

In previous section I defined an *architecture warehose* that contained architectural facts, that is architectural artifacts and their dependencies that were acquired statically and dynamically. Let *software intelligence* denote now a toolset that makes it possible to access the facts using data visualisation and data analysis techniques, hence obtaining a higher level of understanding of those facts, that is obtaining knowdledge. In this section I deepen the definition by several examples.

Fig. 2. Graph-based visualisation of artifacts in jUnit project

Example 9. Figure 2 depicts the graph of all artifacts collected for jUnit software in two different visualisations.

Visualisation of architectural knowledge may be a challenge due to the size of the data set. Such challenges are not unique in computer science, ie. disciplines like computational biology have already developed libraries, frameworks and applications ready for handling and depicting massive data sets. For the proof-of-concept implementation of software visualisation, application *Cytoscape* was selected. It imports data from graph database and supports architects with operations like zooming, panning, rotating, filtering that efficiently implement transformations defined in Section 3.

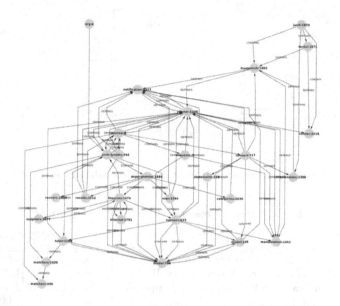

Fig. 3. Subgraph of packages and their dependencies in jUnit project

Analysis of architectural knowledge also poses a challenge due to the size of its data set, especially when assesment of software quality is in question. For the proof-of-concept implementation of software analysis, several metrics were translated into graph model and calculated using graph query language *Gremlin*. The results of the calculation were inserted backwards into the graph model as additional labels attributing vertices representing software artifacts being subject of the calculation.

Example 10. Figures 3 and 4 depict the graph of artifacts collected for jUnit software limited only to classes and packages, respectively.

Though the graph approch to warehousing architectural knowledge introduces new interesting possibilities, it does not limit or prevent software architects from using existing tools and techniques of data analysis. In particular data stored in a graph database can be exported into a tabular format and processed with traditional tools (ie. for charting), examples follow.

Example 11. In Table 1 see results of a sample warehouse query listing vertices and their additional attributes respective for composition of *subgraph* and *filter* transformations with filtering predicate $f(v) : v.labels \ni junit/framework$,

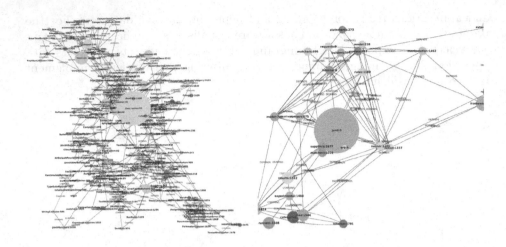

Fig. 4. Graph-based visualisation of metrics calculated for jUnit project

Table 1. Subset of results returned by a graph query

Vertex ID	Path	Type	In	Out	ACC	PR
1960	junit/framework/Assert	class	3	0	1.5128	1.6475
143	junit/framework/AssertionFailedError	class	1	0	1,0000	3,0226
1983	junit/framework/ComparisonCompactor	class	2	1	2,5000	1,2323
2043	junit/framework/ComparisonFailure	class	1	1	1,0000	1,2323
2029	junit/framework/JUnit4TestAdapter	class	1	6	1,1667	1,4472
2017	junit/framework/JUnit4TestAdapterCache	class	2	3	1,5000	5,9435
2010	junit/framework/JUnit4TestCaseFacade	class	1	1	1,0000	1,2323
2008	junit/framework/Protectable	interface	2	0	1,0000	2,8261
124	junit/framework/Test	interface	7	0	1,0000	34,9671
159	junit/framework/TestCase	class	4	2	1,6154	2,6058
1893	junit/framework/TestFailure	class	2	1	1,0000	1,9232
119	junit/framework/TestListener	interface	2	0	1,0000	3,3132
151	junit/framework/TestResult	class	8	3	1,2105	22,1350
162	junit/framework/TestSuite	class	5	3	1,7407	5,7415

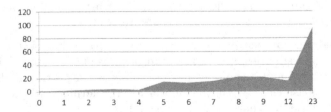

Fig. 5. Classical visualisation of correlation between vertex attributes (in-degree and page rank)

returning vertexes with attributes $\{Path, Type, In, Out\}$ (degrees) and calculated metrics ACC (Average Cyclomatic Complexity), PR (Page Rank).

Example 12. In Figure 5 see a sample chart depicting correlation between the number of edges in-bound for a graph vertex (in this case ranging up to 23) and the importance of software artifacts calculated by PR metric (in this case ranging from $1, 136481406$ to $95, 55763745$).

5   Conclusions

Following the research on architecture of software [11] and software process, I accept an approach that avoids separation between software and software process artifacts as the one worth taking [14]. I demonstrate by example that implementation of such approach has already became feasible - starting with a graph-based model [6], using graph databases [2] as the foundation for artifact representation and using graph visualisation [7] for presentation of the results.

The concept is not an entirely novel one, rather it should be perceived as an attempt to support existing trends with a sound and common foundation. A holistic approach is required for current research to gain proper momentum, as despite many advanced tools, current software projects still suffer from a lack of visible, detailed and complete setting to govern their architecture and evolution.

I am also aware that the scope of research required to turn this idea into an actual contribution to software engineering requires further work. In particular, the following research areas seem to be especially inspiring: assessing further projects in an effort to provide their systematic visualisation and classifications of their artifact and dependency types; designing and calculating graph-based metrics that better assess software quality and software process maturity, in particular combine all software system and process artifacts; classifying existing software and its process according to the model and calculated metrics, and systematically comparing their software quality and process maturity (comparing software projects with one another); defining UML diagrams as reports obtained from the software architecture graph as a combination of its transformations; refining the definition of the graph-based software model and its transformation, designing new components and transformations enriching the model; introducing domain-specific language for quering graph-based architecture warehouses.

References

1. Abreu, F.B., Carapuça, R.: Object-oriented software engineering: Measuring and controlling the development process. In: Proceedings of the 4th International Conference on Software Quality (1994)
2. Angles, R., Gutiérrez, C.: Survey of graph database models. ACM Comput. Surv. 40(1) (2008)
3. Broekstra, J., Kampman, A., van Harmelen, F.: Sesame: A generic architecture for storing and querying rdf and rdf schema. In: International Semantic Web Conference, pp. 54–68 (2002)

4. Chidamber, S.R., Kemerer, C.F.: A metrics suite for object oriented design. IEEE Transactions on Software Engineering 20, 476–493 (1994)
5. Cormen, T.H., Stein, C., Rivest, R.L., Leiserson, C.E.: Introduction to Algorithms, 2nd edn. McGraw-Hill Higher Education (2001)
6. Dąbrowski, R., Stencel, K., Timoszuk, G.: Software Is a Directed Multigraph. In: Crnkovic, I., Gruhn, V., Book, M. (eds.) ECSA 2011. LNCS, vol. 6903, pp. 360–369. Springer, Heidelberg (2011)
7. Dabrowski, R., Stencel, K., Timoszuk, G.: Improving software quality by improving architecture management. In: Rachev, B., Smrikarov, A. (eds.) CompSysTech 2012, Ruse, Bulgaria, pp. 208–215. ACM (2012) ISBN: 978-1-4503-1193-9, http://doi.acm.org/10.1145/2383276.2383308
8. Derrick, J., Wehrheim, H.: Model transformations across views. Science of Computer Programming 75(3), 192–210 (2010)
9. Fleurey, F., Baudry, B., France, R.B., Ghosh, S.: A Generic Approach for Automatic Model Composition. In: Giese, H. (ed.) MODELS 2008. LNCS, vol. 5002, pp. 7–15. Springer, Heidelberg (2008)
10. Gossens, S., Belli, F., Beydeda, S., Cin, M.D.: View graphs for analysis and testing of programs at different abstraction levels. In: HASE, pp. 121–130 (2005)
11. Kruchten, P., Lago, P., van Vliet, H., Wolf, T.: Building up and exploiting architectural knowledge. In: WICSA, pp. 291–292 (2005)
12. Kühne, T., Selic, B., Gervais, M.-P., Terrier, F. (eds.): ECMFA 2010. LNCS, vol. 6138. Springer, Heidelberg (2010)
13. Mens, T., Lanza, M.: A graph-based metamodel for object-oriented software metrics. Electr. Notes Theor. Comput. Sci. 72(2), 57–68 (2002)
14. Osterweil, L.J.: Software processes are software too. In: ICSE, pp. 2–13 (1987)
15. Prud'hommeaux, E., Seaborne, A.: Sparql query language for rdf. w3c recommendation (2008)
16. Roche, J.M.: Software metrics and measurement principles. SIGSOFT Softw. Eng. Notes 19, 77–85 (1994)
17. van Hoorn, A., Waller, J., Hasselbring, W.: Kieker: a framework for application performance monitoring and dynamic software analysis. In: Kaeli, D.R., Rolia, J., John, L.K., Krishnamurthy, D. (eds.) ICPE, pp. 247–248. ACM (2012)
18. Vicknair, C., Macias, M., Zhao, Z., Nan, X., Chen, Y., Wilkins, D.: A comparison of a graph database and a relational database: a data provenance perspective. In: Proceedings of the 48th Annual Southeast Regional Conference, ACM SE, pp. 42:1–42:6. ACM, New York (2010)

The Linkup Data Structure for Heterogeneous Data Integration Platform[*]

Michał Chromiak[1] and Krzysztof Stencel[2]

[1] Institute of Informatics, Maria Curie-Skłodowska University, Lublin, Poland
mchromiak@umcs.pl
[2] Institute of Informatics, University of Warsaw, Warsaw, Poland
stencel@mimuw.edu.pl

Abstract. In modern world the data storage is based on databases. The enormous scatter between the approaches and techniques caused by wide field of database applications brings every system manager to point where integration is required. In this paper we want to challenge the problems of heterogeneous data integration. We discuss a solution that can unify the data integration effort without a need to focus on a data model or schema particularities. The presented polyglot communication based on a network service will focus on an linkup entity that can further be elastically adopted to particular assumptions of the environment to be integrated. The discussed architectural design will depict the most common and well known issues in the area of distributed environment integration, like horizontal, vertical and mixed fragmentation, replication or integrated data storage sparsity problem. The design of the introduced linkup structure brings the benefits of unified platform independence and elastic configuration that later can also bring profits while in distributed environment.

Keywords: database, heterogeneous integration, fragmentation, replication, heterogeneous databases, database integration, distributed database.

1   Introduction

DBMS as the main means of storing data is one of the most significant area of software design and development. As such it provides efficient, reliable, convenient, multi-user safe access storage to massive amounts of persistent data. The databases are behind most of the web sites, telecommunication systems, scientific experiments, deployments of sensors and many, many more other equally vital areas to everyday functioning of present computer systems. Due to this widespread interest in the databases utilization their functioning itself has become diversified considering multiple application flavors. The variety of database applications has influenced its design in all of the aspects mentioned above. Moreover the database enterprise market is also defined by many commercial vendors that tend to promote their proprietary solutions. Therefore, the integration of database systems seems to be a crucial and very complex

[*] Supported by the Polish National Science Centre grant 2011/01/B/ST6/03867.

T.-h. Kim, Y.-h. Lee, and W.-c. Fang (Eds.): FGIT 2012, LNCS 7709, pp. 263–274, 2012.

task to accomplish. This process of database integration can be constrained to general areas formed by progressive level of complexity and abstraction not bounded to their specific use.

In relatively simplest cases the integration itself can be considered in terms of scalability (not only for local grids but also involving distribution) and homogeneous database environment (i.e. based on one vendor's solutions). This tends to be approached and covered by the DBMS vendors across most of the leading enterprise solutions such as Oracle, MS SQL Server, MySQL, PostgreSQL, etc. More complex approach to database integration involves grids. It is based on multiple vendor originated databases. Such heterogeneous nature is imposed by environmental conditions. That assumes integration of many independent data sources that has been already using various database vendors. In that conditions we can consider the data sources as heterogeneous. This is how we refer to heterogeneity. It should be noted that this area has also been heavily investigated as presented in the following section.

Let us move to the last and at the same time the most abstract approach to the integration issue. It covers not only the vendor and the distribution issues, but also must face the problem of data model mismatch between the integrated data sources. In this case, the most well known and reported issue is the problem of impedance mismatch [19]. This issue has been addressed by numerous solutions namely in form of an object-relational mappers (ORM). Under this circumstances the integration procedure must consider the translation between the data models, despite the fact that it becomes a source of system overhead and may cause integration bottlenecks. This situation has been widely accepted as a indispensable condition of a heterogeneous DBMS integration. In this paper we want to propose an improvement for this process of heterogeneous integration in an efficient way.

The paper is organized as follows. Section 2 summarizes the related work. In Section 3 we place our idea in the space of discussed topic's state of art. Section 4 will contain detailed description of the idea of cuboids. Section 6 concludes.

2   Related Work

Current research in the field of database integration is focused around detailed areas without general approach that would be a complete (i.e. independent, extensible by design) and tested concept. Whereas the proposed solution brings the flexibility and abstraction layer enabling unrestricted design for networking and schema customization. The existing research in the domain of integration of heterogeneous databases has provided a diverse array of solutions. The main heterogeneous DB integration issues that are being answered in this research field has been briefly classified in 1995 in [1] and [2]. However, some attempts has take place earlier in 1983 [3]. At present, the main area of interest regarding the integration techniques is basing on XML solutions. It is believed, as mentioned in [4], that the XML has become the undisputable standard both for data exchange and content management, and moreover that is about to become the lingua franca of data interchange. This point of view can be justified by immense number of research papers, like [5,6,7] and many more, trying to utilize the XML technology as the tool for database scheme and data representation. The XML has also become part of many commercial products supported by giants of the software industry like Microsoft [17], Oracle [18] or IBM.

Semantic approach is also present in terms of data integration [7]. Moreover, there also has been some research regarding detection of semantic relevance of entities and in its favor integrate local schemas [8].

The area of interest for database integration is way beyond database itself. In other areas of research the significance of this research has also been encountered and considered. To name just a few scientific disciplines struggling with this problem starting in field of medicine [9] using the ontologies definitions and more [10,11], neuroscience [12], biology [13] ending with agent-oriented analysis for military purposes [14].

Another aspect of significance of the integration research should be considered in the field of enterprise. Since 1992 [15] the concept of data warehouse has been proposed, database vendors have rushed to implement the functionalities for constructing data warehouses. That made on-line analytical processing (OLAP) emerge as a technology for decision support systems. However, problems may arise in building a data warehouse with pre-existing data, since it has various types of heterogeneity. As described in [16], forming the definitions for the problems of semantic conflicts among heterogeneous DB, and requesting local sites to transform the data into XML format and preparing the corresponding XSLT files on the global site. the schema integration problems can be unified and integrated into global view. This integration scheme for data warehouse however had to focus on some conflicts, namely value-to-value, attribute-to-attribute and table-to-table. These conflicts are not exclusive, they may occur in any pair of relations at the same time. Such heterogeneity occurs frequently in two distinct pre-existing databases, when different databases are designed by different designers or driven by different assumptions. This conflicts are resolved only partially or are considered out of scope.

The presented projects' idea is aimed to solve all of the issues and prepare monolithic solution. While in case of published achievements the results can be accessed and classified freely there is still a considerable amount of closed, enterprise solutions that are mainly dedicated for commercial DBMS. Those however are not considered in the scope of this paper.

3   The General Idea

As mentioned above the solutions dedicated to integration tends to focus on data translation utilizing multiple domain-specific languages (DSL) e.g. XSLT or semi-structured data formats like JSON, Object Exchange Model, XML and more. Their persistency is dependent on DBMS, however from historical reasons there is some considerable amount of data still stored in files and moreover spreadsheets are also often considered useful in certain ways. In those cases processing of data is not done through query languages associated with DBMS (e.g. Hadoop).

In each case the idea of integration will imply a need for some unification that would cover all of the possible issues related to such an abstract way of data manipulation. Each of the existing solutions that focus on vendor or data model homogeneous integration repositories or even the classical approach to heterogeneous integration with XML and ORM mechanisms behind, must conform some unification rules. As far as we concern the integration for a known scheme, the integration will focus on conforming such scheme. It is irrelevant whether the scheme is discovered and adopted automatically [20] or if it is imposed by manual configuration from grid administrator [21]. The rule is that the scheme must not vary across the integrated grid.

While this is true, it doesn't give the integration process the flexibility of data manipulation as the scheme must hold. What we want to achieve is not only the possibility to: integrate the conformed scheme, customize data that are supposed to be introduced to the global scheme as its part [21], but also provide total vendor, data model and protocol independence. Moreover, we want the solution to provide a data modification and presentation layer ready to arbitrary manipulations. This would mean that not only the scheme can be conformed. Likewise the data presented from the integrated sources can be exposed in any form of a scheme element and what is more presented as a new global scheme element. Therefore, the integrated scheme would not be strict but freely customizable. This would be possible thanks to the idea of cuboid and architecture designed to utilize it, in what we believe, the optimal way. Existing proposals solve the problem of integrating resources but they do not provide a unified integration platform.

The most complex feature, in the perspective of our solution, is that the scheme constraints must be satisfied at a global grid level only, if it is required for a specific application. In other word scheme consistency is an option not an obligation. The scheme constrained approach is present e.g. in [21] where the data is prepared at a contributory side and then introduced to global integrator instance in preconfigured form and conforming the global scheme. Our approach means that the scheme can also be conformed but moreover it can be created independently of contributory sides' schemes. In such case the integrated sources are not required to carry strictly the global scheme. The global scheme would be something created by administrator regardless of contributory schemes and/or constraints.

4   Distributed Data Structure as a Linkup Node

All of the serious issues mentioned in previous sections focus around complexity of data unified representation. Data representation is sometimes approached in centralized or distributed manner while actually the massive data representation is approached just as a way of showing the physical notion of its existence. In presented solution we want to simply represent the data storage as a service. To fulfill such assumption we need to introduce some polyglot interface to do this. Considering many data sources with different data schemes we want to customize those data to form their arbitrary view that can be accessed by client. The integrated grid will provide data that can (not obligatorily) conform some common scheme. All of scheme-dependent or unrelated data can be referred as data scene that can be freely used for data composition in form of linkup entity. However, this is considered out of scope of this paper and will be elaborated in following papers. For now we are limited in this paper to describe a data scene integration with only scheme-conformed data. In this paper we only introduce the scope of polyglot linkup interface that is a major part for heterogeneous integration platform as a main goal of our research.

4.1   Linkup Entity Definition – Cuboid

The distributed architecture is going to be focused on data as service therefore the data is ought to be obtained from the local contributory sites and customized into a global scheme that becomes a data view for the client (i.e. database instance requesting for data or in some cases service oriented entity). The entire architecture communication will concentrate on client database and linkup entity. The linkup entity is a fastener that serves to join or link the client database to global data scheme. We must remember that the global scheme does not have to conform local schemas however, in this paper we will restrict to mapping local and distributed scheme to a global one. Considering hierarchical structure of a legacy DB, integrated resources would have to be depict and delivered at linkup entity in a way that would be common to all nodes regardless of its data model - virtually integrating data from the underlying resources. This information will let the linkup entity combine the heterogenic data into one integration schema. The integration schema represents the data model, common to all nodes, as a collection of references to all data entities present in the DB grid. Such collection has to address issues common in distributed resources integration (e.g. data fragmentations and replications). Therefore, the mentioned collection would have to benefit from the design addressing these distribution particularities. The idea for overcoming this obstacles will be based on organizing the distributed parts of DB entity in form that can be visualized as an 3D data entity-oriented cuboid as depicted in Fig. 1.

The integration involves simply composing one complete entity object, out of many references to its subobjects distributed across entire cuboid-registered DB grid. This way one complete entity object would form first level vertical plain of the cuboid. Entire cuboid can structurally be referred as a cluster of vertical plains. Some of the entity's parts that will occur to be replicated along the grid will also become part of this cuboid, however as a part of different, successive vertical plain.

Such detailed description for each plain is possible by dint of its definition. As each vertical plain would have to be build according to this definition, the vertical completeness of such plain would be a result of meeting its definition provided in form of Cuboid. Each node providing entity's data could be treated as a next level plain; this however could lead to a sparsity problem. Thus, to reduce the potential sparsity of a cuboid, after having first level vertical plain complete (i.e. all Best Row Ids have their record complete) following plains would have to be populated. The next plains (if replication representation of first plain data present) are being composed out of the next nodes of the registered scheme data and the remains of the previous ones. The main records' integrator of such entity's definition would be the Best Row Id (BRI) that would be essential to composition of each row out of the entity definition (see Fig. 2).

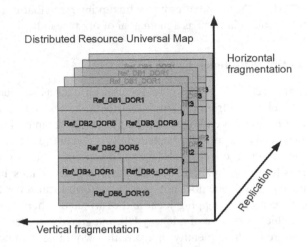

Fig. 1. Distributed Resource Universal Map (DRUM)

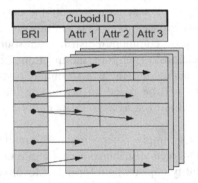

Fig. 2. Cuboid build according to definition

Moreover, in the horizontal plain (slice) section (replication) of the cuboid, the BRI will be the one responsible for identifying the superfluous copies of each entity part. In this manner all the possible fragmentations and replications of an object can be covered and presented in one common interface – Distributed Resource Universal Map (DRUM) in form of cuboid. The cuboid as a global integrating schema, would store only the logical structure of such entities' objects. Each component of such cuboid, would have to include a reference to a complete Fast Access Method (FAM) acquired from each DB legacy node during registration at cuboid . Thus, each contributor participating in global schema for each entity would have to provide its contributory fast access method. Second part of a DB registration in DRUM, would be the export of a fast and native access method for each piece of data present in the integration scheme. Such information enclosed in Database Object Reference (DOR) however, would not be stored as a part of DRUM, but actually as a part of dedicated structure in persistent or volatile form.

Populating linkup entity with data acquired across integrated DB grid is commenced during the registration of each new data source being integrated within the specific DRUM. The content of each drum can however be modified freely in further utilization of a DRUM. This is due to our main goal which is availability over transactional reliability.

4.2   Cuboid – Data Model

As mentioned in previous section the construction of data structures in DRUM is based on the definitions. Let us consider then the system for defining the data structures. The entire solution is going to be based on key-value pairs to identify each part of data. The key would be the unambiguous (in adequate domain) ID of the object and the value would be varied depending on actual type of the DRUM element. The description of this model will proceed from the most detailed pieces of the integration schema to the most general.

For the purpose of such solution there is a need to introduce the most basic structure representing the simplest piece of information in a global scheme – the *Cell*. Let us assume the key-value pair approach for the cell's definition would have to consist of its unambiguous ID (in the domain of all the cells stored in the same Row) and the data storing value i.e. the way of accessing the cell or to be precise its reference. In practice the remote Database Object Reference (rDOR) special object contain essential object address data. The IDL definition of cell is stated as follows:

```
struct cell { key: "name";
              value:   rDOR_John
}
```

The next, in structural order, would be the Tuple. It consists of a key name and the value, that is a map, containing unlimited number of cells. In other word we could call it *SuperCell*:

```
struct tuple{
      key:     "emailAddress";
      value:{
           user:{  key: "user";
                   value: rDOR_john30},
           domain:{key: "domain";
                   value: rDOR_example_com}
      }
}
```

To understand the reason for distinguishing between cell and tuple we need to remember that these resources can be fragmented vertically. Therefore, accessing a tuple may represent not only a logical entity but also may represent fragmentation pattern. Following the structural design next level of complication stage would be a Row:

```
struct row{
      key:"12";//BRI
      value:{
            name:{
                        key:  "name";
                        value: rDOR_john
                  },
            mailAddress:{
                        key:  "emailAddress";
                        value:{
                              user:{    key: "user";
                                        value: rDOR_john30},
                              domain:{  key: "domain";
                                        value:rDOR_example_com}
                        }
            },
            age:{    key:  "age";
                     value: rDOR_30}
            }
}
```

Row will include explicitly a very important piece of information i.e. BRI as its key value. Row could be composed out of cells or tuples however all sharing the common BRI. By sharing the BRI, each cell/tuple would be classified as a component of the Row. In this way all the cells/tuples in each row can be addressed thanks to the same BRI. The value of the Row is the sequence of cells /tuples. For less complex notation the cell/tuple names can be removed to form pure key/value pair and replace the rDOR notation with simple dummy reference providing the appropriate DOR object's value for adequate BRI value:

```
13:{
    name: rDOR_DB1_13_name,
    emailAddress: {user: rDOR_DB2_13_user,
                     domain: rDOR_DB3_13_domain},
    age:  rDOR_DB1_13_age
}
```

Let us consider exemplary DOR. The name DOR can assure the method for accessing all of the names in DB1 using the native query (e.g.: SELECT PK, name FROM Emp;). At this stage, to address the appropriate row we must add WHERE operator defining the right BRI (i.e. the primary key in this case). In consequence the DOR called here rDOR_DB1_13_name would include a query in the following form:

```
SELECT PK, name FROM Emp WHERE PK=13;
```

The three already mentioned elements of the data model however will be referred only as the elements of a basic global scheme entity i.e. the snapshot (otherwise referred as Plain). Snapshot is a complete view of a DB table content, composed out of the distributed resources registered in OLI thanks to rDORs. Snapshot is also key/value scheme dependent. As it is a container for Rows it can be exemplified in the simplified notation as follows:

```
Users:                                    //snapshot key
  1..12:{                                 // rows' keys
    rDOR_DB1                              // SELECT * FROM Emp;
  },
  13:{                      // vertically fragmented rows key
    name: rDOR_DB1_13_name,
                           //SELECT * FROM Emp WHERE PK=13
    emailAddress:{user:  rDOR_DB2_13_user,
                  domain: rDOR_DB3_13_domain},
    age: rDOR_DB1_13_age
  },
  ...
}
```

By dint of the tuple idea, it became possible to overcome the vertical Row fragmentation. However, in this way each remote cell/tuple/row from a DB server would have to be fetched by sending a single query per each. Therefore, for instance requesting for four tuples from remote server would cause need for sending and evaluating four simple queries one per each PK. Sending many simple queries could lead to major inefficiency along with increasing number of tuples per DOR. This problem could be solved by sending one query able to fetch all the requested records from one server at a time.

Up to now the dedicated structures were simply considering the need for distributed heterogeneous integration. However, one last remaining issue has not been addressed yet in terms of data model i.e. the replication. To overcome the problem of replication we propose the idea of **Slice** and **Cuboid**. Cuboid would represent the definition of an entity (see Fig. 3, Fig. 4) whereas the slice would provide the definition of its records' replications.

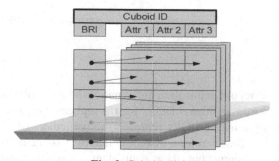

Fig. 3. Cuboid slicing

Each Cuboid would be consisting out of at least one plain (a.k.a. snapshot). This plain would represent all of the data present in one database entity containing integrated data.

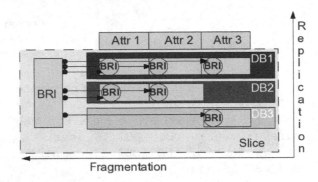

Fig. 4. The way a slice integrate the replication and fragmentation

Let us continue then with the Cuboid as the most general structure. Its key would be the name of a particular distributed entity resource. The value is represented as a map of Plains. The Plains do not have to be complete in terms of their key definitions.

```
Users:{                                        //cuboid key
  Users:{                    // snapshot key; Plain 1
    1..12:{                  // rows' keys at node DB1
       rDOR_DB1                  // SELECT * FROM Emp;
    },
    13:{                     // vertically fragmented row key
       name: rDOR_DB1_13_name,
         emailAddress:{   user: rDOR_DB2_13_user,
                        domain: rDOR_DB3_13_domain},
         age: rDOR_DB1_13_age
    },
    ...
  },
  Users:{...                 // snapshot key; Plain 2
  }
  ...
}
```

Moreover, to add the record replication information in form of slice this structure needs to be enhanced with additional DORs for the replicated data. This will be possible by simply placing a list of DORs representing particular data instead of single Database Object Reference. Therefore, assuming that the first 12 BRIs form the above example have four different but data equivalent locations those rows can be represented as follows:

```
Users:{                                          //cuboid key
   Users:{                              // snapshot key; Plain 1
     1..12:{                            // rows' keys at node DB1
       rDOR_DB1,rDOR_DB12,rDOR_DB7,rDOR_DB9
     },
   ...
}
```

The selection of particular DOR can be based on numerous criteria like first encountered, access or load balancing rules. This way each DOR based part of a snapshot can be accessed by using any of the DOR's replicas. To express the database scheme in terms of cuboid based architecture, the next level of integration can be introduced i.e. the *Keyspace*. Keyspace would be a container for Cuboids representing database scheme.

5   Summary and Future Work

In this paper we have presented a solution that reduces the overhead from intermodel translations in a heterogeneous and potentially distributed database grid. In general, most approaches consider wrapper that plays the role of a mediating actor for each client query to the wrapped resource. The presented architecture however, is focused on overhead reduction. We eliminate this situation. This gain comes with the benefits of the presented architecture design and the general algorithm for direct and native requests to each integrated data source. At this stage we will also focus on belief that if we are after scalability and reduction on the join produced overhead, we must give up some of the transactions' goodness. The detailed research takes us to point where we are trying to get the best of highly reliable and tested solutions and move it to higher level. The presented solution will not reject the existing achievements. It actually embraces what has already been done in field of managing low level storage.

In future papers we will discuss definition scheme for DOR, introduce the grid architecture that incorporate the cuboid idea and employ it as its integrating instance. Furthermore, we will discuss adopting reliable optimization techniques in terms of the presented architecture.

References

1. Hepner, P.: Integrating Heterogeneous Databases: An Overview. School of Computing and Mathematics. Deakin University, Geelong (1995)
2. Gilgor, V.D., Luckenbaugh, G.L.: Interconnecting Heterogeneous Database management System. Computer 17(1) (January 1983)
3. Madnick, S.E.: A Taxonomy for Classifying Commercial Approaches to Information Integration in Heterogeneous Environments. Database Engineering - Special Issues on Database Connectivity 13(2) (June 1990)
4. Rajeswari, V., et al.: Heterogeneous database integration for web applications. International Journal on Computer Science and Engineering 1(3), 227–234 (2009)

5. Tseng, F.S.C.: Heterogeneous database Integration Using XML
6. Shiang, W.J., Ho, M.Y.: An Interactive Tool Based on XML Technology for Data Exchange between Heterogeneous ERP systems. Journal of CIIE 22(4), 273–278 (2005)
7. Rodríguez-Gianolli, P., Mylopoulos, J.: A Semantic Approach to XML-based Data Integration. In: Kunii, H.S., Jajodia, S., Sølvberg, A. (eds.) ER 2001. LNCS, vol. 2224, pp. 117–132. Springer, Heidelberg (2001)
8. Sugandha, L.: Semantic Integration of Heterogeneous Databases in Multidatabase System. Computer Science And Engineering Department Thapar University (2010)
9. Deray, T., Verheyden, P.: Towards a Semantic Integration of Medical Relational Databases by Using Ontologies: A Case Study. In: Meersman, R. (ed.) OTM-WS 2003. LNCS, vol. 2889, pp. 137–150. Springer, Heidelberg (2003)
10. Sujansky, W.: Heterogeneous Database Integration in Biomedicine. Journal of Biomedical Informatics 34, 285–298 (2001)
11. Williams, M.H., Hu, J.: Making heterogeneous medical databases interoperable. Computer Methods and Programs in Biomedicine 43, 275–281 (1994)
12. Lam, H.Y.K., et al.: Using Web Ontology Language to Integrate Heterogeneous Databases in the Neurosciences. In: AMIA Annu. Symp. Proc., pp. 464–468 (2006)
13. Matoba, N., Tanoue, J., et al.: A System for Integration of Heterogeneous Biological XML Data. Genome Informatics 12, 473–474 (2001)
14. McDonald, J.T., Talbert, M.L., DeLoach, S.A.: Heterogeneous Database Integration Using Agent-Oriented Information Systems. In: Proceedings of the International Conference on Artificial Intelligence, pp. 26–29. CSREA Press (2000)
15. Inmon, B.: Building the Data Warehouse. Wiley (1992)
16. Tseng, F.: XML-Based Heterogeneous Database Integration For Data Warehouse Creation. In: PACIS (2005)
17. Microsoft TechNet, http://technet.microsoft.com/en-us/library/ms151835.aspx
18. Basu, J., Chanchani, N.: Heterogeneous XML-based Data Integration, Oracle (2003)
19. Description of SBA and SBQL, http://www.sbql.pl/Topics/ImpedanceMismatch.html
20. Bonifati, A., et al.: Automatic Extraction Of Database Scheme Semantic Properties Using Knowledge Discovery Techniques. Journal of Integrated Design & Process Science archive 3(1), 55–78 (1999)
21. Subieta, K., et al.: Object Database for Rapid Applications (ODRA) Description and programmer manual (2008)

Uncertain OLAP over Multidimensional Data Streams: State-of-the-Art Analysis and Research Perspectives

Alfredo Cuzzocrea

ICAR-CNR and University of Calabria
I-87036 Rende, Cosenza, Italy
cuzzocrea@si.deis.unical.it

Abstract. *Multidimensional data streams* are playing a leading role in next-generation *Data Stream Management Systems* (DSMS). This essentially because real-life data streams are *inherently multidimensional, multi-level and multi-granular in nature*, hence opening the door to a wide spectrum of applications ranging from *environmental sensor networks* to *monitoring* and *tracking systems*, and so forth. As a consequence, there is a need for innovative models and algorithms for representing and processing such streams. Moreover, supporting *OLAP analysis and mining tasks* is a "first-class" issue in the major context of knowledge discovery from streams, for which above-mentioned models and algorithms are baseline components. This issue becomes more problematic when *uncertain and imprecise multidimensional data streams* are considered. Inspired by these critical research challenges, in this paper we present a state-of-the-art technique for supporting OLAP over uncertain multidimensional data streams, and provide research perspectives for future efforts in this scientific field.

1 Introduction

A critical issue in representing, querying and mining data streams consists of the fact that they are *intrinsically multi-level and multidimensional in nature* [5,27], hence they *require to be analyzed by means of multi-level and multi-resolution (analysis) models accordingly*. Furthermore, it is a matter of fact to note that enormous data flows generated by a collection of stream sources *naturally* require to be processed by means of advanced analysis/mining models, beyond traditional solutions provided by primitive SQL-based DBMS interfaces, and very often *high-performance computational infrastructures*, like *Data Grids*, are advocated to provide the necessary support to this end (e.g., [18,17]), also exploiting fortunate *data compression paradigms* (e.g., [10,11,22,20,19,21]). Conventional analysis/mining tools (e.g., DBMS-inspired) cannot carefully take into consideration these kinds of multidimensionality and correlation of real-life data streams, as stated in [5,27]. From this, it follows that, if one tries to process multidimensional and correlated data streams by means of such tools, rough errors

T.-h. Kim, Y.-h. Lee, and W.-c. Fang (Eds.): FGIT 2012, LNCS 7709, pp. 275–282, 2012.

are obtained in practice, thus seriously affecting the quality of decision making processes that found on analytical results mined from streaming data.

Modern data stream applications and systems are also more and more characterized by the presence of *uncertainty* and *imprecision* that make the problem of dealing with *uncertain and imprecise data streams* a leading research challenge. This issue has recently attracted a great deal of attention from both the academic and industrial research community, as confirmed by several research efforts done in this context [8,29,2,9,30,32].

Uncertain and imprecise data streams arise in a plethora of actual application scenarios ranging from *environmental sensor networks* to *logistic networks* and *telecommunication systems*, and so forth. Consider, for instance, the simplest case of a sensor network monitoring the temperature T of a given geographic area W. Here, being T monitoring a natural, real-life measure, it is likely to retrieve an *estimate* of T, denoted by $\widetilde{T}$, with a given *confidence interval*, denoted by $[\widetilde{T}_{min}, \widetilde{T}_{max}]$, such that $\widetilde{T}_{min} < \widetilde{T}_{max}$, having a certain probability p_T, such that $0 \leq p_T \leq 1$, rather than to obtain the *exact value* of T, denoted by $\widehat{T}$. The semantics of this confidence-interval-based model states that the (estimated) value of T, $\widetilde{T}$, ranges between $\widetilde{T}_{min}$ and $\widetilde{T}_{max}$ with probability p_T. Also, a law describing the *probability distribution* according to which *possible values* of T vary over the interval $[\widetilde{T}_{min}, \widetilde{T}_{max}]$ is assumed. Without loss of generality, the *uniform distribution* is very often taken as reference. The uniform distribution states that (possible) values in $[\widetilde{T}_{min}, \widetilde{T}_{max}]$ have *all* the same probability to be the exact value of T, $\widehat{T}$, effectively. Despite the popularity of the normal distribution, the confidence-interval-based model above is prone to incorporate any other kind of probability distribution [31].

Contrary to conventional tools, *multidimensional analysis* provided by *On-Line Analytical Processing* (OLAP) technology [26,6], which has already reached an high-level of maturity, allows us to efficiently exploit and take advantages from multidimensionality and correlation of data streams, with the final aim of improving the quality of both analysis/mining tasks and decision making in streaming environments (e.g., [12,16]). OLAP allows us to aggregate data according to (*i*) a fixed logical schema that can be a *star* or a *snowflake schema* [28], and (*ii*) a given SQL aggregate operator, such as SUM, COUNT, AVG etc. The resulting data structures, called *data cubes* [26], which are usually materialized within *multidimensional arrays*, allow us to meaningfully take advantages from the amenity of querying and mining data according to a multidimensional and a multi-resolution vision of the target domain, and from the rich availability of a wide set of OLAP operators [28], such as *roll-up*, *drill-down*, *slice-&-dice*, *pivot* etc, and OLAP queries, such as *range-*, *top-k*, and *iceberg* queries.

Therefore, the idea of analyzing massive exact and uncertain multidimensional data streams by means of OLAP technology makes sense perfectly, and puts the foundations for novel models and computational paradigms that can be used to efficiently extract summarized, OLAP-like knowledge from data streams, thus overcoming limitations of conventional DBMS-inherited analysis/mining tools.

By meaningfully designing the underlying OLAP (logical) model in dependence on the specific application domain and analysis goals, multidimensional models can efficiently provide support to intelligent tools for a wide set of real-life data stream application scenarios such as weather monitoring systems, environment monitoring systems, systems for controlling telecommunication networks, network traffic monitoring systems, alerting/alarming systems in time-critical applications, sensor network data analysis tools etc, according to similar insights achieved in [5,27]. Indeed, multidimensionality of data streams puts the basis for an extremely variegated collection of stream DW and KD tools with powerful capabilities, even beyond those of conventional ML and DM tools running on transactional data, such as *multidimensional analysis* (e.g., [27]), *correlation analysis* (e.g., [25]), *regression analysis* (e.g., [7]), and so forth. The resulting representation/analysis model constitutes what we call as *OLAP stream model*, which can be reasonably intended as a novel model for processing multidimensional data streams, and supporting multidimensional and multi-resolution analysis and mining tasks over exact and uncertain data streams.

Following these considerations, in this paper we briefly present a state-of-the-art techniques for supporting OLAP over uncertain and imprecise multidimensional data streams, and provide research perspectives for future efforts in this scientific field. The remaining part of the paper is organized as follows. In Section 2, we present a state-of-the-art technique for OLAPing uncertain and imprecise multidimensional data streams [15,14]. In Section 3, we provide and discuss future research perspectives in the investigated topics. Finally, Section 4 summarizes the contributions of this paper and proposes future work in this scientific field.

2   A State-of-the-Art Technique for OLAPing Uncertain and Imprecise Multidimensional Data Streams

In [15,14], we introduce a *novel framework for estimating OLAP queries over uncertain and imprecise multidimensional data streams*. To this end, we first introduce the foundation of our research, i.e. a *probabilistic data stream model* that describes both precise and imprecise multidimensional data stream readings in terms of nice interval-confidence-based *Probability Distribution Functions* (PDF) [31]. Based on this, we then provide the main contribution of our research, i.e. a *possible-world semantics for uncertain and imprecise multidimensional data streams* that is based on an innovative data-driven approach that exploits "natural" features of OLAP data, such as the presence of clusters and high correlations. Finally, we complete our theoretical contributions by means of an innovative approach for *providing theoretically-founded estimates to OLAP queries over uncertain and imprecise multidimensional data streams that exploits the well-recognized probabilistic estimators theory*.

In the reference application scenario of our research proposed in [15,14], a set of multiple data stream sources produce a set of *multiple* uncertain and imprecise multidimensional data streams. The final goal is that of supporting *on-the-fly* OLAP query evaluation over (uncertain and imprecise) multidimensional data stream *readings* in order to provide a *continuous answer* [3] to a *fixed* OLAP query for consumer data-stream-intensive applications and systems. Usually, data stream management systems make use of *buffering techniques* for query efficiency purposes [1], as consumer applications are very often interested in retrieving an *OLAP aggregation* (i.e., the result of an OLAP query) computed over a limited set of *recent* data stream readings [13] rather than querying the "history" of knowledge kept in data stream readings. This query model is also referred in literature as *window-based data stream query model* [1]. The solution consists in making use of a *buffer* storing an appropriately-selected collection of data stream readings (e.g., the last U, with $U > 0$). The problem of meaningfully determining the size of the buffer, denoted by B, is relevant in data stream research [1].

The solution to the problem of OLAPing uncertain and imprecise multidimensional data streams proposed in our research [15,14] builds on some previous results that have been provided by recent research efforts. Particularly, [4], which focuses on static data, introduces a nice PDF-based model that allows us to capture the uncertainty of OLAP measures, whereas the imprecision of OLAP data with respect to *OLAP hierarchies* available in the multidimensional data stream model is meaningfully captured by means of the so-called *possible-world semantics* [4]. This semantics allows us to evaluate OLAP queries over uncertain and imprecise static data, while also ensuring some well-founded theoretical properties, namely *consistency*, *faithfulness* and *correlation-preservation* [4]. Similarly to the PDF-based model, the possible-world semantics is also exploited in our research, and specialized to the more challenging issue of dealing with uncertain and imprecise multidimensional data streams.

Summarizing, in [15,14] we make the following three important contributions: (1) *we introduce a framework for supporting effective OLAP aggregations over uncertain and imprecise multidimensional data streams*; (2) *we provide an innovative possible-world semantics for OLAP aggregations over uncertain and imprecise multidimensional data streams*; (3) *we propose an innovative approach for providing theoretically-founded estimates to OLAP queries over uncertain and imprecise multidimensional data streams, via the probabilistic estimators theory*.

In particular, for what regards the proposed data model for uncertain and imprecise multidimensional data streams, it relies-on and extends the research proposed in [4], which focuses on OLAP over static data. As mentioned above, [4] introduces a nice data model and a theoretically-sound possible-world semantics for OLAP over uncertain and imprecise static data, like those one can find in *probabilistic relational database systems* [23]. Particularly, [4] states that two specific occurrences of *data ambiguity* can arise in a typical OLAP scenario over static data: (i) uncertainty of (OLAP) measures, and (ii) imprecision of dimensional members of (OLAP) hierarchies.

For what regards the proposed possible-world semantics, we provide an innovative approach to solve the relevant problem above, which is based on the well-known evidence stating that *OLAP data (static data as well as streaming data) are usually clustered and (highly) correlated in nature* [7,5,27,13]. On the basis of this evidence, the main idea of the approach we propose consists in *computing the probability of the confidence interval of an imprecise multidimensional data stream reading to be "close" to confidence intervals of its neighboring precise multidimensional data stream readings*, fixed the multidimensional range of the imprecise multidimensional data stream reading, at a certain OLAP hierarchical level, as the reference neighborhood.

For what regards the uncertain and imprecise OLAP query model, we exploit the probabilistic estimator theory, and we provide an innovative ⟨ε, δ⟩-*based probabilistic estimator* [31] that retrieves estimates to OLAP queries via *appropriate statistics* extracted from PDF describing the uncertain and imprecise multidimensional data stream readings.

In order to assess the quality of our research [15,14], in [15,14] we conduct an experimental analysis on several classes of synthetic multidimensional data stream sets. The goal of our analysis consists in evaluating the *accuracy* of retrieved estimates under the ranging of the following critical parameters: (*i*) the percentage of imprecise readings contained by the multidimensional view exploited in the target OLAP analysis; (*ii*) the dimensionality of input uncertain and imprecise multidimensional data streams (this also tests the *scalability* of our proposed framework). Retrieved results clearly confirm the benefits of our framework in the context of modern data stream applications and systems, which are more and more characterized by the presence of uncertainty and imprecision.

3 OLAP over Uncertain and Imprecise Multidimensional Data Streams: Future Research Perspectives

As regards open research problems in the context of OLAP over uncertain and imprecise multidimensional data streams, we firmly believe that, in future years, the following research topics will play a first-class role:

– *Improving the Efficiency of OLAP Cube Computing Algorithms over Uncertain and Imprecise Data Streams* Computing OLAP cubes in distributed environments is still a major problem in this field, due to the excessive computational overheads introduced by this critical task. This issue gets worse when applied to uncertain and imprecise data streams. To face-off this problem, exploiting *MapReduce paradigms* [24] seems a very promising direction of research, still poorly explored.
– *Multidimensional Query Languages for Uncertain and Imprecise Data Streams* This research topic deals with the definition of foundations, syntax and semantics of a proper SQL-like multidimensional query language for uncertain and imprecise data streams, and its integration in modern DSMS architectures.
– *Data Mining languages for Uncertain and Imprecise Multidimensional Data Streams* This research topic extends the previous one and it is focused on

defining a proper procedural Data Mining language for uncertain and imprecise multidimensional data streams, possibly incorporating ad-hoc mining procedures (e.g., frequent itemset mining), along with its integration in modern DSMS architectures.

- *Privacy Preserving Uncertain and Imprecise Data Stream Processing* This research topic deals with the problem of supporting privacy-preserving processing over uncertain and imprecise data streams, as ensuring the privacy of data streams during data management activities (e.g., query evaluation) is one of the most-critical challenge in future critical data stream applications (e.g., health management information systems).

- *Uncertain and Imprecise Data Stream Visualization* This research topic focuses on the definition of models, algorithms and techniques for supporting the visualization of uncertain and imprecise streaming data in the context of scientific and e-life applications and systems, with innovative metaphors like visual data stream sensing and understanding.

4   Conclusions and Future Work

In this paper, we have presented a state-of-the-art technique for supporting OLAP over uncertain multidimensional data streams, and provided research perspectives for future efforts in this scientific field. We discussed both theoretical as well as practical issues in the investigated topics.

Future work should considers two important aspects: (*i*) developing real-life e-science applications based on OLAP over uncertain and imprecise multidimensional data streams – a strong advancement in this research context will be ensured by developing real-life applications focused on novel scenarios such as bio-informatics, genomic computing, social networks, and so forth; (*ii*) further developing and expanding the theory behind uncertain and imprecise multidimensional data stream query algorithms and mining languages.

References

1. Abadi, D.J., Carney, D., Çetintemel, U., Cherniack, M., Convey, C., Lee, S., Stonebraker, M., Tatbul, N., Zdonik, S.B.: Aurora: a new model and architecture for data stream management. VLDB J. 12(2), 120–139 (2003)
2. Aggarwal, C.C., Yu, P.S.: A framework for clustering uncertain data streams. In: ICDE, pp. 150–159 (2008)
3. Babu, S., Widom, J.: Continuous queries over data streams. SIGMOD Record 30(3), 109–120 (2001)
4. Burdick, D., Deshpande, P., Jayram, T.S., Ramakrishnan, R., Vaithyanathan, S.: Olap over uncertain and imprecise data. In: VLDB, pp. 970–981 (2005)
5. Cai, Y.D., Clutter, D., Pape, G., Han, J., Welge, M., Auvil, L.: Maids: Mining alarming incidents from data streams. In: SIGMOD Conference, pp. 919–920 (2004)
6. Chaudhuri, S., Dayal, U.: An overview of data warehousing and olap technology. SIGMOD Record 26(1), 65–74 (1997)

7. Chen, Y., Dong, G., Han, J., Wah, B.W., Wang, J.: Multi-dimensional regression analysis of time-series data streams. In: VLDB, pp. 323–334 (2002)
8. Cormode, G., Garofalakis, M.N.: Sketching probabilistic data streams. In: SIGMOD Conference, pp. 281–292 (2007)
9. Cormode, G., Korn, F., Tirthapura, S.: Exponentially decayed aggregates on data streams. In: ICDE, pp. 1379–1381 (2008)
10. Cuzzocrea, A.: Accuracy control in compressed multidimensional data cubes for quality of answer-based olap tools. In: SSDBM, pp. 301–310 (2006)
11. Cuzzocrea, A.: Improving range-sum query evaluation on data cubes via polynomial approximation. Data Knowl. Eng. 56(2), 85–121 (2006)
12. Cuzzocrea, A.: CAMS: OLAPing Multidimensional Data Streams Efficiently. In: Pedersen, T.B., Mohania, M.K., Tjoa, A.M. (eds.) DaWaK 2009. LNCS, vol. 5691, pp. 48–62. Springer, Heidelberg (2009)
13. Cuzzocrea, A.: Intelligent Techniques for Warehousing and Mining Sensor Network Data. IGI Global (2009)
14. Cuzzocrea, A.: A data-driven approach for olap over uncertain and imprecise multidimensional data streams via possible-world-semantics. In: SUM, pp. 18–26 (2011)
15. Cuzzocrea, A.: Retrieving Accurate Estimates to OLAP Queries over Uncertain and Imprecise Multidimensional Data Streams. In: Bayard Cushing, J., French, J., Bowers, S. (eds.) SSDBM 2011. LNCS, vol. 6809, pp. 575–576. Springer, Heidelberg (2011)
16. Cuzzocrea, A., Chakravarthy, S.: Event-based lossy compression for effective and efficient olap over data streams. Data Knowl. Eng. 69(7), 678–708 (2010)
17. Cuzzocrea, A., Furfaro, F., Greco, S., Masciari, E., Mazzeo, G.M., Saccà, D.: A distributed system for answering range queries on sensor network data. In: PerCom Workshops, pp. 369–373 (2005)
18. Cuzzocrea, A., Furfaro, F., Mazzeo, G.M., Saccá, D.: A Grid Framework for Approximate Aggregate Query Answering on Summarized Sensor Network Readings. In: Meersman, R., Tari, Z., Corsaro, A. (eds.) OTM-WS 2004. LNCS, vol. 3292, pp. 144–153. Springer, Heidelberg (2004)
19. Cuzzocrea, A., Furfaro, F., Saccà, D.: Enabling olap in mobile environments via intelligent data cube compression techniques. J. Intell. Inf. Syst. 33(2), 95–143 (2009)
20. Cuzzocrea, A., Saccà, D., Serafino, P.: Semantics-aware advanced olap visualization of multidimensional data cubes. IJDWM 3(4), 1–30 (2007)
21. Cuzzocrea, A., Serafino, P.: LCS-hist: taming massive high-dimensional data cube compression. In: EDBT, pp. 768–779 (2009)
22. Cuzzocrea, A., Wang, W.: Approximate range-sum query answering on data cubes with probabilistic guarantees. J. Intell. Inf. Syst. 28(2), 161–197 (2007)
23. Dalvi, N.N., Suciu, D.: Efficient query evaluation on probabilistic databases. In: VLDB, pp. 864–875 (2004)
24. Dean, J., Ghemawat, S.: Mapreduce: simplified data processing on large clusters. Commun. ACM 51(1), 107–113 (2008)
25. Gehrke, J., Korn, F., Srivastava, D.: On computing correlated aggregates over continual data streams. In: SIGMOD Conference, pp. 13–24 (2001)
26. Gray, J., Chaudhuri, S., Bosworth, A., Layman, A., Reichart, D., Venkatrao, M., Pellow, F., Pirahesh, H.: Data cube: A relational aggregation operator generalizing group-by, cross-tab, and sub totals. Data Min. Knowl. Discov. 1(1), 29–53 (1997)
27. Han, J., Chen, Y., Dong, G., Pei, J., Wah, B.W., Wang, J., Cai, Y.D.: Stream cube: An architecture for multi-dimensional analysis of data streams. Distributed and Parallel Databases 18(2), 173–197 (2005)

28. Han, J., Kamber, M.: Data Mining: Concepts and Techniques. Morgan Kaufmann (2000)
29. Jayram, T.S., McGregor, A., Muthukrishnan, S., Vee, E.: Estimating statistical aggregates on probabilistic data streams. In: PODS, pp. 243–252 (2007)
30. Jin, C., Yi, K., Chen, L., Yu, J.X., Lin, X.: Sliding-window top-k queries on uncertain streams. PVLDB 1(1), 301–312 (2008)
31. Papoulis, A.: Probability, Random Variables, and Stochastic Processes. McGraw-Hill (1984)
32. Zhang, Q., Li, F., Yi, K.: Finding frequent items in probabilistic data. In: SIGMOD Conference, pp. 819–832 (2008)

Author Index